Paternalism or Partnership?
Family Involvement in the Child

CESS

Studies in Child Protection

LONDON: HMSO

D1422304

Acknowledgements

We are grateful to the many people who have helped us with the research and the report. First of all our thanks are due to Dr Carolyn Davies and her colleagues at the Research and Development Division of the Department of Health for funding the study and for their support and encouragement. We have also benefited greatly from the interest and probing questions of Rupert Hughes and Kathleen Taylor at the Department of Health Community Services Division, and Wendy Rose and Rosemary Arkley of the Social Services Inspectorate.

This study forms part of a wider programme of Department of Health funded research on child protection and we are grateful to the other researchers who have met regularly to try to make sense of our explorations of the subject in different places and from different angles. We were also greatly helped by the advisory group of UEA colleagues and members of the local social work and research community, and by the members of the Norfolk Families in Care group who helped us pilot the interview schedules. Anne Borrett who typed the many versions of the research instruments and report with meticulous care and unfailing good humour; and Arlene Moore who prepared the manuscript for publication; Sarah Mould and Dan Edwards who typed in the data and Jacquie White who analysed it were all essential members of the team to whom we also give our thanks.

The list is long of the many colleagues involved in child protection work, researchers and academics who have helped us to tease out the issues. Foremost among them are the senior staff, social workers and administrators of the seven authorities who trusted us to undertake the research in their areas, and gave us such excellent support as we tried to find our way round different systems and different places. Our lives as well as our knowledge were enriched by these encounters.

Most importantly of all, we thank the parents and children we interviewed and who completed our questionnaires for their willingness to talk to us about these distressing episodes in their lives in order, as so many of them put it, to help others in the future.

Finally we thank our own families for their patience and support.

All have had some influence on this report, but we alone take responsibility for the final contents and for any errors or omissions.

June Thoburn
Ann Lewis
David Shemmings

University of East Anglia
December 1993

Contents

Chapter 1

Introduction

The background to working in partnership

This Guide stresses the need to ensure that the welfare of children is the overriding factor guiding Child Protection work. It also emphasises the importance of professionals working in partnership with parents and other family members or carers and the concept of parental responsibility. . . . (also) the involvement of children and adults in Child Protection conferences will not be effective unless they are fully involved from the outset in all stages of the Child Protection process and unless from the time of referral there is as much openness and honesty as possible between families and professionals. (Working Together, *DH, 1991a*)

This study was commissioned before *Working Together* (1991) was published but after the Children Act 1989 had made it clear that agencies and individual workers should aim to work in partnership with family members in all child care cases. Practice across the country was varied, especially in respect to family involvement in child protection conferences, and there was also inter-professional debate about its desirability. The research examines the issues of participation of the different family members in the different aspects of child protection work from many angles.

Since the first *Working Together* guidelines in 1988 there has been a major change towards involving parents and children in child protection procedures which has implications for the way the professionals from the helping agencies approach and work with families, as well as for the families themselves. To coin a phrase—'It takes two to participate'. Parents and professionals have to work hard in order to achieve participation and partnership and there is much still to be learned from each other.

The child protection procedures are a powerful mechanism intended to ensure the safety of individual children but it is salutary to remember that despite their existence and the commitment of many people to them, the NSPCC predicts that about 190 children may suffer abusive or neglectful deaths each year (Creighton and Gallagher, 1988). Childhood mortality statistics for 1990 (OPCS, 1991) show that a total of 4,491 children died between the ages of 28 days and 14 years in England and Wales. Of these, 34 died from 'homicide and injury purposely inflicted by other persons', 11 from 'child battering and other maltreatment', 67 from 'other violence' and 66 from 'injury undetermined whether accidentally or purposely inflicted' (OPCS, 1991), some 178 altogether.

These are depressing figures about shocking incidents, but it should also be remembered that 322 children were killed in motor vehicle traffic accidents in 1990 and 1,079 children died from Sudden Infant Death Syndrome. Public concern and response to these figures does not hit the headlines in the same way as does a child's death at the hands of his or her carers. Birchall (1989) makes the point that it is apparently not the numbers of children who die that cause public concern but the nature of their deaths which gives rise to our moral indignation.

To keep our anxieties in perspective, it is important also to make a comparison with the figures for the overall child population in England (children under the age of 18). For the year ending March 31 1991 (at the end of the fieldwork for this study), the Department of Health provisional figures (DH, 1992) showed that the number of children on Child Protection Register was 45,200 and that this represented a rate of 4.2 children per thousand in the general population. The number of children on the Register as a rate per 1,000 children under 18 rose from 4.0 at 31 March 1990 to 4.2 at 31 March 1991, although it has since declined to 38,600 in 1992 (a rate of 3.5 per 1000 children under 18). The rate for registrations increased in 1991 from 2.5 to 2.6 and de-registrations from 2.2 to 2.5, but in 1991–92 the rate of registrations went down to 2.2 per 1000 children under 18 and the rate of de-registrations increased to 2.8. It should be emphasised, however, that the Register is not a record of the extent of child abuse as some children are registered because of concern about future abuse and will not have been the victim of actual abuse, whilst other children who have been the victim of abuse will not have been placed on the Register because there was no need for a multi-agency protection plan under child protection procedures.

It should also be noted that, as we shall see from the study, the vast majority of children referred to child protection conferences continued to live with at least one natural parent under no legal order (67 per cent nationally in March 1991, increasing to 73 per cent in 1992).

These are the families who are closely involved in the child protection procedures by reason of the fact that they are in charge of their children daily throughout the year. It is therefore not surprising that the Department of Health has emphasised the importance of involving parents in the meetings which make decisions about protecting their children from harm. Between 1990 and 1992, when this study was undertaken, there was a growing awareness that in order to do this parents need assistance to be participants at child protection conferences and other important meetings and not attenders only. Two parents described their treatment by professionals at a meeting thus:

It was as if we had been asked to play a game of football against a full professional team. We'd only just been told the rules and had no practice. They fielded 11 hand-picked players. (Guernsey's Local Support Group, 1991).

The quote neatly encapsulates the essence of what participation is not!

The practice guidance by the Department of Health (in preparation) lists 15 essential requirements of participatory practice. Information-giving, consultation and involvement in decision-making are basic to participation. They are also basic to clients' rights in social work practice as well as to their rights as citizens. Biehal and Sainsbury (1991) have shown how clients' rights have been derived from the values of social work. They explored the notion of partnership between clients and social workers and the difficulties involved in locating values like 'common sense' and 'practice wisdom' in day-to-day contact with families. They suggest that overlooking the inequalities of the relationship can make the values meaningless and references to clients' rights, little more than a slogan. But they conclude with a list of eight rights related to the early stages of intervention which, if built into standard practice by professionals, would begin to redress the balance in favour of parents' and children's rights in child protection. Biehal and Sainsbury note that the list points more to protecting clients from undue interference than to positively enhancing their rights, but as a practice guide to participation in all agencies, it illustrates social work values in action and suggests that these actions will be visible to research and evaluation.

Their list includes the following rights of clients:

- ' to know the name of the worker responsible and how to make effective contact
- to be told about the worker's role and powers in the specific situation; what she/he has come for (or about)
- to be listened to (i.e. not interrupted, not rationalised)
- to give explicit consent to or to refuse investigation of problems, except in situations where there are statutory responsibilities or there is a need for an assessment of risk before a decision about intervention can be made
- to give explicit consent to or to refuse intervention (except where this conflicts with the rights of dependent others or there is a statutory mandate)
- to be provided with information relevant to making choices
- to share in exploring problems, goals, tasks and criteria of 'successful' outcome
- to know what is said or written about them (except where this conflicts with the rights of others); to have a right to access to records and to the deliberations of professional helpers.' (pp 255-6)

These principles have found expression in several provisions of the Children Act 1989, even though the term 'partnership' does not appear in the Act, and is mentioned but not clearly defined in the Guidance. When planning and carrying out this study we were influenced by the definition offered by the Family Rights Group in the Department of Health commissioned training pack to help social workers and other professionals to integrate partnership principles into their practice.

> *Partnership is marked by:*
> - *respect for one another*
> - *rights to information*
> - *accountability*
> - *competence and value accorded to individual input*
>
> *In short, each partner is seen as having something to contribute, power is shared, decisions are made jointly, roles are not only respected but also backed by legal and moral rights. (FRG, 1991)*

This definition introduces the crucial dimension of power and allows for the possibility that power can be shared to some extent even in circumstances which give rise to child protection conferences when the power held by family members and professionals is manifestly unequal. Nevertheless, the difficulties of **working in partnership,** and in some cases the inappropriateness of doing so, are acknowledged, and the broader concepts of **information sharing, consultation and participation** have been used in this study.

An overview of earlier research

When embarking on new modes of practice it is always useful to look at where and when the ideas originated. Up to the mid-1980s parental participation was not mentioned in the literature on child abuse. The main concern was the management of child abuse and the use of the conference as part of that procedure.

The arguments for and against parental participation appear to have been written up for the first time in 1984 by a student's preliminary study of parental attendance at case conferences with the NSPCC in Coventry (Housiaux, 1984). Housiaux explored the issues of parental attendance at case conferences by interviewing parents who had attended conferences for part or most of the time as well as the professionals involved. She identified most of the factors which have been debated and researched subsequently. They were the parents' and professionals' views about the advantages and disadvantages of parental attendance; of whether decision-making was affected; and parents' views about the procedure and its effect on them. She thought it would be useful to provide written information for families; a pro-forma for written reports to the conference and guidelines for good practice which considered preparation of parents, exclusion clauses, support of parents and the need for agreement by all the professionals to the parents' presence.

There followed a further period when the literature rehearsed the arguments for and against parental participation in case conferences more vociferously and in more detail and it ended with a proliferation of small studies which monitored and evaluated parental participation in practice in the 1990s. One of these (Shemmings and Thoburn, 1990) served as a pilot study for the more extensive research reported in these pages.

It is worth mentioning at this point, before turning to these studies, that there has been a slow but persistent shift towards participation for a much longer time span in the general community, by users of services and buyers of products over a vast range of activities from television viewing to choosing fish fingers. Community social workers and social workers with elderly clients and those with disabilities also embarked upon participatory practice more systematically and earlier than in the field of child care (see especially the work of Croft and Beresford, 1990 and the papers edited by Barnes and Wistow, 1992). This is not to suggest that examples of participatory ideas and practice were missing in child care. On the contrary, there were many in residential children's homes, in statutory child care reviews, in the greater use of Guardians ad Litem in court proceedings and eventually in child protection review conferences. But it has taken the implementation of the Children Act and its vision of partnership with families, as well as the more specific *Working Together* guidelines to accelerate full family participation in child protection work. Some of the major research studies (DH, 1985; 1991b) on child care practice and some smaller, local studies of reviews in child care work with families of children who may be in need of protection have included the dimension of family involvement in their work (Brown, 1984; Sinclair, 1984; Gardner, 1987; Parsloe et al., 1990; Marsh and Fisher, 1992; Owen, 1992). Most of the research which has specifically addressed family involvement in child protection work has been concerned with **parents** at child protection **conferences**. The study reported here is one of a series of studies, mostly commissioned by the Department of Health, which have examined aspects of child protection such as parental control within the family, professional interventions in child sexual abuse, the operation of child protection registers, decision-making, intervention and outcome in child protection work and parental perspectives of suspected child abuse and its aftermath. Although our study and that of Cleaver and Freeman (1995) are the only ones which specifically focus on family involvement, several of the other studies have something to say about it, and reference will be made in the text to some of these.

The arguments against parental participation were well examined by

McGloin and Turnbull (1986) in the context of a pilot scheme to invite parents to review conferences in Greenwich. The recurring themes, which are still produced as reasons for not having participatory practice, were: the inhibiting effect on professionals, the unknown effect on parents, issues of confidentiality and trust, the problems of evidence, conflict, lack of professional skills and fears that the conference might become a pseudo court of law. Phillips and Evans (1986) working through the logical consistency of these arguments found them not to contain flaws as objections. They had intended to present the pros and cons but found themselves fully advocating parental participation. Phillips (1986) went on to list reasons for parental participation in another paper: parents have the right to contribute; decisions should not be made behind closed doors; untested assumptions could be challenged; commitment to plans would be greater; responsibility would be clarified and respect would be engendered.

Morrison and his colleagues (1990), in a paper produced by the NSPCC, were not yet convinced that parents' attendance at all case conferences could be wholeheartedly advocated because in their view major practice requirements would be jeopardised, as would the duty to protect the child. But they thought that greater efforts should be made to involve parents in conferences because of the principles of fairness and good practice. So far as the child's attendance was concerned, they were even more cautious. They thought conferences should retain the child at the centre of their work and have their views and feelings presented, but not necessarily with the child there.

It has taken the efforts of practitioners in the field of child protection as well as some joint projects by local authorities and universities to provide the evaluation of participation in practice at local level. Sixteen of the earlier local studies are considered in this overview although several others have now been completed. They are of grassroots practice, mostly of initial child protection conferences but also of review conferences. They have been carried out in a variety of ways, using a variety of methodological approaches. Some are 'in house', whilst others are conducted by researchers from outside the local authorities. There are personal descriptions of pilot projects, compilations of the views of either parents or of professionals, as well as more detailed analyses using questionnaires, interviews and observations of conferences.

There is no question, though, that all of them conclude positively for the involvement of families in conferences, despite the difficulties, and most consider that parents should normally be invited to the whole of initial and review conferences. Each study concludes with an attempt to answer the question: How can we manage this new way of working and how can we overcome the problems that it is likely to produce? Each contributes something new to the overall picture of participation by family members.

Taking the process in a chronological sequence, parents' and professionals' responses are described as well as some information about children and the conferences themselves. Not all the studies asked the same questions and not all the participation was full, nor all of the conferences initial ones, but there is sufficient congruence to support a positive conclusion.

Parents

Using Housiaux's first list of factors as a guide, parents' views were sought on the written information they received before the conference. Parents in Cleveland, North Tyneside, and at St Gabriel's Family Centre, Brighton, found the leaflets given to be useful (Cleveland Social Services Department 1991; Taylor and Godfrey, 1991; Ely, 1991). In Cumbria (Smith, 1990), 75 per cent of the parents thought the leaflet was satisfactory. Where the reports were shared with parents before the conference, they also thought the practice very good. In North Tyneside parents' responses to a parent pack, which included a leaflet as well as other written information, were mixed. They ranged from parents who thought the pack had painted a more frightening picture than the conference was in reality, to those who thought the social worker had said it all better. A parent said:

> No matter how much is explained to you, you still don't know exactly what to expect. (Lonsdale, 1991)

The majority of the comments about the way the investigation was conducted, the amount of information given about it, parents' rights, social services' rights and powers, and legal information given, were positive, as were responses about being prepared for the conference (Cleveland Social Services Department, 1991; Smith, 1990). In Leeds, a parent said:

> The social worker talked to me about what to expect and my solicitor helped me to write down a statement. (Bell, 1993)

Parents were asked in a variety of ways about the procedures and how they were affected by them. In Calderdale (Calderdale ACPC, 1992) and Dudley, parents felt welcomed in the conferences; in Dudley, 50 per cent of the parents felt they were welcomed very well and 50 per cent well (Dudley Social Services Department, 1991). The majority of the parents questioned in all these studies thought they were able to put their views but they found it more difficult when they were present at only part of a conference (see especially Woodhill and Ashworth, 1989). Entering a room when everyone else had presented their views placed them in a position where they were unaware of what had been said already and therefore uncertain about what they were supposed to say next. The study in Cumbria showed that the alternative policy of asking for parents' views to be presented by the social worker resulted in only 42 per cent giving their views to the social worker.

Parents varied in their response as to whether they thought they were listened to. The Hackney study (Shemmings and Thoburn, 1990) had a high positive response rate, as did Calderdale, where parents thought they had a fair hearing, whereas in Gloucestershire (Burns, 1991) and Lewisham (Shemmings, 1991) the more frequent response was 'not really'. The Hackney study also found that parents thought professionals were open and honest in the conferences.

Did the parents say they understood what was going on in the conferences? Mostly the answer to this question was 'Yes', but Merchant and Luckham (1991) found that in Essex many of the parents had not understood important details about registration. In Leeds (Bell, 1993) a group of parents who had not attended the conferences was compared with a group who had attended. Their understanding of what was happening, the decisions and recommendations made, and whether their views were represented and taken account of, was, by comparison with the parents who had attended, partial or poor.

In Cleveland and Hackney, parents were positive in their response to whether they thought they had influenced decisions, but in four other studies (Bell, 1993; Burns, 1991; Merchant and Luckham, 1991; Shemmings, 1991) the responses were more pessimistic. The St Gabriel's study (Ely, 1991) showed that parents hoped that just by being there they might have had a little influence.

The Calderdale study asked parents about their feelings after the conferences. The most frequently noted feelings were: 'given a fair hearing', 'hopeful', 'positive about the decisions made' and those ticked least often were: 'wasteful of time', 'cynical', 'didn't fully understand', and 'professionals unreasonable'.

The advantages and disadvantages of parental attendance were illustrated in three studies (Bell, 1993; Ely, 1991; Merchant and Luckham, 1991) where parents thought that the professionals had made up their minds beforehand, but nevertheless they found it helpful to be there and were glad they came. In Calderdale, Hackney and Lewisham the majority of parents were glad to have attended:

It was daunting but eased. (Shemmings and Thoburn, 1990).

The clearest message expressed by parents was the advantage of being there the **whole** time. When they were not (as in Cleveland, Cumbria, parts of Essex, St Gabriel's Family Centre, and North Tyneside) they all wished that they could have been. The Essex study is particularly interesting in that an area where there was partial attendance was compared with another part of the county where full attendance was the norm (Merchant and Luckham, 1991). The researchers reached the strong conclusion that full attendance was preferable in most circumstances.

There were a number of telling comments made by parents. Being excluded was threatening and intimidating, and it was particularly stressful to enter a strange room full of people:

> *I would have preferred to have been there and then people have come in. It's less imposing.*
>
> *When I walked into that room, I felt two inches tall. (Merchant and Luckham, 1991).*

It was also stressful to go through all the incidents and allegations:

> *We found it difficult to reply on the spot and when we were waiting for the decisions my husband kept thinking of things we should have said and hadn't. It was awesome for us: so many people there, some not known. (Bell, 1993)*

Researchers also made comments on practice issues: parents' need 'help to attend' and 'want pen, paper and labels'. Cultural factors usually appeared to have been addressed, but parents described a 'them and us' situation, a 'lack of power'. They wanted to tell professionals that their case was individual and different from others' and that they thought it warranted particular consideration. Parents were also aware that they needed to be careful of their demeanour in the conference in case they made things worse for themselves.

Driscoll and Evans in Suffolk (1992) asked parents' views of all the early stages of the protection work, and interviewed parents who did not attend conferences as well as those who did. They received generally very positive feedback from parents about recent changes in practice aimed at increased parental involvement both in the work and in the meetings.

Undoubtedly, from parents' points of view, the experience of participating in conferences is not easy, but nevertheless they want to be there.

Children

Although there has been a rapid acceleration from a complete absence of parents at conferences to full attendance in many authorities, the changes in respect of children have been less marked. This seems to reflect the need to familiarise everyone with the new way of working with parents first and the greater complexity of the issues surrounding the involvement of children. However, there are a few examples of young people attending both initial and review conferences successfully, particularly when the young person is in care or when the alleged abuser has left the family. In Gloucestershire (Burns, 1991) six children attended conferences, and in Calderdale three children attended, one of whom requested that the parents be excluded. Professionals expressed a wish for children to be involved, but also concern at the possible distress which attendance at a conference could cause, though no instances were cited of this actually happening.

The writer of the Bradford report (Fisher, 1990) thought that children should not have to face parents in the child protection arena but that presenting their views was vital. In two others (Berkshire Social Services Department, 1990; Burns, 1991) the professionals felt the focus on the child was maintained in their conferences and in Essex 70 per cent of social workers were in favour of children attending (Merchant and Luckham, 1991). When conferences were observed in North Tyneside (Taylor and Godfrey, 1991) it was found that not all the needs of children were made explicit and their views were not always discussed.

Already, in a number of other areas, positive policies to enable children to participate have been decided upon and plans are being made to put them into practice, taking into account the importance of children having a supporter before, during and after the conference. (See especially the guidelines produced by Wilson (1992) for Avon Social Services Department, and Salford ACPC (undated)).

Professionals

The main overall question was: Does the attendance of parents at child protection conferences affect the participation of the professionals?

Professionals interviewed for most studies thought that information-giving was clearer and that there was less gossip, unsubstantiated evidence and opinion.

Did parents' attendance inhibit others? Some respondents (see Taylor and Godfrey, 1991; North Yorkshire ACPC, 1991) said 'No', but Merchant and Luckham (1991) and Lonsdale (1990) reported that some professionals said that the **other** professionals were inhibited and not themselves!

Was the quality of decision-making affected? The overall response to this question was that professionals were open and honest, did not hold back information and that the decisions were made in the best interests of the child. Also they showed that professionals thought registration and de-registration was satisfactorily dealt with and that the decisions and recommendations were not qualitatively different. No children were reported as not registered when they should have been. Decisions were said not to be adversely affected, the protection plans were said to be better and professionals to perform their tasks adequately (e.g. decision to register, discussion of race). Again, we need to remember that in only a minority of the authorities studied were family members normally present throughout the initial conference.

Did parents help the conference? The Wiltshire study found that 78 per cent of the professionals thought that parents participated, rather than just attended, and that 67 per cent thought it useful or very useful that parents were there. Fifty-three per cent in the Hackney study said 'Yes', though they tended to think that parents were more stressed than they in fact were. Of 233 professionals in Dudley, 223 thought parents' presence helpful or very helpful.

Conferences

In six of the studies, conferences were observed by an independent researcher who was able to make an observation about whether parental and child attendance appeared to affect the conferences. An early study in Sheffield (Woodhill and Ashworth, 1989) found that there was a noticeable amount of intra and inter-professional conflict whether parents were present or not. The opposite question was asked about what effect such disagreement and misunderstanding would have on *parents'* participation? It was thought parents would not understand the nature of such disagreement and therefore feel unable to take part in the discussion. However, the North Yorkshire and Wiltshire studies (which did not observe the conferences) found, from the views of parents and professionals, that conferences could cope with conflict and tension even with parents present and that the group dynamics were not affected detrimentally. The Essex study used an interesting method of categorising interactions in the conference, and found that there was most interaction over information and opinion-giving; that disagreement, tension and antagonism were greater with parents present but also that there were high degrees of enabling and confidence raising with parents present (Merchant and Luckham, 1991).

Finally, the local studies, most notably that of Driscoll and Evans (1992), reveal that, when parents are invited to child protection conferences, many other aspects of practice change, especially in the preparation for conferences. Although the focus of most studies was conferences, they picked up a lot of positive views from professionals and parents about these changes and the way child protection work was being conducted.

It can be seen that several of these reports, as well as *Working Together* which advocated increased parental involvement, were published during the data collection phase of this study, and indeed six of our seven authorities had undertaken evaluations of aspects of their own practice prior to our study, or were doing so concurrently. Additionally, the Children Act 1989 was implemented towards the end of our data collection period and was already affecting practice in the earlier stages. It is hardly surprising that we had the distinct impression as researchers that we were pointing our lenses at and attempting to bring into focus a constantly moving picture, which added to the methodological problems which we describe in the next chapter.

In this research study we have tried to tread a path between misleading over-simplification and an unduly complex account of our findings, resulting from this moving picture and from the range of often differing perspectives on the events we sought to understand, describe and analyse.

Summary

- The Children Act 1989 and the accompanying guidance emphasises the importance of services to children in need and their families (including child protection services) being provided wherever possible in partnership with family members.

- The nature of partnership is discussed in the context of child protection work, and the power differential between professional workers and family members is acknowledged.

- The necessity of attempting to work in partnership with parents is emphasised in view of the large proportion of children on child protection registers (73 per cent in March 1992) living at home with at least one parent.

- Most research on family member involvement in child care and child protection work concentrates on their attendance at meetings—review meetings if the child is looked after by the authority—or child protection conferences.

- Early writing discussed the advantages, disadvantages and the reasons for advocating family involvement in meetings.

- A large number of mainly small 'in house' studies has evaluated the growing practice of inviting parents to decision-making meetings in child care cases. Some have looked also at practice. Family members generally find the experience stressful but consider it essential that they are invited to meetings. They do not like to be invited to only a small part of the meeting, and such practices may serve to alienate them from the protection process. A large majority of professionals support the changes in policy and practice to involve family members, including the attendance of parents at conferences. Opinion is divided about whether they should attend throughout the conference and also about how best to consult and involve children and young people.

- The studies advocated changes in policy and practice and gave guidance about practical ways of achieving increased family involvement. Some of these suggestions had been put into practice already by some of the agencies from which this research sample is drawn.

Chapter 2

The Research Study and the Sample Areas

An Overview of the Methods Used

There is now a growing number of research studies into user involvement in the provision of social work and other social services. The methodological issues for researchers in this field are reviewed by Barnes and Wistow (1992) in their edited collection of papers from a workshop on user involvement. Despite the growing number of studies there is still controversy around ethical issues as well as the technical aspects of data collection and analysis.

The very process of involving users in the design and delivery of services should imply that they are contributing directly to the monitoring and evaluation of those services even without the commissioning of research studies. Research into user involvement is therefore a monitoring and evaluation exercise of a consultation and evaluation process. Despite the growing numbers of such studies both user involvement itself, as a central part of social services provision, and the research into user involvement are in their early stages and thus a qualitative and exploratory methodology is likely to be most appropriate. As our introductory chapter has indicated, there are few studies of user involvement in child protection **work** (as opposed to conferences) and for this reason also a qualitative study is indicated which can tease out the meaning of user involvement policies and practices to those who are on the receiving end and those who are attempting to implement them. An understanding of the purposes of user involvement as perceived by parents and children, workers and managers is essential if we are to provide a description of the process as well as an evaluation of the outcome.

On the other hand, since involving family members in child protection work was still in its early stages, and not accepted as an appropriate strategy in all circles, it was important to be clear whether the cases studied intensively were representative of the total caseload of child protection work. For this reason it was also considered essential to set the qualitative study against a background of a total cohort of cases. This could have been done by ascertaining basic details about the type of abuse and family characteristics of the larger cohort. However, since many of the variables which we hypothe- sised might be relevant to whether the family members were or were not involved in the work concerned attitudes and interpretations rather than facts, we decided also to undertake interviews with social workers, and a detailed records search in respect of all those cases from which the small sample is drawn.

Barnes and Wistow (1992) note that 'both the theory and practice of user involvement have implications for the **conduct** of research no less than the **delivery** of services'. Research design caused problems with which we struggled throughout the data collection phase. These difficulties and our attempts to surmount them are described in this chapter.

The Study Areas

The pilot study in the London Borough of Hackney (Shemmings and Thoburn, 1990) resulted in contacts with several authorities which were interested in involving family members in their child protection conferences and other aspects of the work. Since a major aim of the research was to identify strategies which appeared to be effective in enabling family members to participate, the sample areas were chosen only from those which had expressed a serious intention of attempting to work in partnership with parents and/or children. The seven areas chosen were emphasising different aspects of family involvement and were at different stages of implementation of their policies. All the authorities which were asked if they would be willing to help with this study agreed to do so although in each case only a part of the authority was included. The study was therefore drawn from parts of three London boroughs, one northern district, a midland county, and two counties in the south-east of England. There were established populations of black and ethnic minority families in two of the London boroughs, the northern district and the midland county.

Northtown, with a population of over 450,000, was built historically on the prosperity of the northern woollen industry which left its mark in the fine Victorian buildings of the city centre as well as the functional mill buildings and their remaining eye-catching chimneys. The surrounding rolling hills give a rural backdrop to the busy life of the city streets. The Social Services offices reflect the variety of demographic changes taking place in the manufacturing towns of the north. One was located in a purpose-built modern building, another was part of the rambling departments of the main hospital, and the fourth in the town hall of an adjacent small town. Far from being a traditional English city, Northtown is now a multi-cultural society. The glint of a golden mosque roof and the flash of a chuni blowing in the wind against the millstone grit brightens the urban landscape and is a reminder of the presence and contributions of people who have come and settled there and made it their home.

Westshire, with a population of almost 500,000, is a county where the long roots of history are obvious at every turn of the road. Medieval churches, thatched cottages, Georgian houses, Victorian civic buildings and modern industrial complexes are scattered through the villages, market towns, and the small manufacturing conurbations. A number of ethnic minority communities are established in some of the small towns and evident in the Chinese and Indian restaurants, and the shops selling saris as well as the broad range of vegetables and fruits in local greengrocers. The Social Services offices range from community offices which are easily accessible to the local population, but not so easily accessible to researchers, to the shopfront in a main shopping street and the spacious but now partitioned rooms of two Victorian mansions.

Eastshire is a huge county with a relatively small population of around 750,000 with many communities containing families who have lived there for generations. Tourism plays a part in its economy and has a seasonal effect on its housing and employment. Old fishing industries have declined and not been replaced and more modern developments were being pared down during our study. Arable farming dominates the landscape and in the spring a large patchwork of green wheat and barley, of harsh yellow oil seed rape and roadside verges of poppies, cowparsley and camomile make a colourful picture. The Social Services offices are all in adapted buildings and reasonably accessible to the local communities but with differing degrees of office comfort for the staff. Two offices 'moved house' during the course of the study to more modern and convenient accommodation.

Greenshire, with a population of well over a million, is another huge county with a mixture of rural villages, new towns, and pleasant commuter-dom on the edges of a large city. A circular view of the landscape reveals ancient forestland, concrete tower blocks, undulating farmland and pretty villages annexed to housing estates and criss-crossed by frenetic motorways. The Social Services offices are located in a variety of buildings: one of the municipal towerblocks, the top floor of a funeral parlour, and other adapted houses and offices.

Innerborough, with its population of just under 200,000, is an area of contrasts with its southern edge touching modern architectural develop-ments reminiscent of a Graeco-Roman film set, gracious Georgian squares, mixed housing estates and blocks of flats dating from the 30s and 40s. Many streets are a rabbit-warren of small businesses, warehouses and outlets for anything from shoes to sandwiches. Buildings tend to be barricaded except for small oases like a nursery school with a patch of green grass, child-sized play equipment and coloured murals. The Social Services offices suffer in the same way as other public buildings with grills on the windows and reinforced doors and various graffiti adorning the outside walls. One office has a welcoming child-friendly reception space, whereas the other has only a tiny crowded room.

Midborough has a population of around 225,000 with a socio-economic mix. In the research areas there is an air of a well-settled community in well-maintained 20s and 30s council housing and private housing of various sizes, styles and ages. A cricket pitch and pavilion, parks, hedges and gardens, frequent and friendly local buses add to the impression that this is a well organised borough for its local community. Two of the offices particularly express this commitment to the local community built as neighbourhood offices and accommodating social services as well as housing departments.

The third office, in a large adapted building, accommodates three social work teams, which during the study were reduced to two. It was user-friendly and even had a rustic note sounded by the local cockerel at regular intervals.

Outerborough, with a population of around 170,000, could be one of John Betjemin's Metroland suburbs. It still has an aura of more leisured times with its historic church, leafy parks and well-built suburban houses in substantial gardens. Not all of Outerborough fits this description, of course, but the Social Services office reflected a little of that bygone age, located as it is in a large Edwardian house.

To provide further background for the study there are a number of general pieces of information about the research areas in relation to population, child protection registers and children in care. Where possible, information is given for the time when the sample cases were identified.

Table 2.1 **Population Analysis by Age Bands with Social Services Total Expenditure Analysed by Type of Service**

Sample Authorities	Total population (nearest 000)	Age under 5 %	Age 5–17 %	Total gross expenditure (nearest £000)	Expenditure on children (% gross expenditure)
Northtown	470,000	8	18	58,000	21.4
Westshire	500,000	6	16	37,000	13.6
Eastshire	750,000	6	15	56,000	11.9
Greenshire	1,500,000	6	16	127,000	13.1
Innerborough	200,000	9	17	55,000	31.4
Midborough	230,000	7	16	77,500	28.0
Outerborough	170,000	7	15	19,000	15.0

Source: Adapted from Statistical Information Service, CIPFA 1992.

Table 2.1 shows an analysis of the population in each of the research areas and the amount of money as a percentage of the gross expenditure spent by each Social Services department on its service to children. The percentage of children under 18 in the total population in England in 1990 was 20 per cent (CIPFA, 1992) .

There is a marked difference in the proportion of expenditure on children's services in Outerborough and the shire counties and in the three inner-city authorities despite the numbers of children as a percentage of the total population of the research areas being roughly the same.

Because our sample cases are not drawn from the whole authority covered by population statistics, it is not possible to know to what extent black children and those from other minority ethnic groups are under or over-represented in the sample. For the authorities as a whole the proportion of people from minority ethnic groups ranges between almost a quarter in Innerborough to 1.5 per cent in Eastshire.

Comparing the proportion of young people on registers with the percentage of the gross expenditure of the local authority on children's services, Northtown and Midborough, with between 6 and 7 children per 1000 on registers, also spend the largest sums on their children's services. Innerborough also has a large expenditure on its children's services despite a small proportion of children and young persons on registers. (3.5 per 1000 children under 18). The others all had a rate of fewer than three children per 1000 on registers.

Table 2.2 shows the main categories of abuse as rates per thousand population for the year ended 31 March 1991 in the sample authorities. (The research was conducted in only one, two or three of the offices in each area so these rates do not match the research figures exactly.) These figures reflect the research sample figures. 'Grave concern' was the largest category in all the research areas except for Innerborough where the category of 'physical abuse' was larger. Midborough showed a higher incidence of registration for neglect; Northtown, Innerborough and Midborough for physical abuse; Innerborough and Eastshire for sexual abuse; Westshire and Midborough for emotional abuse; and Northtown for grave concern.

Table 2.2 **Registrations to the Child Protection Registers During the Year ended 31 March 1991 shown in one of the five main categories of abuse, and the Total of Children on the Register by Local Authority**

Sample Authorities	Rate per 000 Population					
	Neglect	Physical Abuse	Sexual Abuse	Emotional Abuse	Grave Concern	Total
Ntown	0.1	0.8	0.3	0.1	2.2	3.4
Wshire	0.2	0.5	0.1	0.3	1.2	2.1
Eshire	0.1	0.3	0.4	0.1	0.9	1.8
Gshire	0.1	0.3	0.2	0.1	0.9	1.6
Iboro	0.1	0.8	0.5	0.1	0.1	1.6
Mboro	0.6	0.8	0.2	0.3	1.5	3.4
Oboro	0.0	0.4	0.1	0.0	0.7	1.2

Source: Children and Young Persons on Child Protection Registers Year Ending 31 March 1991 England, Government Statistical Service, Department of Health, 1992.

Figure 2.1 shows the legal status of the children on the registers and indicates that most of the children remain at home with their families without

Figure 2.1 **Legal status of children on registers by sample authorities (1991)**

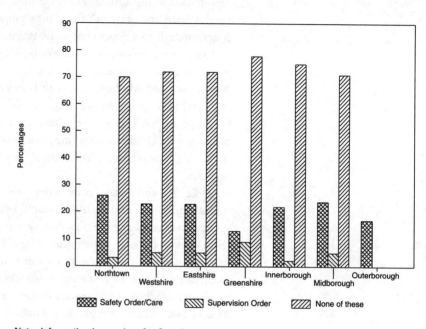

Note. Information incomplete for Outerborough

an order of any kind. Even when there was a Court order the majority remained at home with parent(s), guardian, relative or friend. Greenshire and Innerborough were most likely to have children on registers who were not subject to any legal order, and Northtown was most likely and Greenshire least likely to have children on registers who were also in care. Midborough and Westshire have unusually high figures in the research areas for children returning home under a legal order. (Westshire had a clear policy of using residential care only in very restricted circumstances).

Leaflets

An early observation in the study was the need parents had for written, as well as verbal, information about all stages of the child protection procedures. We therefore ascertained early on what leaflets were available in each authority, as well as information about access to files and complaints procedures. At the start of the study only Outerborough had notices in their waiting-room about access to records and complaints procedures which invited clients to find out more about them.

There was also a friendly notice saying 'If you have been waiting longer than 10 minutes, please return to reception'. All the waiting-rooms had a plethora of notices and leaflets either in racks or on merry-go-round stands, covering every conceivable service from Gingerbread to 'What to do if your child has Sickle-Cell Anaemia or Thalassaemia'. All stocked DSS leaflets, some in ethnic minority languages. Northtown displayed a prominent notice in Urdu, Hindi and Punjabi about how to make enquiries to the social services department. Midborough had a notice saying that anyone wishing to have a woman social worker could ask for one. By the end of the study (December 1991) all the waiting-rooms had notices or leaflets about complaints and access to records. Only one office (in Greenshire) displayed a notice about a Parents' Aid Group.

In analysing the contents of the leaflets produced specifically for child protection procedures, Norfolk Families in Care, a self-help group for parents of children in care or being assessed under child protection procedures, was of great assistance in compiling a list of questions about what they would want to know from the leaflets. They are as follows:

- Will my child be taken away from me? My child has been taken away, how do I get him/her back? What is my legal position?
- What are child protection procedures?
- How do I know what is going on?
- What am I being accused of, and are you labelling me as an abuser?
- What is the list or register and who gets put on it?
- What is a case conference? Can I go to it? Can I have written information?
- Who will help me in all this?
- What should I do next?
- Is there anyone else to turn to apart from social services?
- I want to complain, how do I do it?

The leaflets were assessed on the basis of five standard questions:

- Does the leaflet answer the first list of questions?
- Are the answers clear, straightforward and easy to grasp quickly?
- Is there enough information in the answers given?
- Is there a tone of openness and frankness?
- Are there any implicit or explicit statements in the leaflets as well as basic information? For example, saying that abuse is an offence, or giving reassurance and an intention to help, or that there was a statutory duty to carry out child protection procedures?

In summary, the more leaflets an authority produced the more it was likely to provide answers over the five questions. None of the leaflets addressed the question of the parent feeling accused or labelled, though one acknowledged how difficult such times were for parents. Information was scarce on what to do if the child was received into care or if the child was in care, and there was little reference to what to do if parents wanted to complain, though this was rectified with the separate complaints procedures leaflets produced later. However, all the other questions – about clarity, enough information, implicit or explicit statements – were, on the whole, answered positively.

Three authorities provided straightforward information in a straightforward way which served the purpose, but it was not encouraging in tone. Warmth of language, nonetheless, is immediately recognisable and makes a qualitative difference to the leaflets.

Policies and procedures for child protection

In four of the ACPC Annual Reports there were specific references to the principle of prevention and of the agencies' commitment in those areas to 'preventative work being of the highest priority' despite the climate of economic restraint. Taking account of the diversity of the needs of multi-racial communities was also sensitively addressed. Three of the sample authorities had actively considered publicity to inform the general public about child protection matters and how to seek help, and had issued leaflets and posters. One leaflet was circulated under the auspices of the local free newspaper to every household. This leaflet was suitably low key and informative rather than alarmist. Another sample authority had produced a film for childminders aimed at enabling them to detect signs of abuse and what action to take, as well as guidelines for schools. There were a number of comments in the written procedures about the bonus in understanding gained by professionals when training was in a multi-disciplinary setting.

Each of the local authorities had different ways of putting their child protection policies into action with regard to staffing and organisation. Two had generic social work teams in local social work offices which operated a general duty system. Two had neighbourhood offices, one with specially built offices providing a variety of services to the local community, but with a specialist child care team and duty system, and one with intake and long-term child care team. Three had area or district offices with specialist child care teams and duty systems.

Cases became 'child protection' cases when a referral led to the decision to hold a child protection conference and would continue as such if a child's name was placed on the child protection register and a protection plan devised. If cases were not registered they might be closed immediately or would revert to the status of a child care case and be offered resources on that basis. The decision to hold a conference was taken by the teamleader in conjunction with the social worker, or by the independent chair of the conference with the team leader. The conferences were chaired by independent specialists in three authorities. In one of these, the people who chaired conferences were from the Child Protection Unit; in another area they were child care co-ordinators; and in another area the NSPCC provided the chairperson. The Area manager or District manager (who were semi-independent, in that they were at one remove from the case), chaired conferences in three more authorities, but in one authority the immediate line manager was most often the chairperson. This authority changed its arrangements for chairing after the publication of *Working Together Under the Children Act 1989* to the policy of having conferences chaired by line managers from neighbouring teams.

All of the authorities had policies to address participation in different parts of their children's services, including child care reviews, core groups and planning panels as well as in child protection conferences. At the start of the research study (January 1990) Outerborough, Innerborough and Midborough had established policies, at least in some of their offices, for full parental participation in initial child protection conferences as well as review conferences. Northtown and Westshire had policies for parents to attend the major part of initial conferences and all of review conferences in some of their offices. Greenshire had a policy for partial attendance at initial conferences and full attendance at review conferences and Eastshire had a policy of attendance at a small meeting at the end of the initial conferences but full attendance at reviews.

As the research progressed the issue of family participation in child protection procedures became increasingly the focus of debate in the research areas. This was partly as a result of the research itself and the fact that families and social workers were being interviewed and filling in questionnaires, but also because *Working Together* (1991) stated very clearly that parents and children should be fully involved in the procedures unless there were exceptional circumstances. Therefore the local authorities had to reconsider their policies in relation to the new guidelines.

Two of the sample areas reported:

> *Parents are attending case conferences and reviews in total or in part increasingly frequently.*

> *There has been a vigorous approach to parental participation and our aim is to empower and enable parents within the case conference to participate fully. Whilst we have a long way to go in this objective, we have made significant progress.*

One authority which had not undertaken a pilot scheme of involving family members in conferences sounded a more cautious note:

> *Few of our original concerns about the impact of greater parental involvement appear to have been justified and this realisation has prepared the ground for further steps forward. It is important to be aware, however,*

that at this stage the sub-committee is unable to foresee a time when all
parents will attend the whole of all case conferences.

The 1991 ACPC Annual Reports and Policy documents for five of the seven sample authorities contained positive descriptions of the projects carried out in preparation for increased family attendance at child protection conferences.

Identifying the Families

Discussions with senior child care managers and child protection co-ordinators in each authority resulted in a slightly different method of identifying the families and seeking their agreement to take part. In two areas, as mentioned above, the child protection system and the conferences were managed by specialist child protection advisors and chairs located centrally, and in one of these this service was provided by the NSPCC. In another authority all the conferences were arranged and chaired by two part-time child protection advisors. In the other four authorities, although there were child protection specialists, the child protection system and conferences were managed as part of the child and family social work process.

Arrangements were made for the researchers to be notified of all child protection conferences held after a certain date until the target number had been reached. The aim was to include between 30 and 35 cases from the larger authorities and between 15 and 20 cases from the smaller authorities. It is difficult to predict the number of cases which will reach a child protection conference and in the event the numbers were less even than anticipated. Figure 2.2 gives the proportions from each authority. From this it can be seen that 220 consecutive cases were identified at initial child protection conferences or transfer conferences (8 cases). (In one authority, due to a misunderstanding about cases to be included, a small number of cases involving sexual abuse were omitted.)

Shortly after the conference a letter was sent by the child protection administrator to the parent or main carer on behalf of the researchers giving details of the study and asking him or her if they would be willing to help by completing a questionnaire at a later date, and give permission for a researcher to look at the social services record. Since our main outcome measure would be whether or not the parents and older children were involved in the protection process and the services offered, it was important to obtain their views about the extent of their involvement in as many cases as possible.

In 85 cases (39 per cent) a positive response was received to this letter or a subsequent reminder letter. In 45 cases (20 per cent) the response to the first or the second letter was negative, and in 90 cases (41 per cent) no response was received to either letter.

Figure 2.2 **Percentage of cases from each sample authority**

Sample = 220

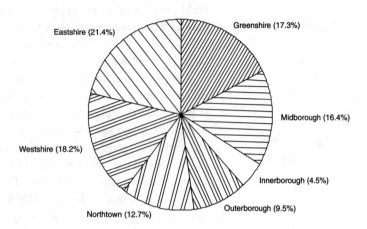

The cohort of 220 cases

Because of the importance attached to having information on a total cohort of cases and yet to gaining parental consent to see any identifiable information in the records, our data on some cases is fuller than on others. The full data set for the cases not involved in the small sample would comprise:

- a schedule completed by a researcher from scrutiny of the case records 6 months after the conference;

- a questionnaire either completed by the social worker and returned by post, or completed by the researcher during the course of an interview with the social worker at the time of case closure or 6 months after the conference;

- a questionnaire completed by the main carer(s).

In some cases questionnaires were completed by young people, non-resident parents or relatives.

The response rate from the social workers was 67 per cent, and in 28 per cent of cases our only source of information was the file. We considered that in 180 cases (82 per cent of the cohort) we had adequate information on which to base our researcher ratings and that in 40 cases (18 per cent of the cohort) the data was deficient in important respects. In six of these cases we had access only to very basic data about the case. The analysis makes this clear and uses a smaller sample size where our data on the remaining cases is inadequate for conclusions to be reached on the issue under consideration. This explains the variation in the total numbers in the tables.

The small sample

Once the data collection process was underway in each area, the conference administrator was asked to notify a researcher of the time and place of child protection conferences. With the permission of the chairperson, and parents who were present, a researcher attended as many of these conferences as possible. Thus the initial criterion for inclusion in the small sample was the logistics of attending a conference at short notice.

A further criterion was the willingness of the main carer to help with the study, except that two cases were included to broaden the range of the small sample, even though it proved impossible to contact a parent. One involved alleged organised abuse where a decision was taken not to tell the main carer about the conference. The other concerned a travelling family. The parents did not attend the conference and indeed their whereabouts were not known at the time of the conference. They reappeared in another borough. Researchers attended both conferences and the keyworkers were interviewed. Of the 33 families in the small sample, two as mentioned did not know of the conference and were not interviewed, and one family refused interviews after agreeing initially. In the remaining 30 families, 28 mothers or stepmothers were interviewed; 15 fathers or stepfathers; and four grandparents and one aunt.

Table 2.3 indicates that the small sample came predominantly from four authorities, this distribution being a feature of the efficiency of the system to notify us of conferences alongside geography which made a difference as to whether we could easily reach the conferences at short notice.

Table 2.3 **Number of Cases from each Participating Authority (Total cohort, small sample, and sample with information from a family member)**

Area	Total cohort		Small sample		Info. from family member	
	No.	%	No.	%	No.	%
Greenshire	38	17	5	15	12	16
Mborough	36	16	8	24	14	19
Iborough	10	5	4	12	4	5
Oborough	21	9	3	9	7	10
Northtown	28	13	1	3	4	5
Westshire	40	18	2	6	12	16
Eastshire	47	21	10	30	20	27
Total	220	100	33	100	73	100

To some extent it also reflects whether or not the main carer attended all or part of the child protection conference since it was more possible to engage family members in the study if we could approach them personally at the conference. Thus one London borough is over-represented in the small sample as is one of the county authorities, whilst the midland county and the northern city are under-represented. We originally did not intend to draw any small sample families from the northern borough, but one parent insisted on being interviewed personally as a precondition for the inclusion of her case in the study.

The proportion of families from minority ethnic groups in the small sample and the main cohort were similar, except that no families were included whose first language was not English. Two were of Afro-Caribbean background, two had one Caribbean parent and one white parent, and the fifth was a travelling family.

In 58 per cent of the small sample cases a child was registered, compared with 62 per cent of the main cohort. Registered cases included two of neglect, seven of physical abuse, four of sexual abuse, four of emotional abuse and two of grave concern. Thus grave concern is under-represented as a category in the small sample and emotional abuse is over-represented, the others being roughly in the same proportions as the main cohort. Thirty-three per cent of the subsample were in the 'severe abuse' categories although none were in the 'severe physical abuse' group. (See Chapter 4 for more details.) Four of these were cases of penetrative sexual abuse, three were in the 'difficult to categorise' severe abuse group, and four involved excessive or repeated physical punishment. Lone mothers were over-represented amongst the main carers in the small sample (64 per cent compared with 54 per cent in the main cohort). There was one case where a grandparent and one where a father was the main carer, and nine cases where the child was living with both parents or a parent and partner.

There were more cases in the small sample where there was no order and the child never left home (70 per cent, compared with 63 per cent in the main cohort). In one case a place of safety order was taken but the child returned home; in two cases a place of safety order became a care order; a child was in voluntary care in four cases, and in two cases a matrimonial supervision order was made. Whilst 23 per cent of the 220 children were in care on a statutory order, this applied to only 9 per cent of the small sample. The main placements for the children in the small sample were similar to those for the whole cohort. Twenty-one per cent lived for most of the period with both parents, 33 per cent lived with the mother only, and 15 per cent with the mother and stepfather or mother's partner. A combination of these factors resulted in a difference between the small sample and the total cohort in terms of the degree of difficulty with which they might have been expected to present social workers who sought to engage them in the protection work and process. Forty-two per cent of the small sample were in our 'best scenario' category (see later in this section for definitions), compared with only 27 per cent in the total cohort, similar proportions were in the middle group, whilst only 12 per cent in the small sample were in the 'worst scenario' group compared with 28 per cent in the cohort of 220 cases.

Thus it can be seen that our qualitative material comes disproportionately from family members where the possibility of working in partnership was higher. However, some of the more severe abuse cases, and some where it might be anticipated that working in partnership would be more difficult were also included. It has already been noted that family members were more likely to take part if approached directly at the conference. Thus a higher proportion of family members who attended for the whole of the initial conference was included in the small sample compared with the full cohort (33 per cent compared with 22 per cent).

The subsample where information is available from the main carer

For some purposes in the report which follows the cases in the small sample are combined with those where we have information from the main carers about the extent to which they were involved, providing a subsample of 73 cases (one-third of the cohort of 220 cases). This subsample differed from the main cohort in similar ways to the small sample. There was a smaller proportion of cases where only one child in the family was abused or alleged to have been abused than in the main cohort; black families were under-represented in this group of respondents and no responses were received from those whose first language was not English; there was a greater likelihood that single carers would respond than those living with a partner, irrespective of the sex of the single parent, and alongside this the main placement was more likely to be with a mother or father living alone than with both natural parents. There were no differences in the type of abuse, or the proportion of cases where the child was registered. However, there was a higher proportion of cases which were registered under the category of physical abuse, and a smaller proportion of registered cases of sexual abuse than in the full cohort. Conversely a larger proportion of parents where the allegation was of sexual abuse but where the child's name was **not** placed on the register was in the parental response sample than was in the cohort of 220 cases. As with the intensive study sample a larger proportion concerned cases which were not rated in the severe abuse categories than was the case with the total cohort. More of the respondents in this group were not implicated in the abuse (36 per cent compared with 30 per cent in the total cohort). However, 38 per cent of the respondents either admitted that they were either responsible or partially responsible for the abuse or neglect. As with the small sample, cases which we placed in the 'worst scenario' group were under-represented (18 per cent compared with 28 per cent in the total cohort), and the main carer was more likely to attend the whole conference (29 per cent compared with 20 per cent in the cohort as a whole).

In addition to the cases where we had direct evidence from a main carer, we had information (from interviews or questionnaires) from children, non-resident parents, or involved relatives about six other cases. We had direct information from 120 members of 79 families—16 children aged 10 or over, and eight children under 10-years of age; 21 non-resident parents (including 11 actual or alleged abusers); two significant relatives; and 73 main parents (a third of the main parents; 22 per cent of the children aged 10 or over; and a quarter of the non-resident parents who might have been involved in the proceedings.)

Collecting the Data

The approach to data collection for the total cohort varied according to whether the main carer responded positively or negatively to the request to help with the study. A questionnaire was sent to those who agreed to help, either shortly after the case was closed, or six months after the child protection conference. In some cases this was supplemented by telephone conversations or letters to the researchers asking for further explanation or expressing an opinion about being contacted by the researchers. Although the original letter was posted by the agency and explained that the researchers were not aware of their identity, some respondents, as may be expected in the confusion and stress of the child protection investigation, were angered by what they thought was a breach of confidentiality. More often, a parent accepted our invitation to telephone for more information, and these phone calls, or the letters explaining why family members were either willing or unwilling to help, were a further source of data about the issues involved in working with family members in child protection. Ten letters were received in addition to the questionnaires ranging in length from one side of notepaper to six sides, and telling us about their family's experiences of the child protection procedures. Eight of the ten were unhappy rehearsals of what the parent perceived as unjust treatment either at the hands of their partner (one letter) or at the hands of social workers (seven letters). Two letters were to say that they had been satisfied with the service they received and hoped they had filled in the questionnaires adequately for us.

The letters and questionnaires were piloted with parents and children known to us who had been involved in child protection proceedings. We were advised at this stage that those who were willing to help us would not be put off by a fairly lengthy questionnaire provided that it was relevant to their concerns. However, we were well aware of the limitations of the postal questionnaires, even when sent to family members who had originally agreed to take part in that they rely on a level of literacy which cannot always be assumed, especially with families whose first language is not English. Translations of the letters were available, and the administrators sending out initial letters were asked to let us know if a letter in a language other than English was needed. Despite their availability none of them was used, nor were we informed of any families where a disability would present problems for written communication. Our attempts to engage families in the research whose first language was not English were not successful. It appears that letters and postal questionnaires are not a satisfactory way of engaging such families in research. Unfortunately no families whose first language was not English were amongst those whose conferences were attended by researchers except the one where the parents were not told of the conference.

When interviewing the social workers at case closure or six months after the conference, we discussed with them whether they would be willing to take a questionnaire to the main carer or the older child in families where there had been no response to the first letter, or a negative response. This produced additional completed questionnaires, some even coming from those who had initially said no to our request. This was not unexpected as the anger aroused by the original investigation in some cases had given way to more positive feelings about the process. A separate questionnaire was used in a small number of cases where the alleged abuser was no longer living in the household. In four cases this was sent to a probation officer who asked the alleged abuser or the person who was in prison on remand or after conviction if he would be willing to assist with the study. In one case a father declined at the time, but said that he would be willing to be interviewed when released from prison. This did indeed take place.

A third questionnaire was designed for use with the older children, with the permission of their parent if they were living at home, or their social worker if they were in care.

We have adequate information from social workers' records, or parents themselves, on 27 parents or parent figures not living in the family home at the time of the conference who were **known to be** implicated in the maltreatment, and a further 25 who were **alleged to be** implicated (52 in total).

We also have information on 25 non-resident parents and 13 relatives (mostly grandparents) who played significant parts in the process but were not implicated in the allegation of maltreatment. It was difficult to contact the non-resident parents, but we had direct information from eight of them, and from two grandparents which offered valuable insights on their views and involvement or otherwise in the protection process.

Table 2.4 shows the extent to which we had direct information from family members. Given the sensitivity of the subject, and the fact that our 220 cases are a total cohort, the response from at least one family member in 79 of the cases (36 per cent) is respectable. Throughout the book we make clear whether our analysis and conclusions are based on the total sample, or on only those cases where we have direct evidence from a family member.

Thirty-one social workers were the prime workers for two cases in the study, eight were the principal social workers for three cases, four for four cases and one for five cases, giving a total of 138 social workers. All except 25 of these (11 per cent) completed questionnaires giving details of their careers and attitudes to family involvement. However, not surprisingly, some wearied of completing questionnaires on more than one case, so that we have detailed information from the social workers about their attitudes to individual cases on only 84 per cent of the cases. The response rate to some of the questions was lower than this. This was a result of the inevitable changes of worker. In some cases the intake worker and the long-term worker completed separate parts of the schedule but in other cases it proved possible to contact only one of the workers, usually the long-term worker, with inevitable gaps in their knowledge about parts of the case with which they were not involved.

Table 2.4 **Extent of data on different family members**

Family member	Information from all sources	Direct information from family members	
		No.	%
Main parent or parenting pair	220	73	33
Children aged 10+	*75	**16	21
Parents not in the family home at the time of conference who were known or alleged to be involved in the maltreatment	***52	11	21
Parents not in the family home at time of conference who were not implicated in the alleged maltreatment	***25	10	40
Grandparents or other involved relatives	13	2	15
Total	385	112	29

   * Includes 3 siblings who were alleged to be involved in the maltreatment.
  ** Impressionistic information also available from conversation with 8 children under the age of 10.
*** Of the parents not in the family home, 9 were mothers or step-mothers and 68 were fathers or step-fathers. This may be an underestimate of the absent parents who might have been appropriately involved in child protection procedures, but information on file about non-resident parents was often sketchy or missing.

Questionnaires and interviews with family members

The questionnaires and guided interview schedules for use with the main carers sought background information about the family, including any previous involvement with the social services departments and any recent experiences of a stressful nature. Respondents were then taken through the various stages of the protection process, and their views were sought about satisfaction with the service, and particularly about the extent to which they considered they had been involved in the decision-making process and the service provided. The covering letter invited the parent to complete those parts of the questionnaire which they considered relevant to their circumstances or to write a letter giving their views on the process, telling us whether they felt they had involved in the decisions. Alternatively, the researchers' telephone numbers were given and respondents were invited to telephone if they would prefer to respond in this way.

Most interviews were tape-recorded. Data on family members in the small sample was collected on two occasions. The first interview was at the time or shortly after the child protection conference, and covered facts and opinions about the early stages of intervention. The second and fuller interview was at case closure or six months after the conference.

Information from the records

A data collection schedule was prepared for the transfer of relevant material from the files. In most cases this process was undertaken by a researcher, but in some cases where the family member had not responded to the second letter, and in all cases where a definite 'no' was received, the schedule was completed by an employee of the local authority, or by the researcher interviewing the social worker with the file available for reference. In only two cases was it not possible either to see the file or to interview the social worker about its contents.

The recording systems and the adequacy of the files both in terms of content and ease of access varied from authority to authority and, indeed, from team to team and worker to worker. However, it was usually possible to learn a great deal from a careful scrutiny of records about how the case developed, how decisions were made, and even about the extent to which family members were involved. The minutes of the child protection conferences were particularly rewarding sources of information about fact and process. In some agencies a separate section was completed about the attitudes and wishes of the family members, whether or not they were present at the conference. Although interviewing the social workers with the file on their desk was a less reliable way of gauging whether certain key procedures were carried out in a way which was likely to involve family members, the researchers asked specific questions such as 'Without giving any names or identifying details, could you read out what it says in the minutes of the conference about the attitudes and wishes of the parents and/or children?' The advantage of interviewing the social workers in this way was, of course, that they were able to tell us of actions and aspects of their practice which facilitated family involvement, but which were not recorded on file. It appears that it is unusual for social workers to record when they have given leaflets or other written information to family members, although some **were** careful to record the giving of leaflets about records and complaints, and to confirm decisions taken jointly by a follow-up letter or in a written agreement.

Questionnaires and interviews with social workers

Two contacts were made with social workers. Shortly after the initial conference there was a telephone interview which served the purpose of establishing contact between the researcher and the social worker to gather basic information about the case, and if there were any particularly sensitive issues about the small sample cases of which the researcher needed to be aware. With the social workers' permission, these telephone interviews were recorded for the cases in the small sample. A questionnaire was sent at the time of case closure or six months after the conference to all those social workers whose cases were not in the small sample. The social work questionnaire and interview followed the case chronologically asking for basic details about the family, which may not have been available in the file, and factual questions about how the investigation and other protection processes were carried out. Questions about the nature of the social work service placed particular emphasis on the extent to which family members were involved in the process and decision-making, and asked about the efforts made by the social workers to engage parents and children in the work. Information was also sought about whether family members were given information about access to records; were involved in the compiling of records; were informed about complaints procedures or made a complaint. Details were sought on written agreements or choices offered about the style and content of social work involvement. Social workers were asked for their opinions about the success of the case; about whether the outcome for the child and the parents was satisfactory; whether they considered that the child had been harmed or helped by the involvement of parents or the child him/ herself, or by lack of involvement; and the extent to which they considered that the parents and child had been involved in the social work process and the decision-making process. Interviews, which were mostly tape-recorded, were particularly helpful to our understanding of the nature of the social work service, and ways in which workers sought to engage family members in the work, or found it impossible or inappropriate to do so.

The reader will by this stage have concluded that our data collection process was somewhat intricate. By confining our study to the 33 small sample cases, and providing only basic information on the full cohort, these complexities could have been avoided. However, for all its complexities, our methodology has resulted in quantitative and qualitative data on a cohort of child protection cases in the context of which the sub-sample of cases where we have information from family members can be set. The researcher ratings have been given greater validity by information and opinion from more than one source in 157 of the cases (71 per cent of the cohort). In 56 cases, information was only available from the social services' file, in seven it was only available from the social worker, and in two the only information available was very basic factual information about the child, the nature of the alleged abuse, and whether or not the child was registered.

Analysis of the Data

Before embarking on the data analysis and coding, the researchers listened to the tapes and read all the questionnaires on some of the fuller files. Key themes around which the data would be analysed were agreed, and the three researchers discussed questions of interpretation and agreed protocols for the researcher ratings on outcome, participation, and whether the child protection conference and registration were necessary. (These ratings will be discussed later in the relevant chapters; and see also Appendix).

Coding sheets and a code book were prepared for computer analysis using the statistical package for the social sciences (SPSS). Apart from basic factual information, the data was post-coded. The three researchers each shared in the coding process, and reliability checks were undertaken in the early stages, as well as discussions about the appropriate coding in cases where the information was ambiguous. Even so, it must be stated that some of our researcher ratings stopped considerably short of 'hard' data. The researcher undertaking the coding of each case also extracted important quotes from either the questionnaires or the tapes, and filed these according to identified themes. Similarly, issues or theoretical points which occurred to the coder were filed under chapter headings for the report.

The frameworks used for analysis

Following our early discussions with child protection workers and family members and our reading of the literature, we devised a hierarchy of family involvement based on Arnstein's 'ladder' (1969). Arnstein's work was essentially concerned with the consumer movement and community work, and therefore we needed to apply it to both practice with individuals and families and to particular circumstances of child protection work where issues of authority and control are to be reckoned with. The following diagram compares the model used for our study with that of Arnstein. Our research outcome measures are based on the second column.

Degrees of consumer involvement	
Arnstein's* Ladder	'Ladder' as adapted for rating of each case
Citizen control	Delegated power
	Involvement in service design
Delegated power	
Partnership	Partnership
	Participation
Placation	Involvement
	Consultation
Consultation	Keeping fully informed
Informing	
Therapy	Placation
Manipulation	Manipulation

* From Arnstein (1969)

We have seen examples of all these except for the first two in the cases studied. Our study was principally concerned with the middle 'rungs' of the ladder. Keeping family members fully informed was a basic requirement if the practice was to be rated as at all participatory, whilst at the top end of the scale 'partnership' **includes** participation, involvement, consultation, and keeping fully informed.

Our major outcome measure, then, was whether or not the different family members were involved in the work and the process. To help us to reach a rating on this we had the views of the social workers, and evidence from their records in a majority of cases, and the view of at least one family member in just over a third of cases. The researcher rating was cross-checked in a sample of cases and there was extensive discussion in the early stages of data analysis. Where a researcher was uncertain, there would be discussion with another researcher at that stage.

Outcome for the child

It would clearly be inappropriate to rate a case as 'successful' if there was any indication that the child had been harmed, or his or her future welfare jeopardised, as a result of attempts to involve family members in the protection process. A researcher rating was therefore agreed in each case for the outcome for the child. Six months after the conference was an early stage at which to consider outcome or likely outcome, so these ratings were especially tentative. Social workers were asked for their views about the outcome for the child, and whether a good outcome, no change, or a poor outcome had, in their view, been contributed to by family involvement, or by lack of family involvement. The researchers made, and cross–checked with each other, a similar rating on the basis of all the evidence. Any subsequent abuse, the child's behaviour, and whether or not there were clear and apparently realistic plans for the child's future, were included in this rating. (See Appendix).

Worst/Best Scenario

It is important to note that in the early stages of child protection work there are few cases where it is **possible** to involve parents fully as partners, many where serious obstacles will be encountered because of the nature of the case, and a small number where even to **attempt** to involve a family member would be inappropriate. We therefore allocated each case to a 'worst scenario', a 'best scenario' or a 'middle' group. Thus if the parents welcomed social work help, accepted that there was a problem, agreed with the social worker about the nature of abuse and the degree of harm, and about the way to proceed to improve the situation, the case was placed in the 'best scenario' group where working in partnership was an achievable objective. On the other hand, if the abuse was of a persistent and deliberate nature, if parents denied responsibility for the abuse, if parents and social workers disagreed about the degree of damage and ways of helping, if parents rejected social work involvement (particularly if they have behaved violently towards social workers or other professionals in the past), the case was allocated to the 'worst scenario' group and even managing to keep family members fully involved could be rated as successful participatory practice.

Although our methodology is essentially descriptive and qualitative, we used the data to explore the different variables and to consider whether any appeared to be associated with involvement of family members. The variables considered included different characteristics of the families; the nature of the abuse or neglect, and the attitudes of the family members towards the abuse and the protection process; the procedures and policies of the agencies and area teams; and the practice of the individual workers. These variables will be discussed in further detail in the chapters which follow.

However, the reader must be aware that the small size of the cohort and the complexity of the variables means that we were unable to hold variables constant. Although we have used chi-squared tests to indicate whether any associations may have resulted from reasons not due to chance, the overlap of variables prevents us from drawing any conclusion about causation.

Summary

- A cohort of 220 consecutive cases which reached child protection conferences was identified from parts of seven authorities, each of which aimed to work in partnership with family members.

- The study aimed to find out the extent to which the social workers succeeded in working in partnership with:

  - 220 parents or parenting pairs who were the main carers during the research period;

  - 77 parents who were not actually living in the home at the time of the allegation but in contact with the child, or who left the household at the time of the investigation;

  - 72 children or young people who were aged ten or over and were the oldest children in the family who were alleged to have been abused or neglected;

  - 3 older siblings of the children who were alleged to have been involved in some way in the abuse or neglect;

  - 13 relatives, mostly grandparents, who played an important part in the care or support of the family.

  Amongst these were 71 parents or 'parenting pairs' who were not implicated in the maltreatment and 216 who were alleged to be or were actually involved in the abuse or neglect comprising:

  - 70 **known** abusers or parents responsible for the neglect;

  - 88 parents or carers who were **alleged** to be responsible for the abuse or neglect;

  - 37 'parenting pairs' where **one partner** was known or alleged to be responsible for the abuse or neglect;

  - 2 parents who were alleged to have colluded with the abuse or neglect;

  - 19 parents who were alleged to have failed to protect the child.

- Data was collected from social workers, parents, a small number of young people, and case files. Some child protection conferences were observed and some managers were interviewed and completed questionnaires.

- More detailed illustrative material was collected from a small sample of 33 cases and was complemented by questionnaires completed by family members. In total we have direct information from 120 members of 79 families.

- Information was collected on a range of variables: about the family; the child; the allegation; the protection process and the social work practice.

- An attempt was made to tease out the extent to which these variables were associated with the involvement or otherwise of family members in the protection and social work process.

- The major 'outcome' measure for this study was the extent to which family members were successfully involved in the work. In addition, there was a 'researcher rating' of the outcome for the child at the six month stage as it would be inappropriate to rate a case as 'successful' in engaging family members if there was evidence that this was achieved at a cost to the child's wellbeing.

- Due to inconsistencies in the content of files there are times when tables and figures are based on totals of less than the 220 cohort cases or the 385 family members. For this reason, a percentage figure frequently supplements the raw data.

Chapter 3   The Parents and Carers

Family profiles

Household composition and marital status

The composition of the families at the time of the allegation of abuse or neglect is shown in Figure 3.1. The main carer was the father in 9 cases (4 per cent), and a woman, usually the mother, in 71 cases (32 per cent). Both parents, or one parent and partner of the opposite sex, were carers in respect of 133 children (60 per cent). Information on the age of the parent was not available in 40 cases. Where this information was known the main carer in 65 cases (36 per cent) was under the age of 25; in 81 cases (45 per cent) the main carer was aged between 25 and 35; and in 32 cases (18 per cent) the main carer was aged 35 or over. In 1989 it was estimated that 1.9 million children lived in single parent households (15 per cent of all children). At 40 per cent the percentage of children in lone parent families in the sample is more than double the percentage in the general population. Figure 3.2 gives the family composition when the child's major residence was with the family after the conference.

Figure 3.1 **Family composition at time of allegation**

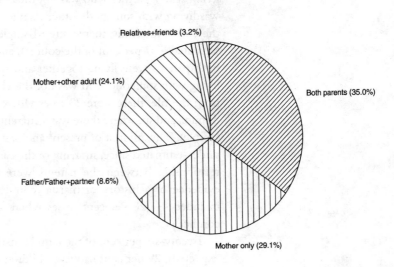

Sample=220

Relatives+friends (3.2%)

Mother+other adult (24.1%)

Both parents (35.0%)

Father/Father+partner (8.6%)

Mother only (29.1%)

Figure 3.2 **Family composition after conference when child's main residence with family**

Sample=177

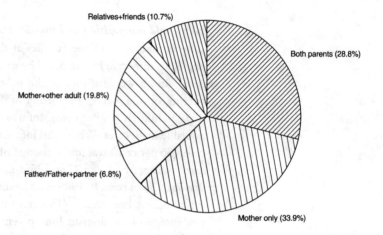

Figures 3.3 give the marital status of the main parent(s) prior to the alleged abuse. At the time of the allegation, 22 were unmarried and living alone (11 per cent), and 46 (22 per cent) were separated or divorced and living alone. In 92 cases (43 per cent) the child's parents, whether married or co-habiting, were living together, and in 48 cases (23 per cent) a parent was married to or living with a partner who was not the child's parent. In seven cases the child was living with somebody other than a parent such as a carer or relative. At the end of the study, there were 81 single parents (26 single, 55 divorced or separated – 37 per cent of the cohort); and there were four fewer cases when both parents were living together and five fewer cases where a parent was living with someone who was not the child's father. As far as could be seen from the file, there were 23 cases where there had been an earlier custody dispute, and six where there was a current custody dispute (17 per cent of the sample). The amount of present and past marital conflict is almost certainly under-estimated since, in many of the case files the matrimonial history and relationship between the parents were not clearly described. There was evidence of a history of marital conflict in 35 per cent of cases. (These included 41 (20 per cent) cases where violence was a part of the marital conflict.)

Twenty-six per cent of the families had only one child (or a first child was expected), 29 per cent had two children and 45 per cent had three or more children.

Figure 3.3   **Marital status of main parent(s) at time of allegation**

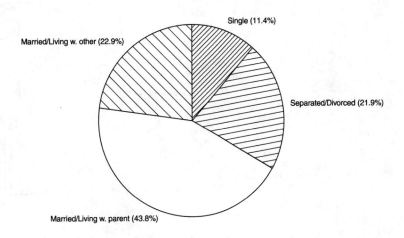

Sample=210

Single (11.4%)

Married/Living w. other (22.9%)

Separated/Divorced (21.9%)

Married/Living w. parent (43.8%)

First language

The racial background of the families will be described in more detail when considering the children. Urdu was the main language of six families, and a European language other than English for two more. In some cases one parent did not speak English and the other did, and agencies differed as to whether an interpreter was used in these cases or communication was through an English speaking family member. It was said that no interpreter was needed in 206 cases. An interpreter was needed but not used in one case, in two cases an interpreter was used on some occasions but not in all contacts with the family members, and in 11 cases an interpreter was needed and used appropriately.

Source of income

Figure 3.4 gives the source of income of the family. From this it can be seen that half were solely dependent on state benefits and/or maintenance payments; 6 per cent alternated between employment and state benefits, and family credit supplemented low wages in 9 per cent of the cases. Seventeen of the 73 parents from whom we had a direct response (nearly a quarter) said that they had had problems resulting from unemployment during the year prior to the allegation. Forty-one per cent said they had had financial problems during this period. In only 36 per cent of cases was income received from

Figure 3.4   **Source of family income at time of allegation**

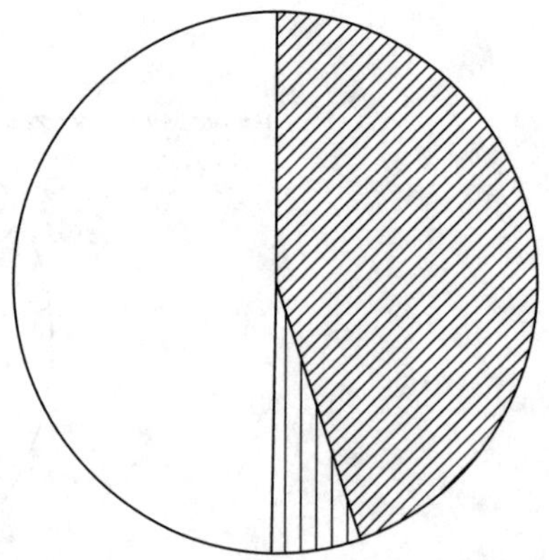

Sample=197

State Benefit (49.7%)

Employment (44.7%)

Irregular Employment (5.6%)

regular employment at a time when, in the population as a whole, the main source of family income for around 60 per cent of families with children was wages or salaries.

Social class

We were also interested to gain an impression of the cultural attributes which tend to be associated with source of income, and therefore asked the social workers to locate the family in more general social class categories. Twenty-six (14 per cent) were described as middle or upper class (one family); 163 (85 per cent) were described as working class. These figures are a reminder of earlier findings that, although upper or middle class families also abuse their children, it is predominantly working class families and those who are dependent on state benefits who are most likely to become involved in the official child protection system.

Housing

In respect of housing tenure, the families were untypical of general populations during this period, where a much larger proportion were owner-occupiers (around 67 per cent). Only 17 per cent of the parents were owner-occupiers. Seven per cent rented private property, and 50 per cent were council tenants or renting from housing associations. Three lived with relatives, nine were in homeless families' accommodation, and there was one traveller family. The details of housing tenure for 43 of the families was not known to the researchers. The families were also at risk of housing instability. Twenty-seven (38 per cent) of the 74 families about whom we had this information had either moved house or had problems with their housing during the previous twelve months.

Other stresses and problems in the family

We were also interested to learn of any other stresses to which parents were exposed, or other problems of the parents which might have had an impact on either the abuse or neglect, or the relationship with the social workers and the professionals. From the questionnaires returned by parents and the detailed interviews, when we were told of stressful events and difficulties which were not reported to us in the social workers' questionnaires, or described in the records, we are clear that the incidence of such problems is under-reported. For example, 37 (52 per cent of the parents who responded) told of a serious loss (by divorce or death) of a close relative during the previous twelve months, and a quarter told of serious illness or accident during this period to one or other parent. A sizeable proportion of families had experienced several adversities in the previous year. For example:

> *In a family with four children there had been a history since 1988 of the parents phoning social services to say that they could not cope with one or other of the children. There had been rigid family patterns for dealing with the children which demanded their total obedience, or the parents would be unable to cope. There had been a series of marital difficulties: the father drinking and frequently leaving home; the mother having a psychotic episode; the father reforming and taking care of her; the mother's arthritis becoming chronic and requiring even more of his care and eventually necessitating a wheelchair. The children seemed secondary to the intense marital relationship. The parents wanted the children removed when things went wrong. The father hit the younger son and cut his lip which led to the father demanding his removal or he'd 'kill him' during the summer holidays when the boy was home from boarding school. Later the focus moved to the daughter when she requested to come into care. The social worker was in regular contact and constantly in communication, but the parents cancelled appointments, became hostile, disagreed, and demanded that the daughter was received into care or they would 'kill her' too. The situation demanded a great deal of patience from the social worker to keep informing and involving them.*

Aggression and violence

In 85 per cent of the 220 cases there was no indication on file or from our interviews that the carer had a history of violent or aggressive behaviour. In

29 cases (13 per cent) there was an allegation of violence or aggressive behaviour, and in 16 of these (7 per cent of the total) this was well substantiated, including one case where there was a conviction for violence. There was substantiating evidence that the partner of the main carer was violent in 25 cases, and there were allegations of violent behaviour in a further six. A previous partner had been violent in five cases. Thus, a quarter of the cohort involved a parent or partner who was known to have a history of violent behaviour. In 61 cases it was not possible to say, but it can be assumed that in most of these any record of aggressive behaviour would have been recorded on file or known to the social worker. It is important to note this, since fear of violence towards a professional worker has often been cited as an argument against inviting family members to conferences.

> *In one family there had been a long history of domestic violence involving the police on several previous occasions. These incidents were usually related to the father being drunk. The parents were separated and there was an injunction against him visiting because of his violence. One evening he came to the family home in a drunken state and was verbally abusive to his wife. He hit one of the seven children and pushed her roughly upstairs, and frightened all the other children who were in a state of undress getting ready for bed. The mother managed to alert her neighbour who called the police. The children crept next door out of the way. Whilst the violence was being sorted out the police took some of the children away on a place of safety order without the mother knowing. She returned to her neighbour's house later to find some of her children had gone.*

Schedule 1 offenders

There were three cases where the parent with whom the child was living was known to be a Schedule 1 offender, and a further six cases where the partner of the parent was a Schedule 1 offender at the time of the conference. These combined to produce a total of nine cases where it was known that a Schedule 1 offender was living in the home at the time of the allegation of abuse or neglect. In most cases the offence was of a sexual nature. (It was interesting to note in our interviews that when social workers use the term they almost always think in terms of sexual offences rather than physical assaults or other crimes against children.)

> *A man who had been convicted of many offences of indecent exposure to young girls was finally imprisoned in 1989 after all possible alternatives had been explored. On discharge he moved in with a young woman and her parents, all of whom had learning difficulties. The young woman became pregnant by him and had a daughter. The Probation Service*

referred the case to social services and a child protection conference was held. The young woman and her parents were unable to perceive any danger to the child and were not upset or perturbed by the offences. The conference decided to review the case each year as the child grew older.

Mental illness and learning disability

In 79 per cent of cases the parents were not described as having a mental illness or learning disability. Nineteen of the parents, and four of the parents' partners, had an emotional difficulty or mental health problem which was described as slight, and 14 parents and ten partners were described as having severe (7 parents and 7 partners) or persistent (7 parents and 3 partners) mental health or emotional difficulty. Five of the parents were described as having a learning disability.

A mother had been causing concern to friends who reported her bizarre behaviour to social services. She had been wearing a white coat, carrying a bleep and telling people that she was a doctor, and then a fashion designer. She said that she did it because she found she got better service for herself because shop assistants thought she was somebody important. One night she left her three children on their own for several hours, and neighbours reported it to the police. This was the incident which led to the child protection procedures and caused her to be admitted compulsorily to a psychiatric hospital. She discharged herself from hospital after a few days and the children went home before the place of safety ordered expired. The initial child protection conference was deferred to enable more information to be gathered. The children were not registered. The crisis enabled the mother to receive help with rehousing, to settle down and to sort herself out.

This case exemplifies the choices which can be made by social workers in cases where the possible harm to a child arises because of mental or physical incapacity of a parent. In similar cases court procedures were initiated.

Substance abuse

We attempted to ascertain whether the parent or partner had histories of substance abuse (including abuse of alcohol). Fourteen parents (14 per cent) and ten partners (8 per cent) were described as having a history of substance abuse, and in 19 cases this was said to be severe.

In a family of five children, the fourth had a serious illness requiring constant hospital treatment and attention which involved the mother staying in hospital with the child. The father had an alcohol problem and had assaulted his wife on a number of previous occasions. She had not complained to the police but her family knew of the violence. Since the illness of the fourth child the father had had to look after the other children and was having difficulties. The house was in an unhygienic state. When he was drunk he became violent to his wife, and an anonymous complaint was made to social services. With a social worker helping, the mother and children left the house and went to a 'homeless families' unit. However, she only stayed there two days before returning to the family home. There had been a social worker working with the family for 18-months providing a range of resources from a fireguard to holidays, but once the child protection procedures were called, and particularly when the children's names were placed on the child protection register, the mother refused to see the social worker, and would not let her into the house. A second social worker who was allocated described the situation as 'a powder-keg'.

Immaturity

Immaturity of personality was recorded in the parent or partner at the time of abuse in 60 cases (33 per cent).

A young 19-year old mother spent four years in care after the death of her mother, when she was 14. Her stepfather was a Schedule 1 offender (sexual offences). Her own baby was born prematurely and concerns were expressed on the special care baby unit about her mothering abilities. Intensive support was given from the unit, the social worker and the health visitor. The mother was not able to settle in her own accommodation, moving many times from place-to-place with the baby and eventually living in a house where there were two Schedule 1 offenders known to procure young people for prostitution. Social services explained to her their reasons for not wishing her to remain there with the baby, and that if the baby was found there they would remove him on a Place of Safety Order. The baby was never found there but the young mother requested voluntary care for the baby eventually because her itinerant lifestyle made it impossible for her to cope with him.

Physical health and illness

The question of the physical health of family members was not well covered in the records and social histories. Of the 73 parents from whom we have direct information, 16 (22 per cent) said they had had an accident or serious ill-health during the previous year.

The separated father in one family had speech and hearing disabilities and when provoked could not control his anger. The mother was placing the children with other carers frequently. Sometimes the baby would be away from home for two weeks at a time. This had happened so often that the other carers thought they had an agreement to adopt the baby. On one occasion the father physically attacked the mother in the street, snatched the 3-year old and ran off with her, and the police had to be called to return her to her mother.

In some cases the physical health of the child contributed to the stress of the parents.

The mother had indicated that she was in need of help by going to her GP, social services, and by taking the baby to hospital three times in the previous six months. No-one had responded adequately to her need. The final crisis came when she knew she was out of control with the baby because he was not feeding properly because of his cleft palate. She put him in a 'cupboard under the stairs' and phoned the Samaritans who in turn contacted social services. The out-of-hours duty system arranged for her to be compulsorily admitted to psychiatric hospital, and the child was removed from home on a place of safety order.

We shall discuss the problems of the children in more detail in the next section.

If these areas of stress or problems were combined, there were only 40 cases where none were reported in the records, questionnaires or interviews, and 100 where at least one of these stress factors or problems was reported to apply in the case of a parent or partner. (Insufficient background information on the parents was available for reliable inclusion of this variable in 80 cases). These factors contributed to a researcher rating of problems of the parents in the early stages of the case. The problem rating for 92 families (44 per cent) was low, that for 78 families (37 per cent) was moderate, and 40 families (18 per cent) were rated as high. (There was insufficient information to rate ten of the families).

Parents' commitment to child

It was evident in our interviews that, despite considerable stress and difficulty, most of the parents were deeply committed to their children. In some cases the extent of their difficulties came in the way of their giving the necessary degree of attention to the needs of their children. In six cases (3 per cent) the researchers considered that from the evidence available the parent was not committed at all to ensuring the child's welfare, and in 13 cases (6 per cent) this was not clear. In around 40 per cent of cases a parent was considered to be committed to the child except at certain times of stress or when incapacitated by mental health problems or addictions. In 113 cases (just over half) at least one carer was always committed to the child's welfare despite, in some cases, the inability for a range of reasons to provide good enough care.

One young mother with a two-year old daughter, Patsy, had a series of complaints made against her in the past by neighbours about the state of her house and garden, and the care of Patsy. Social services arranged 'Home Start' and closed the case in 1990. The complaints had started soon after Patsy's father had left home. In 1991 similar complaints were made again. The housing department visited on a number of occasions and found rubbish piled up in the garden, dog faeces by the back door, the remains of food, fire ashes and soiled nappies in the kitchen and a standard of environmental care which was not acceptable, although the environmental health officers did not consider it to be sufficiently severe to be condemned. The complaints about Patsy were that she was dirty, not dressed appropriately for the weather and not fed regularly so that she was always hungry. Child minding arrangements and an assessment for a day nursery were attempted but did not work. Conditions deteriorated and a decision was made to hold a child protection conference. The issue for the conference was to decide whether Patsy was being neglected. Despite the descriptions of dirt and chaos, mismanagement of finances, and many lodgers and visitors passing through the house, Patsy seemed to be physically fit, developing well in all spheres except speech, and firmly attached to her mother. The conference registered Patsy in the category of neglect and a protection plan was devised which included:

— *Monitoring and support;*
— *Introducing a family aide to achieve what had so far failed and to help budget;*
— *Child minding.*

Following the initial child protection conference Patsy's mother tried very hard to achieve something better at home although she was unsure what standard she was meant to aim at. She and her friends redecorated one room and furniture was made available; the rubbish was cleared, and Patsy had clothes provided and a child minding arrangement once a week. However, the impetus was not maintained and Patsy's mother found herself not coping again and asked for Patsy to be received into voluntary care for a short time. This pattern occurred three times during the following year. On the third occasion Patsy's father heard on the local grapevine that Patsy had been in care. He was very upset and angry to think that he had not been informed either of the child protection conference, or of the occasions when Patsy went to fostercarers. He would willingly have had her to stay with him with his new partner and her children. He had been in contact with Patsy up to six months before the initial child protection conference but had moved house himself and found his visits caused arguments so had stopped visiting. On the third occasion he went to the social services office to complain and immediately found himself involved in her care, contributing to the plan and, ironically, presented with a bill for the two previous occasions when she was in care! Both parents were committed to Patsy and eventually with some mediation and help, were able to work out a satisfactory sharing of her care. Had Patsy's father not taken the initiative to reclaim care of her, Patsy's mother would have needed a more comprehensive protection plan oriented to support and resources to help her cope. Because of the additional support of the father, a less intensive protection plan was arrived at, involving monitoring by a social work assistant.

The extent to which parents were involved in the abuse or neglect

Table 3.1 gives the identity of the abuser(s), alleged abuser(s) or the person primarily said to be responsible for the neglect of the child. From this it can be seen that a male carer was implicated in 54 per cent of cases and a female carer in 45 per cent of cases, sometimes alone and sometimes jointly. (It should be noted that children were statistically at greater risk of being abused by a female since a larger proportion of them lived in single mother households.)

We hypothesised that the attitude of the parent(s) to the abuse, and the extent to which they agreed or disagreed with the social workers and the child protection conference about the degree and nature of the abuse and who was responsible for it, would have an impact on the likelihood of working in partnership with those offering a service. The main carer admitted or accepted responsibility for the abuse or neglect in 43 cases (20 per cent), and partially so in 40 cases (19 per cent). In 66 cases (30 per cent) the main parent was neither an alleged abuser nor said to have failed to protect the child. In 6 per cent of cases the main carer or carers were suspected but explicitly denied being implicated in abusing or neglecting the child, and in 54 cases (25 per cent) they neither accepted the allegation nor denied it.

Relationship of alleged abuser to child

A similar situation is apparent when we pose the question of whether the social worker and the main carer agreed about the **degree** of abuse or severity of neglect. In 37 per cent of the cases they did not agree, in 42 per cent of the cases they were in agreement that abuse or neglect had happened and its seriousness, and in 21 per cent of cases there was partial agreement. In a quarter of cases the social worker and the main carer did not agree on **who was responsible** for the abuse or neglect, but in 57 per cent of cases there was agreement about this and in 18 per cent there was partial agreement.

We combined this information about whether there was agreement as to the nature of and responsibility for the abuse with our information about the difficulties and stresses within the families to produce a researcher rating of the extent to which there would be likely to be difficulties in working in

Table 3.1 **Identity of alleged abuser or person alleged to be responsible for neglect***

Alleged Abuser	No.	%
Mother	65	30.0
Father	65	30.0
Stepmother	2	1.0
Stepfather	23	11.0
Other male carer	4	2.0
Other female carer	1	0.5
Male and female carer jointly	30	14.0
Sibling	4	2.0
Male friend/relative not immediate family	7	3.0
Baby sitter/day carer	2	1.0
Stranger	4	2.0
Multiple	1	0.5
Not clear	12	5.0
Total	220	100.0

*In 46 per cent of cases the alleged abuser was male, 33 per cent female, and in 14 per cent it was a male and a female jointly.

partnership. Each case was allocated to a 'best', 'middle' and 'worst' scenario for working in partnership with the parent. We considered that there were 59 (27 per cent) 'best' scenario cases; 97 (45 per cent) came into our middle group, and 61 (28 per cent) came into the 'worst' scenario group (Figure 3.5). We shall see in later chapters the extent to which our predictions were fulfilled, and whether there was anything about the nature of practice or procedures which made it possible to work in partnership with some families in the 'worst' scenario group, and prevented partnership practice with some families in the 'best' scenario group.

The following case cameos illustrate the variety of ways in which families responded to the procedures. Both were allocated to the 'middle scenario' group.

> *A two-year old girl was referred to social services by the consultant paediatrician because of his concerns at the child's lack of weight gain over a long period of time. Spells in hospital because of gastro-enteritis showed her gaining weight after admission and then losing it on her return home.*

Her older brother had also failed to gain weight at the same age. There was some evidence that the child was not being fed regularly and that the mother did not persevere in feeding her when she did not want it — the mother thought that if she did not want one spoonful, she did not want any food. The cumulative effect of not eating regularly and then not eating sufficiently had made her undemanding and passive. The mother had previously been involved in a programme of handling and learning how to feed her first child at the family centre. She and her husband were angry that a conference was held. They denied abuse or neglect. The conference concluded that the mother did not have the capacity to retain what she had learned with her first child, and would therefore need more input to see her second child through his early years. She was also pregnant. The failure to thrive diagnosis appeared to be because of the mother's ignorance of child care and lack of understanding of the needs of her child despite advice and encouragement from the usual professionals. The consultant paediatrician was certain that registration should have taken place because of his diagnosis. The social assessment from the social worker and health visitor was that the mother was doing her best in the circumstances, and to register would constitute a set back to her. They prevailed, and the child was not registered. The social worker, health visitor and family centre workers continued to offer support and resources despite the parents' refusal to accept that the child protection referral had been appropriate.

Figure 3.5 **Researcher rating of case for potential to work in partnership with main parent(s)**

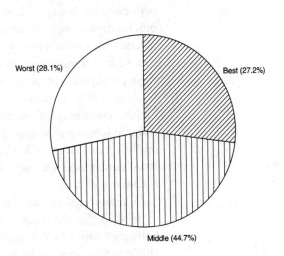

Sample=217

Worst (28.1%)

Best (27.2%)

Middle (44.7%)

A 6-year old boy was still grieving and unable to comprehend the loss of his mother who had left home two years previously. His father and very young stepmother had tried to handle his difficult behaviour as best they could. For example, when he raided the kitchen for food at night, they had erected a barrier over the door-way arch. Undaunted he had climbed up to get over the gap at the top and had cut his toes as he did so. They had regarded that as naughty behaviour and punished him. He had been shut in his bedroom and shut out of the house, as reported by the neighbours. He was under the 10th centile for weight and was always hungry at school. He had stolen other children's packed lunches frequently. He was the same height and weight as his sister who was two years younger. The parents, whilst able, loving and willing to learn, were having great difficulties in handling him. They knew he was grieving, that he had been badly treated by his mother when she was looking after him, and that he had problems, but their response was negative and punitive, and they denied any suggestions of abuse or neglect. The family guidance unit had tried to offer help in the past but had never engaged the family. The intervention by the child protection procedures enabled the parents to agree to help being offered and for the father to be more involved. The child was registered in the category of 'emotional abuse'.

Families where the child continues to live with the person considered responsible for the abuse or neglect

We were particularly interested to know more about the families where the child was living for most of the six months with the alleged abuser(s), or the person(s) believed to be responsible for the neglect. There were 102 children in this group (47 per cent of the cohort). In one mainly rural area 62 per cent were living with an alleged abuser, whilst in an urban area at the other extreme only 30 per cent were living for most of the period with a parent who was in some way held responsible for the abuse or neglect. It seems likely from our discussions with the different areas that differences in these proportions are accounted for by the different thresholds used for the holding of child protection conferences. Those operating a lower threshold for the convening of an initial conference were more likely to include children where a protection plan was not found to be necessary, whilst those operating a higher threshold for entry into the child protection system held more conferences on cases where the alleged abuser or the child left the home.

When more than one child was alleged to be abused or neglected, it was more likely that the children would live at home with the person considered to be responsible ($p < .05$), and this was also more likely to be the case with children who were under three ($p < .01$). Twenty per cent of the children who had not been born at the time of the first conference also remained in the household about which the conference was convened. Other character- istics which marked a difference between those who remained living with the person alleged to be responsible for the abuse or neglect were as follows:

- more boys than girls ($p < .01$);

- living with two parents rather than a single parent **after** the conference ($p < .001$);

- the concern was neglect or emotional abuse (in contrast to only 18 per cent where the allegation was about sexual abuse) ($p < .001$);

- the child's name was not placed on the register ($p < .05$);

- an explanation about the abuse was given by the main carer ($p < .001$);

- the alleged abuser or person believed responsible for the neglect was the mother or the male and female carers jointly ($p < .001$);

- when the carer was implicated in the abuse, he or she accepted responsi- bility for it or did so partially ($p < .001$);

- the case was rated in our 'middle' scenario group ($p < .05$);

- the decision of the initial conference was to take no further action or for the social services or another department to offer assistance but otherwise no action ($p < .01$);

Though not statistically significant there was a trend towards more children living at home if there was an allegation of excessive or repeated punishment and if the allegation was not categorised in any of the 'severe abuse' categories. In 11 of the 15 cases where the main carer was described as having a history of violence, but had no convictions for violent behaviour, the child's major placement was at home. There was a trend towards more children living with a person alleged to be implicated in the abuse if the parents were described as middle-class. Six of the nine children who were living in homeless families' accommodation at the time of the allegation continued to live with a person believed to be responsible for the maltreatment.

Parental attitudes to the child protection process and social work service

Attitudes to allegations of abuse and neglect
The following quotations from the parents' questionnaires and tapes illustrate their attitudes and feelings towards the allegation of abuse or neglect.

The first group describes the parents' view about the abuse or neglect itself. Some agreed that abuse had happened but took a different view from the social worker about its severity or implications:

> <u>A mother</u> *'In my case or family I'd rather have called it cruelty caused by violent temper. I know for sure that because of the nature of my husband's work [long-distance lorry driving] stress caused it.'*
>
> <u>A mother</u> *'It's his [father's] right to hit Mona if she's disobedient. She shouldn't be so insolent to her father. I try and stop my husband but he gets angry because he's frustrated and he has a problem' [mental health].*
>
> <u>A father</u> *'Bringing up two children on my own was difficult as a single male parent, and there were problems with my ex-wife who had been accusing me of not looking after my children properly, which made it worse. Yet she was the one having psychiatric treatment.'*
>
> <u>A mother</u> *'Yes, my social worker and I understood each other but my husband and I felt a small incident had been made a storm in a teacup. Things have settled down naturally but they [the social workers] don't know what's going on under the surface between the children, and my husband and myself. I know it and I'm not saying. The children know it and they're not saying because they don't want to lose their daddy and I don't want to lose my husband.'*

Others accepted that the children were not happy, or indeed were suffering harm, but felt that a child protection investigation was not the way to go about things. These were most often cases where emotional abuse or neglect was alleged, and were often cases which were open to a social worker at the time when a conference was called, or had been in the past. They tended to be in our 'middle-scenario' group. In some cases a small incident triggered a case which was already receiving a service, or was held in the duty system because of repeated requests for help into the child protection arena. Farmer *et al* (1994) and Cleaver and Freeman (1995) have also called attention to the difficulty of handling these cases in a way which the family members can understand, since all too often, if care is not taken to explain that the conference will consider a sequence of events which collectively cause concern, the parental response is 'all that fuss for a smacked bottom'.

The definition of emotional abuse gave ample room for disagreement and was often used when the term 'emotional **neglect**' would be more appropriate and understandable.

> *A father of three children, who was a clinical psychologist, made the point clearly. There was a long history of marital conflict and his wife's depression, which understandably followed the deaths for medical reasons of two children shortly after birth. The mother spoke warmly of social work*

support during this period, and regretted that it was not available when they moved house. The unhappiness at school of one of the daughters and her talking of the impact of marital conflict on herself and her brothers had led to a conference and registration in the emotional abuse category. The father said that he could totally go along with the idea that the children were unhappy and needed help, but that the label of emotional abuse made it all seem much more deliberate than was the case. Both he and his wife knew what the problem was but could not manage to sort things out so that the children would be less unhappy.

Other close relatives were most likely to agree with the social worker about the abuse or neglect. A grandmother said:

I speak with the social worker on many occasions. I phone her. Oh yes, yes it's necessary. Mary, my daughter, just couldn't cope with the boys on her own, not with her illness, plus she doesn't think she's ill. She needs more help than the social worker can give. We clothe and feed them and take them on holiday. It's like bringing up another family, but we couldn't do it without the social worker.

Some, like this non-resident father, accused on the basis of very insubstantial evidence of sexually abusing his 3-year old daughter, insisted that abuse had not taken place, or someone else was responsible:

The worst time of my life was being lied to, forced away from my wife and children, and having the divorce. The second worst time was this case and the thought of not being able to see the children again. My being quizzed by the police was both easy and understandable but frightening at times. Easy because all I had to do was keep telling the truth, understandable because the police have a job to do to protect children. All I have is what I could put in two suitcases and when the house is sold, if it is sold, about £5,000 and, of course, seeing my children every weekend. There are just three questions I'm left with: (1) Was it a genuine mistake? (2) Was it a set-up? (3) Was my daughter interfered with? I think that question three is unlikely. Social services were quite good, but I could have been better informed.

These comments describe the overwhelming feelings of **fear and despair** experienced by some of the parents. The major **fear was of losing the children**:

<u>A mother</u> *'Sheer panic. I just thought I wouldn't have my son anymore, that they'd take him away. I was just all over the place. I didn't know what I was doing, and when I got to social services I just kept saying to her,*

"Where's Nicky, where's Nicky?" I really got paranoid. I just thought they'd got him and they're not going to let me have him. I just thought, "They're not going to take him away over my dead body!" I kept trying to get reassurance from the social workers that they were not going to take him away. She said, "They're going to bring him down in a minute, and they just want to talk to you to find out what happened", but I still kept thinking this is a ploy, and it wasn't until Nicky walked in and I could hold him and I felt secure again. I said to them, "If you're going to take Nicky away from me, you might as well kill me. He's my life".'

A mother *'They were suspicious about the injuries. I was really frightened. It was the fear of being told what I already knew that he'd been abused. In out-patients it was fine, very personal and a curtain, but then we were sent to this ward and once there it was as though all the staff were staring at us. We were taken to a treatment room, no bed, another woman came in to get a bottle, 2½-hours later I decided that we'd waited long enough, and I said we'd go if the final doctor didn't come. We were feeling very uncomfortable and suspected. There was no confidentiality. Other people heard the diagnosis and then there had to be police photographs. When the social worker came, he came in with the police and didn't identify himself. It was appalling, absolutely awful, he nigh on interrogated me. It was the questions he asked, and I wasn't in a fit state to talk to anyone. He was very much accusing.'*

A mother *'Social workers were very rude and I felt that they were accusing me and I wasn't the abuser, my husband was.'*

Others commented about **uncertainty** about their legal rights, and the confusion and anxiety caused when they were not informed at the start of the child protection procedures about their legal position:

A father *'We didn't know what was happening when they turned up at the door; whether we had the right to refuse them entry and what would happen if we did. They said they could have proceedings but no mention of my rights as the accused – never, ever all the way through. No-one explained my legal position or about the child if they were going to take her away from us.'*

The **bewilderment** of parents when the system takes over and they are left without a voice and without any control over the situation also permeated the descriptions of many:

A mother *'I was to be admitted to hospital for a minor operation. I requested for a childminder for the period that I would be in hospital and that started the whole episode. I didn't know the whereabouts of my daughter and the family she was placed with at that period, and I didn't receive any information from the social worker about their decisions on her at the first stage.'*

<u>A mother</u> *'As I was the one who instigated the enquiry, my little girl had an unexplained bruise under her chin, it happened while she was in my boyfriend's care, I went to see my health visitor and it went from there. Incidentally, I still don't know exactly what had happened to her. My boyfriend has always denied bruising her. She was 2½ at the time.'*

Parents' views of the investigation and social work service

Some of the parents were already in contact with a social worker, or made a request for practical help which resulted in child protection investigations:

<u>A mother</u> *'It would have been a lot better if the social services helped me in a way. They were told of my problem about a friend who took over my house, but they didn't help, and that's when the trouble started.'*

<u>A mother</u> *'My social worker came round and said it was a complete mess and what was I going to do about it? I didn't know that was what neglect was. There was no point in saying that I'd spend my last penny on Jamie – that's a bit of a joke to them. She [the social worker] looks round but she doesn't usually say we need to do so-and-so and so-and-so. She did once and when she said it we knew what we had to do. Next time she said "it looks nice". It makes you feel as though you sort of try to cheer yourself up, that she's not satisfied because she's not there to say that it should be done like that, or you should do it like this. She isn't exactly saying "Hm, that's better, you could improve it", but it's her standard and after all she's not the one who's got to live here. It's not how she wants it'.*

This father wished he had received advice and support **before** or instead of the investigation:

Social services only seemed to be involved as a last resort when problems became noticeable. You hear of social services doing work but don't know what they could do for you unless you're referred to them. Although they are there to help, you only seem to get it if you're extremely desperate. If the system had better facilities it might get to help you before things get to a head. If more advice was given to parents to help them with problems before they got to a serious stage things would be a lot better. They'd probably be better off financially as well.

For some families, the social work service was initiated by a child abuse investigation, and took the form of an assessment, in this case based on what was referred to often by social workers and even parents as 'the Orange Book'

(DH, 1988). This mother differentiates between the social worker as a helper, and the assessment process.

> *I suppose they'd call it support, but all they did was come in with their programmes set out. They were always very open, nothing done behind our back. That's when I began to appreciate they weren't just social workers, but also friends. It was more a friendly chat over a cup of coffee. We'd just moved here and didn't know anyone and then we got in touch with our church again, and I made friends there. All the children went to new schools and they've made friends now, and they talk to their teachers. Once I'd got myself sorted out it got back to normal. The social workers observed us, and the children were happy and out playing and it was summer, and some children moved in next door. They [social workers] didn't touch on us as parents. They gave us a couple of booklets on the problems of puberty. We were always seen on our own, no family sessions. It was dreadfully boring and farcical and my husband would say, 'Don't open your big mouth'.*

The frustrations at not being listened to or understood figured prominently in some interviews:

> <u>A mother and father</u> *'These units [residential] don't work. They wrote us off. We were never informed till later that Julie had taken an overdose, nor when she'd been shoplifting. We never had knowledge of her medical either. She was on the pill because of period problems and they took her off without telling us.'*

> <u>A mother</u> *'The emergency social worker didn't listen to what I said. She said I swore about the kids. I didn't. My neighbour said I didn't. I was upset. I got the impression that she thought I didn't care about my kids. She was a bit abrupt and she asked all sorts of questions on the phone [no visit]'.*

This mother and father show how parents behaved strategically, planning out how to give the social workers the right answer:

> *At least this time we got the information before the case conference. Previously no, we didn't actually have a look at the information. If you're seen as defending what you've done you're seen as minimising it not accepting it. It's a bit like a guy getting out of Broadmoor. What he has to do is to say "I'm terribly, terribly sorry about the whole thing. I'll never ever do it again." And he's got to convince everyone of that, because if he doesn't he's never going to get out. What he can't do is say, "No, it wasn't like that, that's not actually how it happened. What's happened to me has been wrong or unfair" or anything like that. Because if he says that, he's*

going to get another four or five years in Broadmoor, and it's very much the same kind of feeling. Also if you try and challenge anyone's preconceptions about what's happening, then you get the feeling as though you're going to be seen as difficult and uncooperative, and all of that, which again is going to land you in the cart. You're in a no-win situation – double-bind. If you say nothing you're sunk, if you challenge you're sunk.

Some parents had more mixed views, with positive comments mixed with suggestions about how the social worker could have been more helpful:

<u>A mother and father</u> *'We never heard from anyone in social services apart from Trish [their social worker] to exonerate us. She didn't have to come round about it but she did. We would have liked a letter of acknowledgement of what had happened, and why social services acted as they did.'*

<u>A father</u> *'It's not easy to apply all the questions to my case. When allegations came about I went to social services A and they got the children on the list. Then I was swopped to social services B while my wife was living in social services C area. Although the work done by the social services B at my end was of a good standard and I was very pleased, there was not a very good liaison between the different offices. My children are now off the register at both addresses but I was pretty disgusted with social services C. They not only refused to let me attend their final conference but they didn't even invite a single social worker from my team's area. I don't think my team leader was too pleased either. I did also ask for minutes of meetings but haven't had a thing. My son had no representation nor was anyone at that meeting [who knew him] and it's my view that the social services C just wanted to close the case and just get on with something else instead.'*

<u>A mother</u> *'Me and the social worker haven't seen much of each other recently. All I'm getting is on my personal life. I call her a Christian. She's on a different level. She's into my private life, not reality. She seems to speak to me as though she's trying to convert me. To begin with it was brilliant and then all of a sudden, if you're not getting on with your boyfriend kick him out. I don't thinks she's a very good social worker myself. She's not into the reality of what goes on.'*

Others could find little positive to say, but had suggestions for a different approach:

I think instead of involving the police and putting us through a trial and the result being my husband was sentenced to 18 months, I think we should have tried to solve the problems and rehabilitate the children sooner.

> *They just said that if I didn't get myself together and they had one more phone call about the children, they would go straight into care. There should be a more friendler talk about things and offer some kind of help.*

Finally, this group of comments shows how grateful parents are when they have an understanding social worker:

> *She was very friendly, a likeable person, constructive and not accusative and it came through genuinely. She made us talk about things that made us think and that really we should have talked about before.*

> *She was compassionate, she listened to us, she was very supportive and understanding, especially over the allegations. She was terrific. We trusted her because when she said she would do something she did. She always phoned and left a message for us and told us when she would be unable to see us because of working part-time or holidays.*

Parents not living in the family home

We have information about 77 of the parents or carers no longer living in the family home or, if still in the home, not taking any active part in parenting the child. This included direct information in questionnaire or interview form from 19 non-resident parents (all fathers or stepfathers). Amongst these were 11 who were, or were alleged to be, responsible for the maltreatment of the child. Most of the 77 parents or carers were men (52 fathers and 16 stepfathers) but there were also eight mothers and one stepmother. They were in three groups: those who left the family home at the time of the investigation and were usually implicated in the allegation; those who had left the family home some time previously and were alleged to have been maltreating the child during contact visits; and those who had left the family home some time previously and were not implicated in the allegation.

Parents who left home at the time of the abuse allegation

Where it was possible to contact these non-resident parents, who were all fathers or father-figures, mostly resident in prison, we sent a specific questionnaire to seek their views. There were six responses out of nine. One of the respondents was illiterate and his probation officer filled it in on his behalf. For all six, the first contact they had about the child protection procedures was with the police. Three thought the police were frank and honest, and three did not. The probation officer commented that she knew that her client did not understand what 'incest' meant at the time, so despite the honesty of the police, her client did not comprehend the reason for the police action. Five of the fathers wanted help and support at the time, but only two considered they were offered it, in both cases by solicitors, one of whom had arranged for a psychiatrist to see his client. A question about who would have been the best person to offer help and support at this time produced three answers: 'a doctor for mental disorders for my wife, no-one for myself' (this from the unhappily separated father); 'I don't really know'; and 'someone who knows about sex offenders and the procedures'.

From our discussions with social workers, parents and probation officers we realised that the possibility of help and support for alleged abusers, particularly for sexual abusers, was rare during the early weeks of investigation and assessment. Social workers we interviewed seemed to have given little thought to a possible role with the abusers, and those who had, or were asked to think about it during the research interviews, said it would not be appropriate. In the few cases where probation officers did attend the child protection conferences they made an important contribution. The view was expressed by the two probation officers interviewed that the service could play an important role at this early stage, but that the emphasis and resources were all placed on their work later on, particularly the provision of group work for abusers in prison and on discharge from prison. They believed that help with practical issues and the adjustment to dramatically changed circumstances in the first days and weeks could improve the chances of work directed at changing offending behaviour at a later stage.

We asked our respondents whether they thought the first contact about the allegation could have been handled any differently. Four thought it could and two thought not. In reply to how it could have been different, the probation officer who wrote on behalf of her client said that he should have been helped to understand what he had been accused of. Another respondent wrote he would have liked 'A more caring approach. I was treated as if I had actually been found guilty.' And a third respondent wrote enigmatically, 'I could have had help when a 17-year old asked a 5-year old to take her pants off', perhaps referring to an occasion in his past when he first started abusive behaviour. Some of these points are illustrated by the case of Melanie.

Jim had been the stepfather of 9-year old Melanie since she was three. Her father, whom she had not seen for eight years, lived in America and Mandy, aged three, was the child of the marriage. Melanie's mother, Jennie, came home from her evening job to find a very distressed youngster who told her that Jim had sexually assaulted her. The police were immediately informed and Jim was taken into custody that night. He was in custody for about 12 months before and after his trial. It was his wife who asked for him to be seen by a probation officer because, although she wanted nothing more to do with him either for herself or her children, she was fearful for his mental health. This was one of the few cases where a probation officer was at the initial child protection conference and was in close contact with his colleague in the prison. The prison probation officer was interviewed for the research and confirmed what Jim had told us on his release from prison about this early stage of the case. As well as being concerned for himself and, as with many such abusers, putting a less negative construction on his behaviour, he was concerned about the practicalities of life such as the income of the family, and access to money in the bank as he was the only signatory for the bank account. He was also concerned for and missing Mandy. The social worker did not consider that it was any part of her role to see him, but did contact the prison probation officer at the request of Jennie. She also said that she did not believe it would be appropriate for her to be in direct contact with him, at least in the early stages, as this might reduce the trust that Melanie had in her.

The prison probation officer commented on the importance of being involved with Jim from an early stage and regretted that this rarely happened and would not have happened in this case if Jennie had not requested it.

Later during his prison sentence and on release, Jim was involved in a group for sexual offenders which he told us he did not find helpful because of the diversity of the group membership (again, a common comment of offenders who attend such groups). After release he was discussing with his solicitor the possibility of applying for a contact order with Mandy.

Non-resident parents implicated in the allegation because of something that happened during a contact visit

Although it is believed to be rare for false allegations to be made by the child, there are indications that when false allegations **do** occur they are most likely to do so in disputed custody and access cases. When the allegation is not made by the child, but the resident parent alerts the authorities to what she considers to be signs of distress, the situation is even more difficult to deal with. On the one hand there is a risk of a child being harmed by contact with an abusing parent; on the other hand there is the possibility of a child being harmed by the unnecessary loss of contact with a loved and loving parent. These three cases illustrate the issues. A non-resident father said:

The social worker took me to the police station in his car. It was just a discussion, just an inquiry. The police officer asked me some questions then he took my shoe laces out and I was locked up for two hours and cautioned. I waited 'til the solicitor came. The police phoned for a duty solicitor. She told me to say what had happened and they taped me. When I got out I was ashamed. I had to go back to work and explain to all my friends where I'd been. It was a shock.

Ted was separated from his wife, Wendy, but had regular weekend access visits to his two children at his parents' home. He felt he had been forced out of the marital home because of Wendy's dissatisfaction with him and that he had 'lost' his home, its contents, the family car, and – after the allegation of sexual abuse against his two year old daughter – both his children because his access visits were stopped. The allegation rested on whether there was forensic evidence of semen from Katy's nappy but the delay in Wendy contacting the police made this allegation impossible to substantiate. Ted was certain that Wendy had made the allegation to finally remove him from the family scene. The lack of access for Katy and her brother following the allegation has meant that they were suddenly deprived of a father and their grandparents. Ted said that he thought it unlikely that any explanation was given to the children by Wendy.

Peter was a very boisterous 4-year old who lived with his mother in homeless families' accommodation. There had been previous allegations of neglect, largely due to lack of supervision. Peter stayed with his father from time to time in order to give his mother a break. When he returned home with a bruised bottom, the mother reported this to the social services department with whom she was already in contact. The police were notified of the complaint and Mike, the father, was interviewed. He denied smacking Peter, at least heavily enough to cause a bruise, and said that he thought that his ex-wife was always hitting Peter but that he could understand this as Peter was such a handful. At the child protection conference the police officer said that it was very difficult to come to any conclusion and that no charges would be pressed. The mother was present at the conference but the father was not invited. It was not until about two months after the conference that a letter was sent to him telling him of the conclusions. The social worker did not have any direct contact with him, other than a phone conversation. During the research interview the worker said that on reflection he thought that it would have been useful to have interviewed Mike at an earlier stage as he would have learned more about the family which might have been helpful in the provision of longer-term support.

It was difficult with such small numbers to reach conclusions about what usually happened if no evidence was found to support allegations of abuse by non-resident parents. Only two respondents received information that the case had been closed in these circumstances. None of the six knew how to complain had they wished to. One respondent knew that social services kept a written record of what had happened and none knew what happened to those records subsequently. This information would be particularly important for those against whom the allegation was unsubstantiated.

Non-resident fathers not implicated in the abuse

Some of these non-resident parents had not been in contact with their children for many years, whilst others were in regular contact. It was rare for such parents to be contacted early in the investigation stage and to be invited to the child protection conference. There are, indeed, some difficulties about this in that much of the information given to the conference will be confidential information about the daily life of the parent caring for the child, and perhaps her present partner. However, some workers and conference chairs did demonstrate that it was possible to involve absent partners in the conferences and also retain confidentiality.

> *Susie suffered a mental breakdown during her first year at university and could not complete her course. Over the next ten years during her periods of recovery she lived with three different partners and had three children. A child protection conference was held on her last baby because Susie's partner, the father of the baby, was suffering from a psychotic illness and had threatened to kill the baby. Susie left him and moved house and area so the case was transferred into the research area. The social worker allocated to the case was concerned because of allegations made by Susie to the children that their fathers were not their real fathers. The older two children were becoming confused and unhappy. A transfer child protection conference on all three children was held. There was regular access to their fathers by the older two children and supervised access for the father of the baby. All three fathers were invited to the conference and they attended. Separate waiting areas were arranged for them and they were invited to that part of the conference which considered their child, thus preserving confidentiality but allowing maximum participation within the parameters of the confidential information.*

For the more serious cases, especially when children went into care and there were court proceedings, the pattern was for the non-resident parent to be contacted some time during the assessment stage.

> *Three boys were removed from their mother's care when one told a casualty officer that the serious burn on his arm had been deliberately inflicted by his mother with an iron. The father was a caring parent in regular contact with his sons, aware of the stresses within the family, and wanting to do all he could to support the children remaining with their mother. He was not present at the child protection conference, but was subsequently contacted when the children were in care.*

The implications of the Children Act 1989 should mean that non-resident parents are involved earlier in such cases, and invited to play a fuller part in the earlier planning.

Parents who had been away from the family home for several years and were not apparently in contact with the children were rarely involved in the investigation or assessment. However, to return to the case of Melanie described earlier:

> *After discussions with the social worker, Jennie and Melanie decided that it would be appropriate to contact her father in America. This resulted in letter and telephone contact between him, Jennie and Melanie, and there was also phone and letter contact between the father (who still had parental responsibility as Melanie had not been adopted by her stepfather) and the social worker. Melanie decided to revert to using her legal name and was hopeful of having some contact with her father.*

There were important issues also for children in the family who were not alleged to have been abused, but who lost a father as a result of the allegation.

> *Mandy lost a father overnight when Jim went into custody. Although the conference expressed concerns about whether she had been abused, and concluded that she had not, no concern was expressed at the impact on her well-being of suddenly losing a father who had been a significant and, as far as one could tell, appropriately loving and caring parent figure to whom she was attached. She had not seen him since going to bed on the night when the abuse of her sister came to light.*

The extended family

At some stage during the investigation or the first six months after the conference, 18 of the children (8 per cent) lived with a relative or friend, and a further nine lived with a parent at the home of a relative or friend. These case cameos show the extent of involvement of some members of the extended family.

> *A paternal aunt who had brought up two children of her own on her own, and knew the difficulties of lack of money and support, offered care and resources to the mother as well as the children. She was the only one in the family to commit herself to the children in the foster home by visiting two or three times a week and considering custodianship or guardianship. She had been involved and participated throughout—at case conferences and reviews, contacting foster carers and social worker. She had high commitment to the children. The mother became more settled and asked for the return of children. The participatory practice of the social worker had created an atmosphere for sharing decisions and the care of the children.*
>
> *A 10-year old girl was diagnosed as suffering from gross vulvitis. Her mother suspected her father of sexual abuse on access visits. The child was*

sensitively helped through investigative interviews by social services and police. The mother was very upset by events and the implications, and in need of support. The social worker phoned every time there was an interview to check how everything was. With the mother's agreement the social worker saw the maternal grandparents and the mother's sister to explain what had happened so they could support the family as much as possible too. At the mother's request the social worker also contacted the local Roman Catholic priest who knew the family well.

A mother alleged to her health visitor that she thought her separated husband had sexually abused her 4-year old daughter. There was an acrimonious divorce in process. The husband's parents were very supportive of him and the children, and there were long letters on file offering the same weekend access arrangements for the father as had previously been in existence, but at their home. They pointed to the wife's role in the situation: how she wanted the divorce, and her husband out of the house. As they saw it, the mother gained the house, the contents, the car, the children, and their son was left with nothing. The allegation of sexual abuse was the last straw. They asked for 'fairness': that if he was investigated by the police then so should she (this eventually happened, influenced by their letter); that if she had a visit from a social worker then so should he (this was done by phone rather than face-to-face). Had the father not had such an articulate mother (she had been a local councillor) who wrote and contacted social services on his behalf, he may well not have fought for continued contact. He was so shocked by the allegations and appeared to be helpless once his access to the children was stopped. His parents' insistence on participating and being sure that he was treated fairly added another dimension to the picture when it was first presented to social services, and cast doubts on the mother's allegation. The investigation could find no indication from the child of abuse and the decisions were handed over to the Matrimonial Court to resolve.

We have no way of knowing in how many other cases members of the extended family might have had a role to play if they had been encouraged to do so. Our study suggests that the encouragement given by the Children Act 1989 to greater involvement of members of the extended family may pay dividends.

Summary

- This chapter gives detailed information about the family composition and characteristics, and the views of the family members about the child protection system, and the social work service.

- At the time of the allegation 60 per cent of the children were living with both parents or a parent and step-parent.

- For 80 per cent of the index children (the oldest child known or alleged to be abused) the major residence during the six months following the conference was with at least one parent. In 39 per cent of these 177 cases the child lived with a single parent.

- Forty-seven per cent of the children lived for all or most of this time with at least one person who was alleged to have been implicated in the maltreatment. A male carer was alleged to be implicated in the maltreatment in 34 per cent of cases, and a female (sometimes jointly) in 45 per cent of cases.

- In only 36 per cent of cases was income received from regular employment of one or both parents.

- All social classes were represented, but 85 per cent were described by social workers as 'working class' and a quarter of the cohort were on the fringes of society with little hope of gaining employment.

- In 14 families at least one parent was not fluent in English and an interpreter was needed, though not always provided. Both parents of the index children were white in 81 per cent of the families, both parents were from a minority ethnic group in 12 per cent of cases, and 6 per cent of the children were of mixed race parentage.

- Files were unreliable sources of information on family circumstances in the year prior to referral, but half of the parents who responded described a serious loss by death or divorce in the preceding year and a quarter told of serious accidents or illness.

- In about a quarter of the families there was a history of aggressive behaviour. There were nine cases where a parent had a Schedule 1 conviction for a physical or sexual assault on a child.

- Mental health problems, substance abuse, immaturity of personality or learning disability featured alone or in combination in at least half of the family histories. (This figure is almost certainly an underestimate due to poor recording of family histories).

- Difficulties in the family and the extent of agreement with the social worker about extent and responsibility for maltreatment were combined to produce a 'researcher rating' of the likelihood that it would be possible to work in partnership with the different family members. Twenty-seven per cent were allocated to a 'best scenario' group; 45 per cent to a 'middle' group, and 28 per cent were in a 'worst scenario' group.

- The reactions and attitudes of the main parents, the children, non-resident parents (including alleged abusers) and significant relatives to the allegation of abuse and the protection and social work process are described in detail.

- The opinions expressed confirm the findings of other consumer studies of child care social work. All family members stressed the importance of being cared about as people. They could understand that the professional had a job to do, and that procedures were necessary but strongly objected to workers in whatever profession who did not appear to listen, did not show warmth or concern, and 'just did things by the book'. These opinions were common to parents who were implicated in the abuse and to those who were not.

- We were left with the clear impression that a sizeable proportion of these families could more appropriately have been helped at an earlier stage without the need for the child protection system. Earlier requests for help had been brushed off by a low level response or none at all. When the cases came into the system services were provided which were often warmly welcomed by parents and children, provided that the worker managed to break through the hostility or anxiety which most felt to the child protection system.

- The satisfaction of family members with the service is inextricably merged with the way they were treated as people, and the extent to which they were informed and involved in the process. This issue is explored in detail in the chapters which follow.

Chapter 4

The Children

Background characteristics

The description which follows of the 220 index children who made up the cohort of consecutive cases is of interest because it gives a more detailed picture of day-to-day child protection work than is normally available in annual reports or Department of Health statistics. Where appropriate, data will be compared with statistics from the local authorities from which the sample was drawn, and with Department of Health statistics. It should be noted that these cases are a small proportion of the total child protection workload in that only those cases which actually reached a child protection conference have been included. Gibbons et al. (1994) have estimated that cases reaching conferences are only about 25 per cent of the total number of cases where a child protection referral is made. Our sample areas were selected to include urban and rural areas, and we would expect the cases included in the cohort to be representative of those which occur in routine child protection work. Any bias in our sample because of our selection methods will occur in the way in which the agencies and social workers worked with the cases, rather than with the cases themselves, since we specifically selected areas which were making serious attempts to work in partnership with family members.

The main focus of our study was on the extent to which parents and children were involved in the protection process and the social work and other services offered. For that reason, if more than one child in a family was the subject of protection procedures, we identified the oldest child who was alleged to have been abused or neglected as the index child to be studied. In a quarter of the cases there was only one child in the family, in 30 per cent there were two children, in a quarter there were three children, and in 20 per cent of cases there were four or more children (Figure 4.1). Not all of the other children were alleged to have been abused, however. In three-quarters of the cases only one child was alleged to have been abused compared with a quarter in which two or more children were the subject of the protection procedures. Five conferences were in respect of unborn children (Figure 4.2)

Thirteen per cent of the index children were under one year of age at the time of the conference, 20 per cent were aged between one and four, a third were aged between five and eleven, and almost a third were twelve or over at the time of the conference (Figure 4.3). Fifty-six per cent were girls and 43 per cent were boys.

The proportion of children from minority ethnic groups is higher than the 9 per cent for the population of children under 18 in England and Wales as a

Figure 4.1 **Number of children in family**

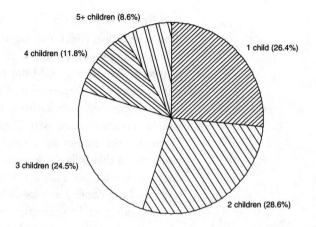

Sample = 220

Figure 4.2 **Number of children alleged to be maltreated**

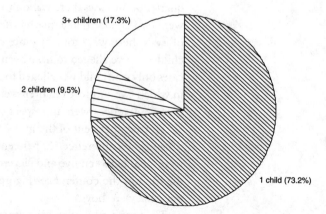

Sample = 220

Figure 4.3 Age of index child at time of allegation

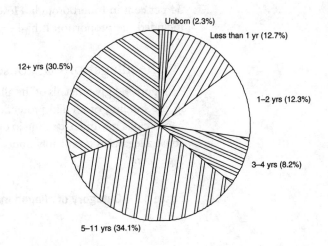

Sample = 220

Unborn (2.3%)
Less than 1 yr (12.7%)
12+ yrs (30.5%)
1–2 yrs (12.3%)
3–4 yrs (8.2%)
5–11 yrs (34.1%)

whole, and children of mixed racial parentage appear to be particularly over-represented (the latest known statistics on children of mixed race parentage for the population as a whole is about 1 per cent). Both parents of the index child were white in 81 per cent of cases, both were black or of another

Table 4.1 Ethnic origin of children

Ethnic Origin	Number	%
White British	178	81
African Caribbean	9	4
African	5	2
Indian	1	0.5
Pakistani or Bangladeshi	7	3
Middle Eastern	1	1
1 Caribbean, 1 white parent	7	3
1 South Asian, 1 white parent	4	2
1 East Asian, 1 white parent	3	1
Mixed race parentage, both parents black	3	1
Not known	2	1
Total	220	100

minority ethnic group in 12 per cent of the cases, and in 14 cases (6 per cent) the children had one black and one white parent (Table 4.1). The proportion of people from minority ethnic groups in the authorities studied at the time of the research was 14 per cent, and varied between 1 per cent in Eastshire to 34 per cent in Innerborough. However, if only young people under 18 were included the proportion is higher (OPCS, 1993).

The allegations of abuse or neglect

Figure 4.4 gives details of the allegation of abuse or neglect which resulted in the holding of a child protection conference. We should note here that because of a misunderstanding in one of our authorities, the number of sexual abuse allegations is probably under-estimated to the extent of between 1 and 2 per cent.

Figure 4.4   **Category of alleged maltreatment (main categories only)**

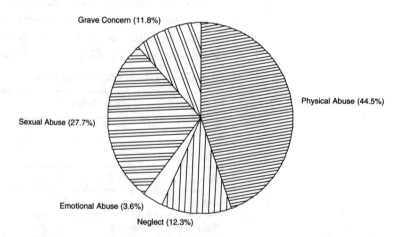

The initial conference led to the names of 61 per cent of the children being placed on the child protection register, and in 35 per cent of the cases a decision was taken not to register (Figure 4.5). This need not necessarily mean that the child had not been abused or neglected, but rather, following the Department of Health guidelines, that conference members concluded that an interagency plan under child protection procedures was not needed. In eight cases the conference members decided to defer a decision about registration, and in two of these the child was subsequently registered resulting in a registration total of 137 (62 per cent). The registration rates varied between authorities, with Middleborough and Outerborough registering 41 and 43 per cent respectively, and the others registering between 66 and 71 per cent. It should be noted that the registration rate is affected by the ease or difficulty with which cases cross the threshold to a child protection conference as well as the nature or severity of referrals and the interpretation placed by conference members on the criteria for registration.

Figure 4.5   **Decision of initial conference on registration**

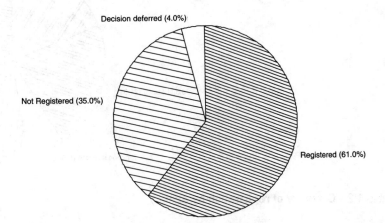

It can be seen from Figures 4.4 and and 4.6 that the discussion in the conference led to changes in the way the abuse or neglect was perceived, the main effect being that a higher proportion of the registered cases was included in the 'grave concern' category after the conference than at referral. Some agencies only used this category alongside another more specific one so that the registration would be in terms of 'grave concern' of sexual abuse or neglect, whilst others used it as a more free-floating category without stating specifically in the conference minutes exactly what form of abuse or neglect they were gravely concerned about. In one of our sample agencies this category was not in use and it should be noted that 'grave concern' is no longer used following the 1991 version of 'Working Together'. The proportion of cases referred in the 'grave concern' category ranged from between 0 and 3 per cent in Innerborough, Greenshire and Middleborough to 11 and 22 per cent in Eastshire and Midshire.

Table 4.2 gives the **registration** categories for the cohort of children in the different agencies. Whilst there are many different reasons for differential rates of holding conferences, as discussed above, one would expect fewer differences between agencies in using the criteria for registration in the 1988 version of *Working Together* in use at the time.

Figure 4.7 gives the proportion of children registered under different categories for the sample agencies as a whole and in England. It can be seen that the proportions in our study are similar except for a much higher

72

Paternalism or Partnership?

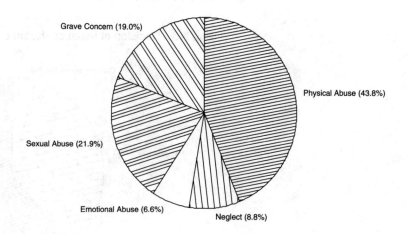

Figure 4.6 **Categories of maltreatment of registered children (main categories only)**

Sample = 137

Table 4.2 **Category of registration by agency**

(n = 137 registered cases)

Category	Ntown		Wshire		Eshire		Gshire		Iboro		Mboro		Oboro	
	No	%	No	%	No	%	No	%	No	%	No	%	No	%
Physical	14	74	12	41	5	19	13	42	5	71	6	40	6	67
Neglect	2	11	2	7	2	7	3	10	0	0	3	20	0	0
Emotional	0	0	1	3	2	7	5	16	0	0	1	7	0	0
Sexual	1	*5	4	14	12	44	6	19	2	29	2	13	2	22
Grave concern	2	11	10	34	6	22	4	13	0	0	3	20	1	11
Total	19	100	29	100	27	100	31	100	7	100	15	100	9	100

*This percentage (Sexual – Ntown) is slightly lower than it should be due to a misunderstanding about whether cases of sexual abuse should be included.

percentage nationally in the 'grave concern' group, and consequent reductions in physical and sexual abuse categories. (Similar proportions have been found by Gibbons et al. (1994) in a much larger study of registers). In each area, except for Innerborough, 'grave concern' registrations are underrepresented in our sample. This may be because, when we collected our data towards the end of 1991, agencies had already started to make less use of this category having realised that it was likely to be removed from the Department of Health categories.

Figure 4.7 **Categories of maltreatment of registered children (England)**

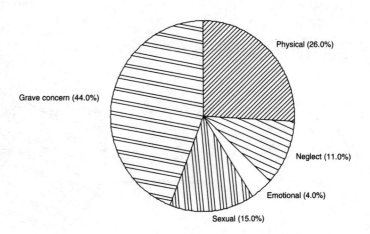

Severity ratings

It seemed also important to consider in respect of this cohort, which we believe to be representative of child protection work, whether the allegations were of a more or less severe nature. This is not to imply that **any** form of abuse or neglect does not have adverse consequences for the children concerned, but rather to paint a realistic picture of the extent to which it might be possible to work in partnership when the allegations are of a severe nature. Figure 4.8 shows that 130 of the cases (60 per cent) did not come into the severe abuse categories, but 29 per cent were considered to be cases of severe abuse, whilst 11 per cent came in the category of excessive or repeated physical punishment. In our discussion with parents and social workers we found a distinction was made between physical abuse which resulted from a hostile attack on the child with the intention of causing harm, or a loss of control, and physical harm which was caused when the intention was to punish the child, in the belief that this was appropriate parenting behaviour. It was suggested to us that there might be differences in the way parents viewed the child protection process and were enabled or otherwise to take part in the protection process when the allegation was of physical punishment. Figure 4.9 shows that agencies varied in the proportion of severely abused children registered from 15 per cent in Outerborough to 45 per cent in Westshire. The proportions of sexual abuse cases were similar in each area. (The proportions in Innerborough are unreliable because of the small total number.) The proportions where excessive punishment was the reason for registration varied from 0 per cent in Greenshire to 30 per cent in Northtown.

Figure 4.8 **Severity of alleged abuse**

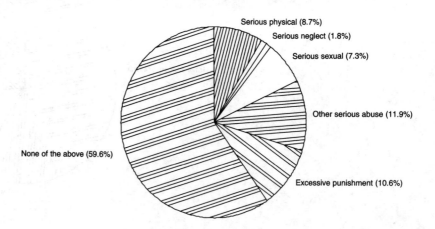

Sample = 218

Serious physical (8.7%)

Serious neglect (1.8%)

Serious sexual (7.3%)

Other serious abuse (11.9%)

Excessive punishment (10.6%)

None of the above (59.6%)

Figure 4.9 **Severity of alleged abuse by agency. N = 218 index children**

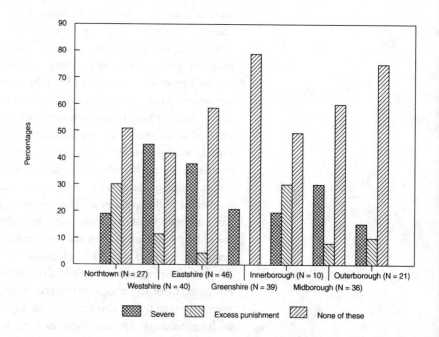

Percentages

Northtown (N = 27)   Eastshire (N = 46)   Innerborough (N = 10)   Outerborough (N = 21)

Westshire (N = 40)   Greenshire (N = 39)   Midborough (N = 36)

Severe   Excess punishment   None of these

Some examples of the cases from each of these categories will illustrate the ratings.

The child who died was resident in the sample authority for the major part of his life. His mother and father were separated and his care was the responsibility mainly of his mother, although he had regular contact with his father. She took the child away on holiday for three weeks to another area and whilst there he was physically and sexually abused and died as a result of his injuries. (A man was charged with murder and the mother with wilful neglect). A child protection conference was held in the other area and the child was registered after his death. The mother returned to her home in the sample authority and a transfer conference was held because of future concerns were she to have another child in her care. The conference recommended counselling to be offered to both mother and father.

The 'serious injury' category included skull fractures or multiple fractures. Most such injuries were to babies. So, for example, one baby had a fractured skull; and twin babies, one a fractured skull and the other fractured ribs and tibia; another baby had a fracture of humerus, petechial bruising on the neck, face, under the eyes, and at the wrists; and another baby had a fractured wrist and ankle.

The 'moderate injury' category included single fractures of the limbs or burns and included a child scalded on a small area of her arm caused deliberately by her mother's boyfriend; a two-year old with bruising to the left ear and hairline fracture above the ear; a three-year old with a series of bruises to the face and arms where the father admitted to picking her up by her cheeks; and a two-month old with a spiral fracture of the right humerus.

The category of 'persistent or deliberate' abuse included an unborn baby of a Schedule 1 offender, and two older girls aged five and ten of a previous marriage now in his family, where the Schedule 1 offender had been charged with causing 23 areas of bruising on his 6-month old baby of his previous partnership; and a 10-year old boy with severe bruising to the leg inflicted by both his mother and his father, together with an allegation that he was made to eat his meals from the floor like a dog.

The 'severe neglect' category included two children of one and two who were failing to thrive being left alone at night, whose mother was illiterate and unable to keep the house in a satisfactory condition to provide for the children; and three children of six, two and one being left alone during the day and night with the oldest child described in terms of 'frozen watchfulness'.

The category of 'penetrative sexual abuse' depended on an unambiguous statement from the children or a medical diagnosis. The presenting symptoms were varied. For example, it included a 9-year old with gross vulvitis and no hymen who eventually disclosed that her father had been sexually abusing her; a 16-year old who told a friend that her father was sexually abusing her; a 4-year old with a sore vagina who was found at medical examination to have been penetrated; and five children in one family who, with their mother, were systematically abused and terrorised by their father.

The category of 'other serious abuse' included three children who came downstairs one night and wrecked the kitchen. Their mother was stressed and ill and hit the 8-year old boy about the head with a shoe, washed his mouth out with soap, and then put all three children outside in the garden; two boys of 6 and 8 who had severe bruising on their legs where they had been hit by their father with a slipper; and a very small 1-year old baby failing to thrive but thought to have a deficiency in growth hormones. When admitted to hospital she put on two pounds in a week.

The 'excessive or repeated punishment' category was added to distinguish what might be cultural difference or differences of opinion about the discipline of children. It included a 13-year old boy who exposed himself to his mother's friend so his mother hit him repeatedly with a slipper; a 10-year old boy hit with a bamboo cane; two girls of 12 and 5 hit with a leather belt.

The remaining category of 'none of these' has by far the greatest number of cases in it and these included a 15-year old slapped by her father in temper who fell against a door handle; two children of one and four caught between their fighting parents who were having a violent argument; the sexualized behaviour of a 6-year old girl after access visits to her father but for which no clear reason could be identified; and a 4-year old with a bruised bottom.

Problems or disabilities of the children

We were also interested to know whether the child had any particular difficulties prior to the conference. We have already mentioned that five of the children were about to be born to a parent who had seriously abused or neglected previous children, or was believed to have done so. Thirteen children were in voluntary care at the time of the conference.

Figure 4.10 show that in 118 cases (just over half) the child was described as having no problems or only mild problems or difficulties at the time of the conference. However, 35 (16 per cent) had behaviour problems and 31 (15 per cent) had emotional problems. Others had a learning disability, or a health, growth or nutrition problem.

Social worker *'There was no real discipline, no real idea of the children's needs. They [the parents] couldn't cope with the rebelliousness of the children so the children became totally unruly. They were referred to the family centre to give them an understanding of handling. They did attend, but didn't learn much. They certainly did everything they were asked. They tried half-heartedly and then gave up. They were just not capable. It got to the stage where the children were really unruly and school were having a really hard time. The bruise was the reason we decided to conference.'*

Figure 4.10   **Problems of children at or prior to allegation**

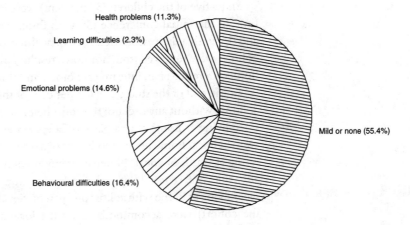

Figure 4.11   **Contact with social services department prior to this allegation**

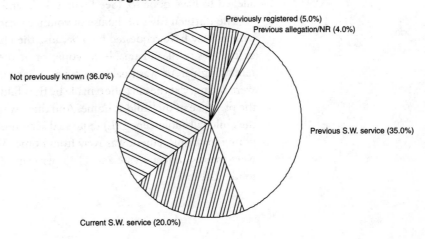

In 19 cases it is known that there had been a previous allegation of abuse, or neglect and the child was known to have been previously registered in ten of these. Support services had been or were being offered, either because of concern about abuse or neglect, or for the purposes of offering support to the family in 64 per cent of the cases, and one in five of the children or families was receiving social work services at the time of the abuse or neglect allegation (Figure 4.11). Fourteen children were subject to supervision orders at the time of the allegation, and three were wards of court. One was living at home under the terms of a care order. Many of the children, along with their parents, suffered deprivations resulting from low income, poor housing, and the loss of people, including fathers or mothers, who were close to them.

Placement of the children and legal status

Sixty-five of the children (30 per cent) were living away from home at the time of the initial conference (39 with foster parents, 11 in residential care, and 15 with relatives or friends). Forty-three of these (20 per cent of the cohort) were removed from home as a result of place of safety orders, four left home as a result of an interim care order, and three as a result of a care order.

At the end of the study, 139 (63 per cent of the whole sample) were living at home without any order of the court being sought during this period, nine were living at home after a place of safety order was allowed to lapse, seven were living at home under conditions of a supervision order, and nine were at home as wards of court. Nineteen were in voluntary care or accommodated after the conference. Thus at the end of the study 70 per cent of the children were living at home with at least one parent. Seventeen of those (8 per cent of the cohort) were accommodated by the local authority for a brief period (either on a Place of Safety order or in voluntary care) but were mainly living at home. In almost half of the cases (47 per cent) the child's major placement was at home with the person who had abused or neglected them, or was alleged to have done so. (See Figures 4.12, and 4.13).

The thirteen cases of the use of voluntary care fall into three groups. The parents may have requested help because the child was beyond their control or they were ill and unable to cope; or at the time of the allegation the remaining parent was unable to cope. A second group was of parents who were so angry at the allegation made by the child they were unable to tolerate the presence of the child at home. And there was a third smaller group where the child (all adolescent girls) requested accommodation for herself. Of those whose major placement was away from home, 31 (14 per cent of the cohort) were mainly in foster care and 11 (5 per cent of the cohort) were mainly in residential care.

Voluntary Care

> *One adolescent girl of mixed race parentage had been adopted as a baby and had presented behavioural problems during the previous year. She had anorexic symptoms and was being violent to her adoptive sisters, and finally she refused to go to school. Her parents sought help from social services. When the social worker eventually interviewed her at school, she alleged sexual abuse by her adoptive father. The girl and her family chose voluntary care as a time-out intervention pending the child protection conference.*

> *Another adolescent girl left home following persistent requests by her father to masturbate him. She randomly took a bus and because of her obvious distress the other bus passengers took her to the police station. The police took a place of safety order and the girl was placed with foster carers. After her father was interviewed by the police he took an overdose and was admitted to hospital leaving her mother in a state of shock and unable to cope. By agreement the girl remained with foster carers under a voluntary care arrangement both before the child protection conference and afterwards.*

Figure 4.12   **Court orders obtained during 6-month period (*More than 220 as in some cases there were 2 orders during the 6-month period)**

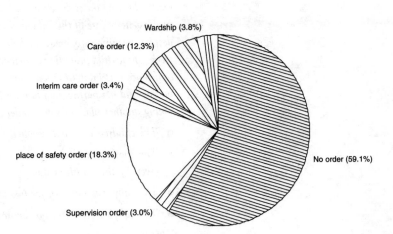

Sample = 235

Wardship (3.8%)

Care order (12.3%)

Interim care order (3.4%)

place of safety order (18.3%)

No order (59.1%)

Supervision order (3.0%)

A third family with two children aged 2 and 1 had requested voluntary care because of their mother's ill health. There had been a number of concerns about the care of the children from the health visitor and then the hospital at the time of the birth of the second baby. There had also been a case conference some months before because of a diagnosis of bruising and a cigarette burn as non-accidental injuries at the casualty department at the hospital, but the children were returned home. Some months later the police took a place of safety order because the baby had been left with a very young lodger who was unable to cope with her. This was allowed to lapse but as their mother became increasingly unwell she requested voluntary care. It was whilst the baby was with foster carers that a spiral fracture of the elbow was diagnosed and the child protection conference held.

Use of place of safety order

A neighbour phoned the police late one night to say that two children aged 2 years and 5 months had been left on their own for two hours already. The neighbour knew that the children had been left on previous occasions too. The police phoned the emergency social services and the children were removed on a place of safety order, first to the police station where they were fed and medically examined and then to foster parents. A note was left on the door by the police in the early hours of the morning for the mother who had still not returned. It was not until the next day that she reported to the police station asking where her children were. She was visited later the same day by a social worker and police officer. An initial child protection conference was convened within three days and the children registered under the category of neglect. Very clear statements were made about the level of improvement which needed to take place if the children were to be returned home. The mother and her partner agreed to a family support worker helping them three times a week to sort out the house, budget and in the general care of the baby and the children were returned. However, despite the support offered, the baby was admitted to hospital within six weeks of the child protection conference as failing to thrive. The review case conference was brought forward and it outlined specific criteria which the mother and her partner had to meet if they wished to avoid social services taking another place of safety order. The order would be sought if:

- *The children were not weighed regularly.*

- *The mother did not co-operate with the baby's feeding programme given by the health visitor.*

- *The baby was not seen for two weeks.*

- *The baby's weight did not improve within six weeks.*

This threat of statutory intervention seemed to gain the response which social services required and an order was not sought nor care proceedings initiated.

Figure 4.13   **Major placement of child during 6-months after conference**

Sample = 219

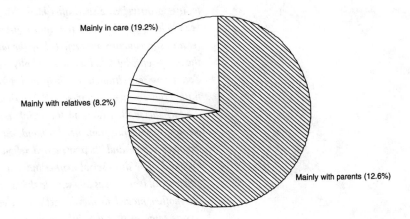

Mainly in care (19.2%)

Mainly with relatives (8.2%)

Mainly with parents (12.6%)

Voluntary care followed by court proceedings

The oldest of three little girls aged 7, 5 and 3 was seen at school to have extensive bruising on her legs. There had been concern in the past about the care of the children because of their mother's drinking habits, her lack of parenting skills and comments by the children which raised concerns about possible sexual abuse by their mother's boyfriend. The child was registered in the category of physical abuse at the initial child protection conference and her sisters in the category of grave concern. After the conference a package of family sessions and assessment was arranged at the family centre. There had been concerns about the middle child's development and she had recently been referred to the paediatric child development unit. The family attended twice a week for three months. A request from the mother for voluntary care for the middle child because she was being excessively difficult and not sleeping at night was agreed to. The placement was planned and arranged. The first night proved traumatic for the foster carers because of her nightmares, wetting, tears and highly distressed state which resulted finally in the disclosure of serious sexual abuse over many months to her and her sisters. Social services immediately called another child protection conference and the registration was altered to sexual abuse of all three girls. Place of safety orders were taken on the other two children and then all three placed together in foster care. Gradually the full extent of the abuse became evident and, because the severity was considered to preclude the possibility of the children being returned to their mother, care proceedings were initiated.

Voluntary care used at a later stage

> The health visitor had been concerned about the health and development of the children because of evidence that they were being neglected and because previously the oldest child had been diagnosed as a 'non-organic failure to thrive' case soon after birth. A child protection conference had been held at the time and the child registered. The help offered by social services subsequently was rejected by the father. He was very angry about the interference by social services and physically threatened the family aide. Social services withdrew the help and de-registered a year later after no further concerns were expressed. When the children were aged 3 years and 2 years the mother came to the social services office and requested help because of violence from her husband. She was supported to go to the women's refuge and then requested rehousing elsewhere away from her husband. The duty social worker made a referral for further involvement and a social worker was allocated to the family. Anxieties rose higher when the mother moved to the district's homeless family accommodation and reports came in that the children were being left alone and not fed. The social worker visited daily and the concerns about the care of the children increased and were confirmed by the warden and health visitor. An initial child protection conference was held after three weeks and voluntary care was offered to the mother which she accepted. The children were not registered. The children's aunt who had accompanied the mother to the initial child protection conference was also very worried but could not at that stage offer to care for the children herself. The children and their mother visited the foster carers' home in preparation for the placement and they were placed the next day. All this was within a month of the original self referral. Access was arranged regularly at the foster carers' home for mother and for the aunt. After a month of the children being there the mother began to refuse to make the access visits and then she disappeared for four weeks. Child care reviews were held but the mother did not attend although invited and arrangements were being made to support the children's aunt in providing a home for them for the future. However four months after the children were placed in foster care the mother wrote requesting their return to her, so new plans had to be made since she had met a new boyfriend and was settling down and was making it clear that she wished to have her children with her.

Access arrangements for four of the 73 children who were in care at some stage are not known, but of the remaining 69, 15 (22 per cent) did not have contact with the parent during this period. In seven cases contact was not allowed, in four the parents did not ask for contact, and in four cases the child either did not ask for or did not want contact. In the 69 cases where there was contact with family members, it was known to have been supervised in nine cases. Where contact was arranged, it appeared to be working satisfactorily in all except six cases.

Of the children who were in care at any stage, 22 did not have siblings. Twenty-two were in care whilst all their siblings remained at home, 26 were in care with a sibling, and 11 had one or more siblings at home and one or more siblings in care.

Outcome for the child

Any assessment of outcome only six months following the child protection conference must of necessity be tentative. However, it was part of our research design that a case should not be seen as satisfactory if there was evidence that the outcome for the child was poorer as a result of the involvement of family members in the process. The researchers allocated cases to the different outcome groups according to answers to the following questions:

- Do the child's living and parenting arrangements appear to be settled?
- Is the child either living with or in contact with parents and other adults who are important to him/her, and is this contact arranged in a way which makes it a positive experience? If there is no family contact are there clear reasons why contact would be harmful to the child?
- Are there any indications that the child is making developmental progress or is slipping backwards?
- Are there indications that any emotional or behavioural problems are diminishing or increasing?
- Does it appear that the protection plan is offering protection for the child?
- Does the protection plan appear to be working as intended for the overall benefit of the child?
- Is the professional contact for the child and carers at an appropriate level in view of the problems identified?

As well as a general rating on outcome, and our collection of information about those children who came into care, we considered the extent to which children were re-abused during the research period. Four were seriously re-abused, and ten suffered minor injuries or neglect. One was **suspected** of being again seriously abused, and 18 were suspected of being abused in a less serious way. Four were abused by a different person, and four were abused whilst in care. Two of the children whose major placement was with a person who was thought to be responsible for the abuse or neglect were seriously re-abused during the period as were two of those not living with the person alledged to have ill-treated them. However, a greater proportion of the first group (27 per cent compared with 10 per cent of those living away from the abuser) either received minor injuries or were **suspected** of having been abused again or neglected during this period. (Six were abused or suspected of being abused whilst being looked after by the local authority). This information was not known in respect of 14 children. Thus one in five were actually or suspected of being reabused, although in eight cases this was by a different person.

Figure 4.14 shows that in 65 per cent of cases the interim outcome for the child was rated as good (33 per cent) or moderately good (32 per cent). In a quarter of cases there appeared to be no change from the time when the case conference was held, and in 10 per cent of cases the outcome for the child was rated as 'poor'. In five cases there was too little information on which to attempt a rating. Cross-tabulations were undertaken to allow us to consider the relationship between variables and outcome.

Figure 4.14   **Interim outcome for child (researcher ratings)**

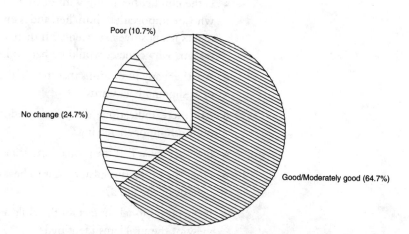

Because of overlapping variables, figures are used descriptively. We report trends rather than statistically significant findings, and are certainly not able to make statements about causation. For example, there are more positive outcomes when the child remains living with the alleged abuser than living away from home, but much of this difference is likely to be accounted for by the fact that in most cases where the abuse was unsubstantiated, or when the child's behaviour was not problematic, the child remained at home. Teenagers were more likely to have poor outcomes and more likely to be away from home. Cases were only allocated to the 'middle' (no change) category if they could not be appropriately allocated to the 'good' or the 'poor' group. Most were children whose living circumstances changed little after the conference, and who were not actually suffering significant harm at the time of the conference.

Figure 4.15 lists the variable which were associated with 'good' or 'moderately good' ratings or 'poor' ratings. Numbers are small in any one category, variables overlap, and numbers are too small to control for key variables such as severity of abuse.

When outcome was related to agency, there were 18 and 20 per cent of children with a 'poor' outcome in two authorities (Innerborough and Northtown) compared with 5 per cent in two others (Midborough and Outerborough). As with registration rates, this probably had more to do with differential thresholds for holding conferences than with quality of practice (Figure 4.16).

Figure 4.15 **Variables associated with a 'good' or 'poor' outcome for child (researcher rating of outcome – 'good' and 'moderately good' ratings combined)**

VARIABLES ABOUT THE CHILD OR PLACEMENT

Poor	If there are 4 or more children in family	$< .05$
Poor	If child is over the age of 5	$< .01$
Poor	If child is of mixed race parentage	$< .05$
Poor	If the child is in care and there are siblings still at home	$< .0001$
Poor	If child's major placement was away from home	$< .0001$
Poor	If child rated as having behaviour or other problems	$< .001$
Good or Poor	If the child was away from home during investigation, outcome tended to polarise; if child was at home during investigation, it was more likely that the outcome would be rated in the 'no change' category.	$< .001$

VARIABLES ABOUT THE FAMILY OR THE ABUSE

Poor	If child registered as sexually abused	$< .05$
Poor	If allegation made by child	$< .05$
Poor	If parents' problems were rated as high	$< .05$
Good	If main parent not implicated in abuse or admitted involvement at least partially	$< .05$
Good	If main carer and social worker agree about whether abuse/neglect has happened and its severity	$< .01$
Good	If main parents took part in drawing up protection plan	$< .01$
Good	If main parents involved in decisions about protection plan	$< .01$

Good	If child rated as taking part or being a partner	< .05
Good	If main parents agreed with assessment	< .01
Good	If main parents were satisfied with help given	< .01

VARIABLES ABOUT THE AGENCY AND SOCIAL WORK

Poor	If decision of initial conference was to apply for a care order	< .001
Poor	If child away from home at time of assessment; more of those not away were in the 'no change' category	< .0001
Poor	If help wanted by parent but not offered. 'Good' outcome if help wanted and provided. No change if not wanted and not provided	< .01
Poor	If overall main help or services given to child rather than whole family	< .01
Good	If investigation process was rated as participatory	< .05
Good	If conference stage was rated as participatory	< .01
Good	If social work rated as at least adequate	< .01
Good	If social worker rated their work as successfully involving the main carers	< .05
Good	If work of agency and social worker was rated as participatory	< .01
Good	If main parent was consulted about change needed	< .05
Good	If main parent contributed to plan	< .01
Good	If main parent said they were involved or involved to some extent (only 73 cases included where there was a response from main parent). 42% were in 'poor' outcome when main parent responded that they were definitely not involved.	< .01
Good	If researcher rated that main parent was involved; but there were no 'poor' outcomes when main carer was rated as not involved.	< .0001
Good	If supportive relationship provided for main parent	< .01
Good	If practical help provided for main parent	< .01
Good	If service was focused mainly on child's well-being	< .05
Good	If type of assessment was a more comprehensive one than child protection	< .01
Good	If social worker had spent more than 5 but less than 10 years as a social worker	< .05
Good	or Poor (Not 'no change') if work had a long term focus	< .01

Figure 4.16 **Outcome for child (researcher rating) by agency**

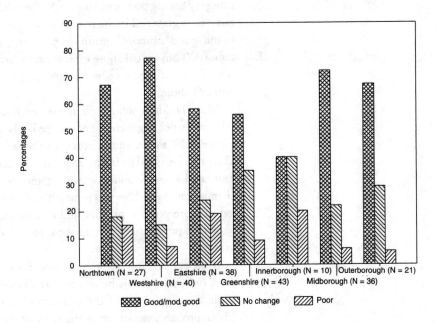

Child and abuse related factors and outcome

Outcome was rated as 'poor' for four of the 11 children of mixed racial parentage (36 per cent compared with 10 per cent for the cohort as a whole). Although more girls than boys were rated as having poor outcomes (12 per cent compared to 9 per cent) this difference was not statistically significant.

It has already been noted that some **children** were experiencing difficulties or had health or behaviour problems before the child protection conference. Forty-two per cent of those whose problems were described as 'mild' or 'not at all apparent' were in the 'good' outcomes group, and only 4 per cent in the 'poor' outcomes group. There was a similar pattern for those described as having moderate behaviour difficulties. However, the 11 who were described as having severe behaviour problems and the 31 as having emotional problems were more likely to be rated in the 'poor' outcomes categories than those without problems (27 per cent of those with severe behavioural difficulties, and 23 per cent of those described as having emotional problems). Three of the five described as having learning difficulties were in the 'poor' outcomes category, and none was described as having a 'good' outcome.

Several of those who had behaviour difficulties at the time of the conference subsequently left home, and it has already been noted that those whose major placement was away from home were more likely than the others to be in the 'poor' outcomes group. There was a difference between children referred for different types of abuse, with 17 per cent of those *referred* in the sexual abuse category and 27 per cent of those actually registered in that category having poor outcomes. On the other hand, those who were referred but **not registered** in the sexual abuse category were more likely to be rated in the 'good' outcome group (38 per cent compared with 33 per cent for the cohort). Thus sexual abuse cases seem to have either good or poor outcomes with fewer in the 'no change' group than those referred because of other types of abuse.

More children who were registered had 'good' outcomes, whilst those who were not registered were more likely to be in the 'no change' group. Figure 4.17 shows the children in the severe abuse categories were more likely to have good or moderately good interim outcomes and children in the 'not rated as severe abuse or neglect' group were more likely to be in the 'no change' category. This was probably because the greater clarity in those cases led to more positive practice and case management. Those in the 'severe or persistent punishment' group were more likely to be in the poor outcome group.

If no explanation about the cause for concern was offered by the main carer (whether or not he or she was alleged to be involved in the abuse or neglect), 23 per cent of the children were rated as having poor outcomes. This is probably explained by the fact that they tended to be older children for whom the outcome tended to be rated as poor.

Not surprisingly, where the main carer was not believed to be involved in the abuse, 44 per cent of cases came into the 'good' outcomes group but there is also a fairly positive picture in those cases where a parent was alleged to have colluded or failed to protect the child (9 out of 19 (47 per cent) were in the good outcome group).

This could indicate that the labels of 'failure to protect' or 'colluder' were wrongly assigned to an appropriately caring parent in some cases, and our interviews lend support to the conclusion that this sometimes happened. There was a statistically significant difference in outcomes between those children whose main carer was clearly involved to some extent in the abuse or neglect and agreed that this was the case, and those where there was good evidence that the carer was involved but did not accept this to be so. Twenty-one per cent of those in the latter group were in the 'poor' outcomes category whilst 48 per cent of those in the first group were in the 'good' outcomes category. On the other hand, none of the 13 main carers who were accused of but explicitly denied being the abuser and where the evidence was still unclear after six months, had children in the 'poor' outcome group. In some of these cases it seemed probable that the allegation was ill-founded though it was rarely possible to be totally certain.

There was a similar finding in terms of those who agreed or disagreed with the social worker about the seriousness of the abuse. In the 77 cases where there was disagreement between the social worker and the main carer about

Figure 4.17   **Outcome for child (researcher rating) by severity of alleged abuse (p<.01)**

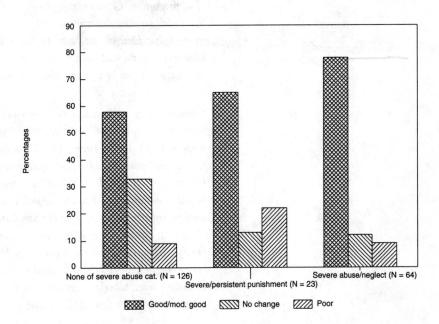

the **degree** of abuse, 14 per cent had 'poor' outcomes compared with only 5 per cent when the social worker and carer **agreed** about the degree of abuse. There was a similar but less marked difference depending on whether the social worker and the main carer agreed about **who** was responsible for the abuse or neglect. Although there was a tendency for more cases to be allocated to the 'poor' outcomes categories where social workers disagreed with the main carers about the nature, extent, and culpability for abuse, it should also be noted that several cases in these categories were allocated to the 'good' outcomes groups. In 15 per cent of cases where they did not agree about whether abuse had occurred or its extent, outcome was rated in the 'good' category. In at least some of these cases it seemed likely on the evidence available to the researchers that the allegation was not well founded, or that the parents' interpretations of severity was closer to the truth than that of the workers.

Gerald and Charlotte represent two cases where there was a dispute between the social worker and parents but which fell into our 'good outcome' group.

Gerald, aged 8, had behaved badly at home and according to his mother, Karen, had been 'asking for it' because he was 'winding up' Karen's partner, Douggie. Douggie hit Gerald on his upper arm to punish him, and as well as bruising him there were cuts to his shoulder from Douggie's rings. The bruising was noticed by Gerald's teacher at school. Child protection procedures ensued and Karen thought that the incident grew out of all proportion. Gerald was registered and an assessment undertaken by the social services department. Many months later Gerald was still worried that Douggie might go to prison for hitting and bruising him. However, Gerald had moved school where he was less bullied because of his mixed race and he was according to Karen happy, doing well at school, and achieving better.

Charlotte's step-father was a strict Jehovah's Witness and his method and manner of disciplining Charlotte, aged 15 years, led her to run away from home and ask for fostercare. Despite attempts by the social worker to resolve the issues of adolescent independence and find a compromise between parents and child, Charlotte's step-father denied he was at fault in his punishment of her and objected to what he regarded as social services' interference in their family life. Charlotte's older brother had run away from home some months previously and lived independently of the family. Charlotte's mother seemed unable to modify her husband's behaviour to protect Charlotte and felt Charlotte would be better in voluntary care. Charlotte settled well in foster care and became more cheerful and positive about the future.

Moving on to look at the children's care histories, a quarter of those where place of safety orders preceded coming into care and the child remained away from home after the place of safety order were rated as having 'poor' outcomes, as were a quarter of those received into voluntary care without the use of a place of safety order. The cases were most likely to involve adolescent girls whose parents denied the allegation of abuse or its seriousness, resulting in them being pushed out or deciding to leave the family home; or where the allegation of abuse was just one of many difficulties experienced by the parents and young person. Whether they were on a care order or in voluntary care, the outcome for these young people, estranged from their parents and exposed to the many risks of being isolated in care, was usually bleak. Some social workers struggled against all the odds to provide care and support, but a poor long-term outcome looked inevitable. On the other hand, none of those where a place of safety order was taken and lapsed were in 'poor' outcome groups and half were in the 'good' outcomes category. Cases where the alleged abuser was now out of the home were usually in this group. Only 5 per cent of those where there was neither a court order nor did the child come into voluntary care were rated in the 'poor' outcomes category.

Of the 21 who were in care and had a sibling still living at home, almost half had a 'poor' outcome. Again, this may be because these were usually adolescents at odds with their parents. On the other hand, there was a significantly higher number of cases rated in the 'good' outcome category if the mother and child were living with a relative. Fifty-one per cent of those whose main placement was with the mother alone had 'good' outcomes compared with only 3 per cent who had poor outcomes. Those living with both parents for most of the time were more likely to be in the 'no change' group, and those whose major placements were away from the family home were more likely to be in the 'poor' outcomes group (29 per cent of those with foster parents, 22 per cent of those with relatives or friends, and 40 per cent of the ten who were known to have spent most of the six months in residential care).

It has already been noted that 47 per cent of the children were placed for most of the time with parents who included the alleged abuser or person who was alleged to have neglected them. Only 3 per cent in this group had a 'poor' outcome, and 33 per cent were described as having a 'good' outcome, 31 per cent in the 'moderately good' group, and 33 per cent were in the 'no change' category. Two of the children whose major placement was with a person who was thought to be responsible for the abuse or neglect were seriously re-abused during the period as were two of those not living with the person alledged to have ill-treated them. However, a greater proportion of the first group (27 per cent compared with 10 per cent of those living away from the abuser) either received minor injuries or were **suspected** of having been abused again or neglected during this period. (Six were abused or suspected of being abused whilst being looked after by the local authority). Thirty-four per cent of those whose main placement was not with the alleged abuser were described as having a 'good' outcome (the average for the cohort), and 16 per cent in this group were in the 'poor' outcome category—i.e. those not living with the alleged abuser for most of the six month period were most likely to be in the 'poor' outcomes group. The age factor again has to be borne in mind, since many of these were older girls. There also appeared to be concern about the outcome for children living with the father and a female partner since in 30 per cent of these cases the outcome for the child was rated as poor. No child under four had a poor outcome, whilst 17 per cent of those aged 12 or over had poor outcomes.

Parent related variables and outcome

Our data almost certainly under-estimates the extent of mental illness amongst the parents since this is often not recorded unless it was of a severe nature. It was interesting to note that a quarter of the 32 where the main carer was described as having some degree of mental illness were in the 'good' outcomes category, and five (16 per cent) in the 'poor' outcomes category. Four of the five whose parents were described as having a learning disability were in the 'good' or 'quite good' outcomes categories and none in the 'poor' group. There was a similar pattern when it was the partner of the main carer who was described as having a mental illness or a learning disability. Thus, although on average outcomes were less favourable if parents had a mental illness or a learning disability, this was not invariably so.

In six cases it was considered that the parent was not committed at all to the welfare of the child, and in two of these six there was a 'poor' outcome. On the other hand, where the carer was assessed as being always committed to the welfare of the child, in only 5 per cent of cases was the case allocated to the 'poor' outcome group and 39 per cent were in the 'good' outcome category.

Turning to material circumstances, outcome was not clearly related to social class or income source, although there is a trend towards a polarisation, with children from middle class backgrounds less likely to be in the 'no change' category. Four of the 24 who came from middle class background (17 per cent) were in the 'poor' outcomes category, and ten of the 24 middle class children (42 per cent) were in the 'good' outcomes group. Fifteen per cent of the children whose parents were dependent on benefits were in the 'poor' outcomes category, and a quarter in the 'good' group. The outcome was rated as 'good' for 45 per cent of those where the mother had a regular job. In other respects, income source appeared to make little difference. It is interesting to note that 18 per cent of those whose parents were owner-occupiers were in the 'poor' outcome group, whilst four of the nine in homeless families' accommodation at the time of the case conference (44 per cent) were in the 'good' outcomes group, as were seven of the 15 in private rented accommodation. The explanation for this rather surprising conclusion may be that the materially adverse circumstances led to child protection conferences being held on families when the major problem resulted from stress due to poor housing or income. The additional support and practical help at the time of referral led to better outcomes for the children. In some of these cases we would dispute the necessity for child protection proceedings as simply help to secure improved accommodation would have been just as satisfactory and avoided the stress of the conference as well as the cost in professional time.

It is to be expected that better outcomes would be seen when the case appeared to offer a positive set of circumstances for the involvement of family members. Fifty-four per cent of those in the 'best' scenario group had 'good' outcomes but it should also be noted that 10 per cent had 'poor' outcomes. On the other hand, rather surprisingly, only 6 per cent of those where the case was in the 'worst' scenario group for achieving family involvement were in the 'poor' outcomes group and these were not under-represented in the 'good' outcomes group. The possible reasons for this will be considered later when we consider in more detail the factors associated with family involvement.

Moving on to the decisions of the child protection conference, there were no 'poor' outcomes where the decision was taken to take no further action (17 cases). Similarly, there were proportionately more 'good' outcomes (49 per cent) amongst those who had not previously been known to the social services department, and only 6 per cent of these were in the 'poor' outcomes group. We shall return to the question of the investigation and social work practice with children, but it is interesting to note here that ten (21 per cent) of the 47 children who were interviewed without the permission of their parents were included in the 'poor' outcomes group. This may be partly explained by the fact that more of the children where the allegation was of excessive or severe punishment were in the 'poor' outcome group (22 per cent), and these, and older children, were most likely to be interviewed without consent of parents.

Twenty-five per cent of the 40 where the problem rating of the parents was high were in the 'poor' category, and only 15 per cent of those where the families' problem rating was high were in the 'good' outcomes category. When the outcome for the main parent was 'poor', the outcome for the child also tended to be rated as 'poor' (47 per cent of these cases). In contrast, where the outcome for the parent was 'good', the outcome for the child was rated as 'good' in 84 per cent of the cases.

Variables related to social work and protection process

The outcome was described as 'good' for the six children whose names were taken off the register four months after registration. Three of the 17 who were deregistered between four and six months after the conference were in the 'poor' outcomes group. Outcome was also described as 'poor' for seven of the 74 who were never registered and not in care, and for the only two who were never registered because they were in care.

Figure 4.18 indicates that there was not a statistically significant association between the interim outcome for the child and the attendance of the main parent at all or most of the initial conference. This may suggest that social workers tried hard to involve the main parent at least to some extent and to include them in the conference in the more difficult cases where the outcome for the child was most likely to be poor. The relationship between family member involvement in the work, the nature of the social work service and the outcome for the child will be discussed in more detail in the next section. From Figure 4.15 it can be seen that there were more cases in the good interim outcome group if services were offered to the whole family, but with the focus of the work being the child's well-being. Practical help and a supportive relationship also figured more highly in the cases which were allocated to the good interim outcome group.

Figure 4.18 **Attendance of main parent at initial child protection conference by outcome for child (researcher rating) (not significant)**

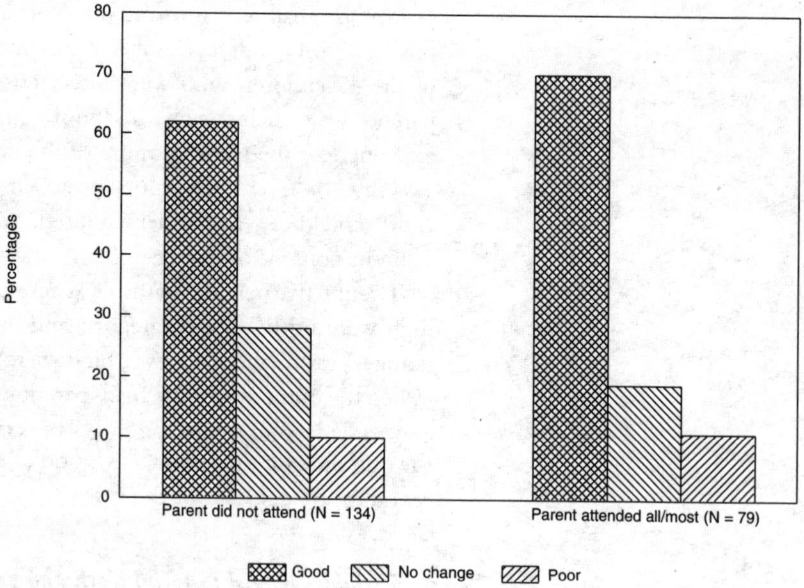

Attitudes of the children to the social work and child protection process

Questionnaires were completed by ten of the young people, and a further 14 were interviewed as part of the small sample. The research instruments also covered several areas of social work practice with the children which will be considered in Chapters 5 and 6.

In the 10 questionnaires returned by young people in the sample, five said that the social worker was the person who listened most, and seven said that the social worker treated them alright, compared with four who thought foster carers had treated them well, four who thought teachers had, and four who thought the police had. Three spoke positively of the support they had received from their family, friends and neighbours. On balance, there seems to have been a reasonably open exchange between the young person and their social workers with three thinking they had been able to be open and honest with the social worker, five to some extent and two not at all. Three thought the social worker was open and honest with **them**, six to some extent and one not at all.

Six of them were in care at some stage during the six months following the child protection conference. Of the other four, all were well supported by their families; two of them felt their social workers were very helpful but two were at odds with them. One young person writes vividly of the tussle she had with her social worker about being allowed to remain at home with support from friends and neighbours rather than being received into care. It is worth including her quote in full:

When my mother was ill and had to be admitted to hospital, the only help that my social worker offered was that me, my brother and sister was to go into a residential home or a foster family. When we said we didn't want to go, we wanted to stay with our family, she said it wasn't up to us—either my dad or me—to say where we wanted to go. She said it was entirely up to her. The only help or comfort she can offer is telling my little sister and brother that they weren't going to be staying with mummy for long, that they were going to go to a new family and putting worry on them. Now my mother is back in hospital and us three kids are staying with neighbours because she can't get her own way by putting us in care. She's now taking out a court case against my mother who's mentally ill which can't be helped, and my father who's doing his best to keep our family together. All she or they I should say are one big problem. Every time they pop up they cause disturbance. She's been asking around my neighbourhood for people who know us well to act as witnesses in the court case that she's been setting up behind my dad's back. The only way we found out was by friends and next-door neighbours telling us social services keep ringing up and pleading them to stand up against my mum and dad so that she can finally get what she wants—us three kids all in a happy foster family where she thinks we'll live happily ever after. She never ever listens to our point of view, to who we want to stay with even if it's our family. She'd rather have us with some strange people who we've never met from Adam. She talks my dad into signing papers and gets him wrapped round her little finger. She tries it on with me too and my brother and sister, but they don't really understand. I could see what she was trying to do from the start. She got my mum put in hospital, I said it to her face; but all I got told was that I was talking a lot of nonsense and stop hiding things from her. I don't agree with social services, well not in this case in which they're not really necessary. I believe they should be helping poverty-stricken families or teenagers with no homes or kids being beaten and even sexually abused by their own parents—none of which goes on in my family. My mum's illness and the children's welfare is the only reason they say they come for, well they can leave my mum's illness to the hospital and doctors, and leave us where we are now.

The 14 children who were interviewed had a number of telling things to say about the procedures. Their replies cluster around five themes:

- What they thought about being called out of class and interviewed at school.
- Their comments about not being listened to and about being 'quizzed'.
- Their relief about being allowed to talk openly about what had happened.
- Wanting to hear what was said, and their views about the register.
- Their comments about their social workers.

What they thought about being called out of class and interviewed at school
10 year old Ali said, 'They just come to visit us at school. The teachers come up to you and say, "Come on, there are two social workers come to see you" which sometimes is . . . [grimace]. Sometimes it got me really annoyed. They just kept on doing it.'

Maura, aged 9 said, 'They come round quite often at school. Sometimes it's embarrassing. Sometimes it isn't. When I'm doing my work and I have to stop doing it.'

14 year old Andy said, 'The second time the secretary came to the classroom and said "Two police officers are here." They took me out of history class so all the class knew. It was embarrassing, and it happened ten days afterwards when it was all calming down at school.'

Their comments about not being listened to and about being 'quizzed'
Jim aged 10 said, 'We had to listen to them and they didn't listen to us. I wanted to do my school work. They tried to give us little presents and stuff so they could ask us questions instead of giving us something to do like paper to draw on. They always gave us sweets.'

Imelda aged 14 said, 'My social worker never talked about what happened. She just queried my social life. I didn't have any particular difficulties but the social worker was more interested in my private life than helping me overcome what had happened to me.'

15 year old Ben said, 'I didn't like it because they tried to make me answer questions whilst they wrote notes. My second social worker listens, she doesn't ask questions. She helps you with your problem.'

Their relief about being allowed to talk openly about what had happened
A thirteen year old girl said, 'I'm glad it was a woman. I don't think I'd have been very comfortable with a man. You don't want to talk about some things to a man. Even if I'd been a boy I think it would be easier to talk to a lady.'

Martin aged 11 said, 'They didn't keep pushing me. They let me say what I wanted to say. They talked about other things as well, they didn't just harp on all the time about what had happened to me.'

A sixteen year old girl, whose father was in prison after being convicted of incest told us: 'I saw her once a week for about three weeks, and then my problems started getting worser at home because of my mum. She and my sister were pushing me to one side, so I stayed with my nan for a week to try and sort it out. Then I went back home to see if it was better, but it got worser. So I told my nan and my nan got in touch with Janet and she came round and she suggested two places for me to stay, and I suggested one place. We looked nearer and at foster parents here, but I stayed in — house and I liked it. I can't go back home because my mum don't want me back there. It was suggested that me nan should adopt me and my little sister. I'd have liked that, and my sister would have been together. I missed my sister. Me and Janet are still working on it. There's a lot of hurt still inside my mum and she's taking it out on me. I'll keep trying but if it don't work out I'll just leave it. It's been a bad year.'

Wanting to hear what was said, and their views about the register

Most of the young people living at home expressed curiosity about the conference and were pleased if their parents went, but did not want to go themselves. One or two, like this thirteen year old, did!

'It isn't really fair that they talked about us at a conference. I would have liked to have gone.'

A 13 year old boy said about the child protection register, 'I was told a few days ago about the register. I thought we'd been taken off it years ago. My second social worker told me it was because dad hit me.'

Their comments about their social workers

Mary, aged 14 had two younger siblings who remained in care but she was allowed home after court. Asked what it was like having a social worker, she said after a long pause and a big sigh 'It's been hard' and then 'It's not fair, no I couldn't talk to anyone. They said we'd be about a week at — [residential home] but it was three months.'

Sixteen year old Anna said: 'I was frightened at first and then they told me what would happen, and I wasn't so afraid then. The social worker was the main person who told me what would happen next.

Usha, aged 13 said: 'My social worker was very helpful so I hope this questionnaire will help you.

Summary

- About a third of the index children were under 5 (including five not yet born), a third were aged between 5 and 11, and a third were aged 12 or over. Fifty-six per cent were girls and 44 per cent boys. Just under a half had health, emotional, or behavioural problems or learning disabilities at the time of the conference. (The 'index' child was the oldest child in the family who was alleged to have been maltreated).

- The abuse was rated as severe in 29 per cent of cases, 11 per cent were described as excessive or repeated physical punishment, and 60 per cent came into neither of these categories.

- Sixty-two per cent of the conferences resulted in the child's name being placed on the child protection register, with a range between 41 per cent and 71 per cent for the different agencies.

- One in five of the index children left home as a result of an order at the time of the allegation and a further 10 per cent went to relatives or were in voluntary care. At the end of the study, 70 per cent were at home but some of those originally away had gone home, and others who were at home at the time of the conference had left.

- The researchers allocated the interim outcome for the children six months after the conferences to four groups (see Appendix for rationale and criteria): 33 per cent were rated in the 'good' group; 32 per cent as 'moderately good; in a quarter there appeared to be no change; and 10 per cent were allocated to the 'poor' outcome group. Because of the interaction between variables it was not possible to tease out clear associations between variables and outcome. However, teenage girls, where the allegation was sexual abuse or over-chastisement and who left home, were most likely to be in the 'poor' outcome group, and cases were more likely to be in the 'good' outcome group when the main parent was not implicated in the maltreatment.

- Four children were seriously re-abused during the six month period, and 10 suffered minor injuries or neglect. Suspicions were aroused in respect of 19 others.

- Children expressed very similar opinions about the process to those of their parents, but one very strong message was that most of them strongly objected to being interviewed on school premises, and especially to being taken out of classes.

Chapter 5

Social Work Practice and Agency Policy

An overview of the social workers and their practice

Ethnic origin, gender, qualification and age

It has already been noted that some social workers were responsible for more than one case, with two being the key workers in five cases. Consequently, 138 different workers were the main workers for these 220 cases although many more were involved at some stage, including the team leaders. Even allowing for a greater proportion of women in social work posts, they were over-represented in that 113 of the workers were women and 25 were men. One hundred and ten of the workers (80 per cent) were white British; six were white of another European country or American origin; ten were black of Caribbean ethnic origin; and three were of south Asian ethnic origin. The ethnic origin of nine was not known. Figure 5.1 and Tables 5.1 show that of the 125 whose qualifications were known, only eight did not hold a recognised child care social work qualification (including the two CSS holders who had not followed a child care option). Over a half were additionally graduates, including 16 per cent who had higher degrees. Nor did they fit the stereotype of a young worker lacking in life experience. None was under 25, and only 18 were aged under 30. Almost a half were aged 40 or over.

Table 5.1 **Professional qualification of main social workers**

Professional Qualification	Number	%
CQSW or equivalent	110	88
CSS (child care option)	7	6
CSS (other option)	2	2
Unqualified	6	5
Total	125	100

[Not known 13]

Social work experience

It is not, therefore, surprising, given the age distribution, to discover that almost three-quarters had been practising as social workers for five or more years, and that almost a half had been qualified social workers for ten years or more. Whilst it is to be regretted that any social worker with less than two years' postqualifying experience is the investigating or keyworker in child protection cases, it is encouraging that this applied to only seven of the workers in these cases (Figure 5.2)

Child care experience

They were also likely to be experienced **child care** workers, with only ten having less than two years' experience of child care work after qualification and 42 per cent having worked with child care cases for ten or more years. The move to specialisation in child care work was apparent in that 59 per cent worked for the whole of their time with child care cases. A further third worked for between half and the whole of their time on child care cases, with only three (2 per cent) working for less than a quarter of their time in this area of practice. (Figure 5.3). A quarter of the workers estimated that they had worked with over one hundred child protection cases, and a further 48 per cent had been accountable for twenty or more such cases. Only three had worked with fewer than five child protection cases.

Figure 5.1 **Academic qualifications of main social worker**

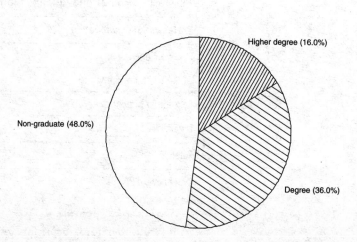

Sample = 492

Figure 5.2 **Length of time in social work since qualifying**

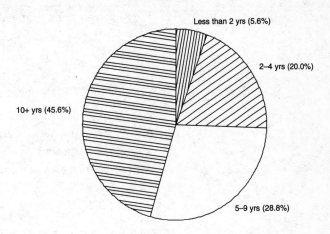

Figure 5.3 **Length of time in child care since qualifying**

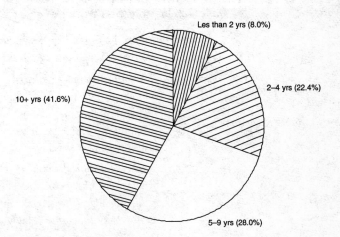

Child protection investigation

Information was sought on how they went about their child protection investigations, and in particular whether they made use of checklists. Whilst 21 said they did not, and seven said that they worked out a different plan in each case, the majority said that they made use of a checklist to guide them through the process. In half, however, the checklist was kept in their heads, whilst a quarter used a written checklist. Most referred to the child protection guidelines, and those who used written checklists based them on the guidelines.

> *I regularly refer to the procedures for guidance and clarification.*

> *I use the child protection procedures as a checklist to ensure that no important area is left uncovered.*

A typical response to the question about what was on their own checklist was:

> *Seek for information for assessment; establish risk/ protection issues and action needed. Procedures including liaison requirements; share what I'm doing and thinking with the family.*

Differences between child care work and child protection work

Half of the workers indicated that they did not see social work in child protection as being substantially different from general child care social work practice, although 11 (8 per cent) thought there were major differences between child protection cases and their other work with children and families. These quotes illustrate answers which referred to positive and negative differences. Most referred to both positive and negative features of child protection work.

> *I think I am probably clearer and more focused in my work with a child protection component due to the structure of the agency and procedures.*

> *The conflict and anger directed at you and the agency. Court appearances and giving evidence. The possibility of making a mistake — the guilt of failing to protect the child or intervening wrongly and damaging family relationships. Having your career and/or personal life wrecked by making a mistake and being subject to an enquiry.*

> *There is the difficulty of living with uncertainty. What if something goes wrong, have I been observant or objective enough? That the anxiety level is high would, I hope, make me extra conscientious and vigilant. The team is very supportive usually.*

Differences between child protection work and child and family social work were often explained in terms of attempts to involve family members. Sixty-two per cent of the workers considered that involving family members was more difficult in child protection cases compared with 37 per cent who thought it did not make much difference.

The relationship initially tends to be more formal in child protection work. In non-statutory work it is more acceptable for families to 'opt out', there is more negotiation about benefits of having social work involvement. Families have less choice in child protection work. Social work involvement may well continue even if they object – both social worker and family are aware of this.

There are the risks to one's self as a worker – the risks of leaving children at home after quite serious abuse, or making the wrong decision on legal action. The poor social work image in the media means that the families' suspicions can lead to non-disclosure of relevant information.

I worry that a parent or other adult may harm the child because I am unable to visit often enough – that is every day to help protect the child. I worry also about lies and fob-offs used against me or threatening behaviour towards me.

In some cases the workers made clear that they exercised choices about whether to work with a case already known to them on the basis of providing voluntary support, or to bring child protection procedures into play. When asked why the child protection system had been used in a case where support services were already being offered and the parent was asking for help a social worker responded:

In other similar cases I wouldn't use child protection procedures. Here, I don't think we could ignore the child protection system because there were few supports in the family, and there were other issues such as having two previous children in care who she had not been able to parent. When I read through the file there were other indicators that it needed to go through the child protection system. Had it been another team, they would probably not have used the child protection procedures after what seemed like just a smacked bottom.

Another worker found the child protection label helpful in limiting her caseload.

I would only take on so many child protection cases. It would not go over the limit. It's very time-consuming.

Is practice child–centred?

The Children Act and Guidance and all professional commentators on the subject note the importance of ensuring that the child's welfare and safety are paramount. To some workers and practitioners this means that the service must be child centred, if necessary at the expense of the service to the parent. Another perspective, which fits more closely with the principles and practice guide accompanying the Children Act (DH, 1989), is that, whilst the child's welfare must always be put first if there is any conflict of interest, there is also the obligation to offer a caring and concerned service to parents, if necessary by the allocation of another worker. There was sufficient information about 80 of the social workers to rate them in terms of the extent to which they appeared to be primarily child-centred in their practice. None was rated as totally child-centred, 11 (14 per cent) were considered to be mainly child-centred, and 12 (15 per cent) to be mainly parent-centred. Fifty-seven (71 per cent) were considered to be focusing their concern and service on the whole family or on the non-abusing parent and the child. Two contrasting comments lend weight to the ideas of Fox-Harding (1991) on the continuum of child care workers' attitudes about the place of the child within the family.

> *I'm keen on children's rights. Children have the right to fit parenting. It worries me that I'm asked to improve parenting. I don't think children should wait. I don't think we have the right to put them through the mill to wait.*

> *I do not like taking children into care. I have a huge horror of it. Children do not thrive in care. Even if he had gained weight in hospital, he has a family who loves him.*

It was often in the context of discussions about the advantages of working with the family or taking action to place the child in care that these differences were most apparent.

Social workers' attitudes to working in partnership with family members

Agency policy

All the workers responded that they were aware of their agencies' policy on the involvement of family members either fully (57 per cent) or mostly (43 per cent). None said that they were only partially aware of it or hardly at all. Figure 5.4 and Table 5.5 gives the main influences on their attitudes to the involvement of family members. When interviewed, several either gave examples of a particular tutor or teamleader who had had a strong influence, or, even more likely, a case which had made them realise the importance of seeking to involve family members as much as possible.

Most workers (60 per cent) considered that there were no differences between their own attitudes towards working in partnership and those of the agency, although some noted a difference between their agency's policy and that of other agencies or the ACPC.

> *I suspect that most within the agency actually share similar views. The ACPC policy is however, different and it is other agencies that hold it back.*

Figure 5.4   **Main influence on social workers' views about client involvement in cohort cases**

Sample = 189

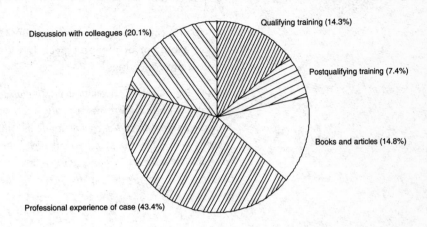

Discussion with colleagues (20.1%)

Qualifying training (14.3%)

Postqualifying training (7.4%)

Books and articles (14.8%)

Professional experience of case (43.4%)

For 30 per cent of social workers there were minor differences, but in 12 cases (10 per cent) social workers spoke of major differences between their own view about the importance and ways of working in partnership with family members, and those of the agency for which they worked. The following quotes give the range of social workers' general views on working in partnership with family members in child protection cases.

Parental participation – it's the best thing since sliced bread. They know exactly what we are talking about and it's all clear.

Initially I felt very sceptical about parental participation mainly because of my own fear that parents would become very upset, angry or violent. I was also concerned that other professionals would be unwilling to be honest with the families about their concerns for the children and therefore their contribution would be limited. However, I am happy to say that none of my fears have been realised. I now view parental participation as very positive, indeed essential in most cases in order that an effective plan can be formalised for ongoing work with the family.

On balance I'd much prefer the family to be there. I've always believed it. I've thought it ludicrous to discuss a family without involving them but there are some circumstances where you <u>cannot</u> *or* <u>should</u> *not.*

I think sometimes professionals need to have a space where they can express things without clients being present. It's always been a way of working. It's not easy to be open in that official kind of way with people, and it takes some time to get used to it and working towards being as open as possible with people. I've not been in a position of saying something that I wouldn't have said to clients face-to-face. It's been an historical thing about the power we have and what we think is 'good' for people. Things are changing and it's right they're changing and at the end of the day I think it's got to be healthier for relationships between ourselves and clients.

This worker represents the minority of those interviewed who had some doubts about family involvement, especially at the information sharing stage of child protection meetings.

I think that has to be looked at depending on the family – their ability, their state of mind, there are so many factors there. There's going to be things said that directly affect the family and they ought to be there but when you're discussing plans, possibilities, options and things like that then it's not necessary. It's only when you come to saying we will do this and this that may be the parents should be there to say whether they're prepared to do it.

Value positions

The workers were asked to rate themselves in terms of the priority they gave to attempting to work in partnership with family members. None said they gave it a low priority, only two gave it a low to medium priority, seven said that it varied according to the case, and the remaining workers rated themselves as medium to high on this dimension. When asked about the extent to which they had thought actively about how to involve family members in their work, just over half said that they had thought a great deal about this, and only nine said that they only occasionally thought about it or not at all. In our early discussions with child protection workers and managers, six statements were identified which covered the range of arguments for or against inviting parents to child protection conferences. Workers were asked whether they agreed or disagreed with these statements and Table 5.2 gives their responses. The statements were:

- Parents of children who may have been abused have rights as citizens not to have major decisions taken about them or their children without the opportunity of hearing what it is that concerns the professionals, and of putting their point of view. (The rights argument.)
- When an allegation of child abuse is made, parents suffer a loss of power and self-esteem and this has a negative effect on their parenting skills. When the parents participate their sense of powerlessness is lessened and their positive abilities are likely to be enhanced. (The therapeutic argument.)

- In the majority of cases a co-operative working relationship is of central importance in protecting children. Parental participation is likely to make for more professional practice. (The effectiveness argument.)
- Parental participation is a good idea in principle, but in practice there is a risk that it will impede professionals in their work.
- Parents find it too distressing and difficult to discuss abuse situations and their best interests are not served by involving them in child protection procedures, such as case conferences.
- Parents and professionals build up trust in order to work together. Complete openness about abuse situations is impossible if trusting relationships are to be preserved.

Table 5.2   **Social workers' agreement with arguments for or against parental attendance at conferences**

Argument	Strongly agree		Agree		Disagree		Strongly disagree	
	No.	%	No.	%	No.	%	No.	%
Rights	90	76	27	23	1	1	0	0
Therapeutic	39	34	72	62	5	4	0	0
Effectiveness	74	63	44	37	0	0	0	0
Good idea in principle, but some risks	0	0	25	21	66	57	26	22
Too upsetting for parents	1	1	4	3	58	49	55	46
Participation risks destroying trust	1	1	8	7	65	55	44	37

[Response varied between 116 and 118]

From the table it can be seen that the vast majority of the workers supported the attendance of family members at conferences, and that the rights and effectiveness arguments were particularly persuasive.

> *I am totally in favour of parents attending and being involved. It is only in exceptional circumstances that they should be excluded. Such involvement helps establish the openness and trust essential to good protection work.*
>
> *I've always been against parents coming in only at the end of the conference. I think that's silly. I've been keen on participation since we introduced it here, it keeps you on your toes. You discuss it all with parents and say "You can disagree and you can have your say." They have a pad and a pen and can take notes too. I say "Don't talk when someone else is talking – just make a note." It's about honesty.*

However, almost a quarter thought that although family attendance at conferences was a good idea in principle there were some risks attached, and a small minority considered that it could be too upsetting for parents or interfere with the development of trust between worker and parents. When asked to choose one statement with which they were most strongly in agreement, 49 per cent chose the effectiveness argument, 38 per cent favoured the rights argument, and 9 per cent the therapeutic argument. Although 21 per cent had agreed with the statement that it was a good idea in principle but that there were some risks attached, none said that this was the statement which was closest to their own position. One gave priority to the statement that parental attendance was too upsetting for parents, whilst two were most in agreement with the statement that participation risks destroying trust. This answer has traces of the effectiveness and therapeutic arguments:

> *I've always been honest with him and told him that if he wasn't pulling his weight I'd see he got off his backside!! We tried to arrange things around his job like we had the meeting during his lunchhour. It did him good because he has a part to play.*

This worker's concern for the harm to a parent and to the effectiveness of the work appears to come from a feeling that the conference could have been arranged differently:

> *Well, good because of the openness of it and helping people to see social services work differently and they'd see themselves as more involved. And bad because I've had several experiences where the client was confronted by 16 individuals in a room where it was damaging. There was this 19-year old mum – it alienated her and she felt she was being told she wasn't a good parent.*

Some differentiated between different types of abuse:

> *I am sure that involvement early on by **parents** in physical abuse cases helps co-operation and improves relations – but for sexual abuse many other issues need to be addressed. I feel (also) there must be **some** time put aside in CCs to air professional views which cannot be stated in front of parents – e.g. unsubstantiated allegations or hunches.*

The workers interviewed were strongly committed to involving **children** in their work, but were unsure about whether they should attend conferences.

> *I do, however, have some reservations about children attending the child protection conference as in my own experience most of the children would be too young to understand the issues discussed with the parents and*

would not be appropriate for the children to be involved with. So far I have not had any children present at the conferences, and I'm not sure if I would view this as a positive step.

Table 5.3 **Workers' agreement or otherwise with statements about their attitudes and practice with respect to involving family members in their work**

Statement	Hardly applies		Applies to some extent		Applies		Highly Applicable	
	No.	%	No.	%	No.	%	No.	%
I am strongly in favour of the principle of participation	0	0	5	4	21	19	86	77
I am participatory in my practice	1	1	5	19	70	63	35	31
Certain situations in child protection work make it difficult for me to facilitate family participation	18	16	50	45	29	26	35	31
Agency policy makes it more difficult for me to facilitate family participation	62	57	19	17	23	21	4	4
I share information with parents as a matter of course	0	0	11	10	50	45	51	45
I seek parents' views routinely about decisions to be made	1	1	5	4	49	44	56	50
When the child's protection is at risk participation is a low priority	33	32	22	21	34	33	14	14

[Response varied between 103 and 112]

Ratings on participation

Workers were also asked to consider the extent to which each of seven statements was applicable to their values and practice in respect of involving parents in their **day-to-day** child protection work. The response rate to these questions varied between 103 and 112. The question focused on family members generally and did not specifically refer to children. This was because at the time when the research started few agencies had systematically developed their policies for involving children in child protection work. However, detailed questions were asked about the extent to which children were involved in the different aspects of the work, and the responses will be reported later in this chapter.

It can be seen from Table 5.3 that although 77 per cent were strongly in favour of the principle of participation, only 31 per cent could strongly agree that they succeeded in being participatory in their practice. In our interviews with social workers this difference seemed to lie in their undervaluing their own contribution to the process of participation if it did not lead to obvious and full participation by parents. Yet in many situations social workers had initiated participatory practice and had continued to do so against the odds. Thirty-one per cent strongly agreed with the statement that certain situations in child protection work made it difficult for them to facilitate family participation, 14 per cent appeared to be suggesting that they saw some conflict between attempting to involve family members and child protection in some cases. Since the agencies had been chosen because of their interest in making attempts to involve family members in their practice, it is not surprising that the majority of the workers did not consider that agency policy made it more difficult for them to facilitate family participation. However, 25 per cent did agree with this statement, as some of the following quotes indicate.

> *I would like not to see a difference between child protection work and other work, but that's not how the agency sees it.*

> *We seem to differ on the resource issue. I'm not sure how committed the agency is to involving the family.*

A high proportion of workers rated themselves positively on **sharing information** with parents as a matter of course, and routinely consulting them about decisions to be made. The following quotes give details of how they sought to do this.

> *Openness and honesty about the concerns; sharing information; clearly explaining where the information is coming from if not directly from social services, and liaising carefully and factually with other agencies. Helping other agencies to raise issues directly with the parents; involving family in plans and discussions; advocacy and explaining what the department can and can't do and what we will do or not do depending on the family's response and their actions. Clear cut boundaries and warnings, and helping parents accept we want to work together for the sake of the child protection issues.*

> *Work by written agreements; operate in an honest manner and with clarity; specify the issues, the concerns, the possible causes of action and the implications. I try to be more careful to be honest. The reason being that the legal issues are greater, the power issues are more explicit, and the only hope of people trusting me and working with me is that they know exactly what is going on and why.*

In the light of their responses, and the researchers' awareness of the extent to which the worker had attempted to work in partnership with family members in the study case(s), the researchers rated each worker in terms of the extent to which their practice was likely to lead to working in partnership. Seventy-five (60 per cent) were rated as strongly participatory in their practice and attitudes; 47 (38 per cent) were rated as moderately so; and three (2 per cent) were rated as hardly participatory at all. None were rated as being opposed to involving family members in their work. Insufficient information was available for the purposes of rating the social workers in 13 cases.

The views of managers

Twenty-four managers in the research areas responded to a questionnaire. Most of them were team leaders or team managers of the social workers for the 220 families in the large study. Others were the child protection co-ordinators who chaired the conferences in the areas. The questionnaire was brief and sought to discover the managers' views on past and present practice with regard to participation, their value positions, what had influenced their thinking about participation, the practical consequences of parental partici-pation and whether child protection procedures created pressure for their social workers.

We asked managers first of all whether it was any different involving the families in child protection in the 1990s compared with involving families in child care in the past. There was an assumption here that 'past' would mean an equal period of time for all the managers, and it clearly did not. Most of them did have a belief that there were real differences between past and present practice. Fifteen said 'Yes, it was different', ten of whom contrasted the secrecy and the paternalism of the past with the present better opportunities for parents to participate in meetings, and for social workers to aim at partnership:

> *Now it ensures* <u>everyone</u> *should be straight and honest with parents and that parents hear what is said and its not filtered through their social worker. Professionals have to be more careful about what they say.*

> *It 'feels' more active now because of parents presence in the child protection conferences as valued and respected members.*

Two said the specific guidelines alter current practice and one that the child protection conference itself was a barrier not present in previous casework. Two said that it was different now because of the police involve-ment and so much legal action.

Four managers thought there was no difference:

> *The ideas have been around for a long time.*

Five managers answered 'Yes' *and* 'No' for various reasons:

> *In theory 'no', in practice 'yes' – involving parents in the investigation of sexual abuse is extremely difficult and hasn't been properly addressed in the research or guidelines.*

About participation in Conferences

We therefore asked the managers to rate themselves on the series of statements about parental participation in conferences discussed earlier in this Chapter.

The two statements which accrued the largest number of agreements (24 for each) concerned citizens' rights, and effectiveness of social work practice. Four managers identified their own position with both of these statements together.

The statement with which most disagreed (23) was the assertion that parents would find involvement in the procedures too distressing.

The other statement which attracted nearly as much disagreement (21) expressed doubts about whether trust can be maintained in abuse situations if there is complete openness.

Their views more or less reflected the views of the social workers in the whole sample giving a picture of workers and managers being in tune with each other's value positions and with current policy about family involvement.

As with the social workers, the majority of managers (16) rated their professional experience of a particularly difficult case as the main influence. Books and articles, however, rated far more highly for managers (over half) than for social workers (less than a quarter) and their 'other' comments included such individual influences as 'the enthusiasm of our child care co-ordinator' and 'my life experience of racism and lack of power'.

When asked what sort of priority family member participation held for them, 18 managers said it was 'high' or 'top' and one linked it with 'along with surviving the job'! If they did not specifically say 'high' or 'top' their comments indicated that participation was central to their thinking:

> *Most of the cases in my team where the children are on the register live at home with their parents. We need their active participation if protection is to work.*

but one manager said –

> *I have doubts about the distribution of power between the participants.*

The early literature on participation (Housiaux, 1984; Phillips and Evans, 1986; Brown and Waters, 1986; Morrison et al., 1990) contained many anxieties and cautious queries about what effect the presence of parents would have on the conferences. We asked this as an open question to the managers and just over half of the responses (13) were that the presence of parents resulted in less gossip, fewer value judgements, and more accurate and clear information.

Another group of positive responses (9) included that the conference was a more honest meeting, more professional and more focused because of the presence of parents. Some managers thought that the conferences were better organised because of written reports (4); that parents had a greater under-standing of and responsibility for the decisions made (6); and that the 'group' nature of the decisions was more obvious to parents (4). The negative replies contained views that the conference was more contentious, uncomfortable and longer (6); that it was daunting for parents (2); that some professionals colluded publicly with parents or browbeat them (2); and that there was a risk of parents needs overwhelming the children's (1). The largest group of negative responses (7) suggested that the professionals were inhibited by the presence of parents. When the managers were asked, on balance, whether the parents' presence was positive or negative they over-whelmingly stated that they thought it was positive (22) with one negative view including a proviso 'But in future when its positively planned it will be positive' and one 'don't know'. They said —

> *I feared agencies not sharing important information but in practice have not been aware of this*

and

> *Parents presence gives a feeling of completeness.*

Managers were asked if they thought it necessary for there to be additional training — 19 said 'yes' and specifically mentioned training for all professionals attending.

> *'All those attending need to be able to live with the fact that they may have to say unpalatable things in front of clients* _and_ *still maintain relations with them.'*

Four managers in addition suggested training for people who chair conferences and four suggested 'training' for parents. Eleven of the managers said they did not have the resources to meet those training needs but ten said that they did. Two did not know and one did not answer the question, so a reasonably clear picture emerges of respondents being committed to the idea of further training with nearly half of them believing the resources existed to do it.

Recording policies and leaflets

Even though an agency may have fulfilled the requirement to offer access to records, complaints procedures and explanations about child protection procedures, the information is useless unless it is disseminated. Social workers like anyone else are often enthusiastic at the start of a new scheme but persisting with it presents problems in ensuring that the leaflets reach the people for whom they are written.

Our question was 'How do you ensure leaflets are used by your staff?' Eleven of the managers said they reminded their staff from time to time either in team meetings or in supervision. One said the leaflets were sent to parents with the invitations to the conference. Three said that complaints leaflets were available in reception and two said they relied on staff to give them to clients whilst four replied with disarming honesty that they didn't have a system at all! It was clear from the study that both verbal and written information for parents was a key to their participation in the procedure. Unless they had information about what was happening any attempt to enable them to take a full part was seriously undermined. Therefore the use of leaflets played an important part in preparing the ground for participation and partnership.

Whilst visiting the offices in the seven areas (to attend child protection conferences and look at files), the researchers were aware of the pace of work and the bombardment of cases. We asked managers whether they thought their social workers were under greater pressure because of the child protection procedures. Thirteen replied 'Yes', six 'No' and three 'Yes and No'. Their reasons reflected the mixed blessings of such procedures and guidelines. Ten thought that they increased the volume of work whereas nine felt they offered a helpful framework and guidance. Two thought they protected social workers but three thought they could get in the way of professional judgement and could have the effect of creating obstacles to catch out staff.

> *The procedures cannot be seen as an end in themselves because at the end of the day we must still rely on sound professional judgement to protect children adequately.*

Four managers thought that the pressure came from the public rather than the procedures. One comment was tinged with cynicism or perhaps harsh reality:

> *Child protection procedures are largely about protecting the local authority and senior managers in the event of a tragedy or serious incident. The local authority and senior managers absolve themselves of responsibility by creating new procedures for any given situation for an already hard pressed*

and overworked social worker to follow. Thus in the event of a tragedy hopefully a low level scapegoat can be easily identified.

A final section in the questionnaire asked for other comments. We noted in particular the commitment of managers to the partnership philosophy of the Children Act, which they were about to implement. As well as responses about the need to prepare parents well and support them in order to move towards partnership, the managers suggested there must be consumer feedback before it could become an equal partnership.

Some wrote of the importance of recognising cultural and ethnic differences in conferences and the careful use of language. Others mentioned the problems of involving children and the conflict between parents and children which might arise. One argued in favour of time for the professionals to discuss things on their own; another gave a warning that having a conference and registering does not make a child safe, and a sigh that the pace of change in child protection had been too great. There was one strong comment about the unfairness of the system for parents:

I believe the conference system is intrinsically unjust. Parents do not have the means to compete with the professionals often ranged against them. Parental participation reduces arbitrary power but too often conferences remain a quasi-judicial setting. I'm not convinced that registration of children either reduces 'abuse' or strengthens family functioning.

Several respondents wrote similarly about what they regarded as the limitations of the procedures, including the conferences. Although the guidelines provide a way to manage abuse and neglect, the complexity of carrying them out, especially if it is 'to the letter', may profoundly affect the lives of families who come within their orbit, in a way which can swiftly cancel out participation and partnership and further decrease family self-respect and power. As a group the managers appeared to be more aware of this than the social workers, and expressed more strongly the view that much remains to be improved in relation to family participation in child protection procedures.

To conclude this section, we add our impression that morale amongst the workers we interviewed was generally high despite the pressures that they were under. First line managers were most likely to describe anxiety and pressure, whereas the morale of those whose role was mainly to chair conferences (mainly recently appointed after policies for involving parents had been adopted) was usually high. This appeared to be because of the congruence between their professional values and the way they were working.

Summary

- There were 138 different workers who held principal responsibility for these 220 cases. 80 per cent were white British, six were white people from another country and 13 were Afro-Caribbean or Asian. Only 8 did not hold a recognised child care social work qualification. None was under 25 and almost half were over 40. Three quarters had been working as qualified social workers for at least five years. Most worked in child care for most or all of their time, and almost two thirds had been the key worker with more than 20 child protection cases.

- Although 77 per cent were strongly in favour of working in partnership with family members, and the rest were generally in favour of it but had some reservations, only 31 per cent strongly agreed that they usually succeeded in working in partnership.

- All were strongly committed to attempting to involving children in their work, but most were unsure about whether they should attend child protection conferences.

- On the basis of their answers and their work on the cases the researchers rated 60 per cent as strongly participatory in their attitudes and only 2 per cent were rated as hardly participatory at all.

- The 24 managers and conference chairs who were interviewed or completed questionnaires were supportive of the attempts of workers to involve family members, but a minority expressed more reservations than the workers about the extent to which this was possible in some child protection cases.

- Morale amongst workers and managers was generally high, and this was especially so for those who spent a large proportion of their time chairing child protection conferences when parents were present. Workers and managers did however talk of the stress and anxiety which was a part of their professional lives and came not so much from their work with parents and children but from the fear of failing to protect a child.

- Most of the workers and managers were strongly in favour of parents being present throughout child protection conferences unless there were clearly stated reasons why this should not happen. Where this was not ACPC policy they were trying to persuade the ACPC to move in this direction. Their major reasons for this were that conferences were more effective if parents were present and they also believed that parents had rights to hear what was being said and to give their own account and put their point of view to the conference before important decisions were made.

Chapter 6

Social Work Practice in the 220 Cases

Overview of the protection process

Details have already been given in Chapter 4 of the abuse or neglect which led to the conference. The questionnaire and the interview sought information about the social workers' approach to child and family social work and child protection work, and whether they saw any difference between the two; and asked for a detailed account and analysis of the work with this particular case. Checklists were used to gain a view of the different services offered, covering questions about the social work relationship with the family members, any practical assistance offered, and any therapeutic approaches or casework methods used. Information from the social workers was complemented by material from the records, and from the family questionnaires or interviews. In a few cases it was also possible to observe the interaction between the social worker and the parents or children if members came to the child protection conference attended by a researcher. In other cases where family members did not attend, the researcher went with the social worker after the conference to invite parents to help with the study, and hear how the conference conclusions were described to the parents.

The questions about practice were divided into three stages – the investigation stage and the work around the conference; the more detailed assessment stage if the case remained open after the conference; and, merging with this, any supportive or therapeutic work aimed at improving the situation for the child or the other family members. Workers were asked to describe their practice at these various stages in their own words. The researchers categorised the work as a whole in the light of the different sources of information. Categories used were the descriptive/analytical categories devised by Hardiker and her colleagues (1991) to describe preventive social work practice, but with two additional categories.

> **Backs to the Wall** was a term used to illustrate preventive work which is undertaken 'against the odds' because either agency resources are inadequate or the family is not successfully engaged in the work.
>
> **Preventive Packages** referred to the range and diversity of resources and services orchestrated in attempts to keep a family together in the community, the emphasis being on resources rather than relationship-based help or therapy.
>
> **De-labelling or Down-Tariffing** was used to describe one aspect of what Hardiker describes as 'the new orthodoxy in social

services – i.e. diversion, minimum necessary intervention and preventing agency dependency.'

Family Casework Hardiker describes as 'a form of practice which most social workers will recognise: it was the backbone of the post-war childcare services and it still continues. It combines the purposive use of a helping relationship with a range of therapeutic and practical resources.'

The following two categories apply more specifically to protection work:

Labelling/Up-Tariffing describes multidisciplinary work with the intention of collecting systematic evidence in cases where it is suspected that abuse or neglect are causing significant harm to the child, but where parents are not specifically asking for help. This work may aim at removal of the child or at convincing parents that there is a problem with which they or the child need help.

Child Protection or Child Therapy were used to indicate that protection and long-term or short-term help for the child/ren was the major focus of all the work. Help for the parents played no part in the work, or was minimal and incidental to the service offered to the child/ren.

Factual information about the frequency of visits, whether children were seen separately or with their parents, and where the visits took place was gained from the record and details about average length of visits were provided by the workers. As mentioned in Chapter 2, we had information directly from 116 of the 138 social workers, either through interviews or questionnaires. In some other cases it was possible for the researcher to complete the schedule after reading the record, so that our numbers for analysis vary between 116 and 138. When analysis is on a case basis rather than a social worker basis, the possible total is either 220 for work with the main carer, or 385 when work with any family member is referred to.

Before considering the detail of the protection and social work service, it should be noted that it was not unusual to find discrepancies between the information given by the social workers, different family members, and that which was available from the records. In some cases there was clear evidence about what did happen, and an explanation was apparent about why the discrepancy occurred. When several meetings were held about a particular situation, it was possible for family members to be confused about precisely which meeting we were asking them about. In other cases the stress around a particularly traumatic investigation might have led a parent or child to obliterate a detailed memory of the event. In one case, for instance, it was clear that a parent had attended a child protection conference since her contribution to the conference was noted in detail in the minutes. However, she assured the interviewer that she had not been there; not (it was considered in the light of the totality of the conversation) with the intention of deceiving the interviewer but because her recall of events around that traumatic week was extremely confused.

In other cases the family member had made notes or a tape-recording of a particular event or conversation, but a social worker gave a different account which, in the light of information from the parents and the file, was a less accurate one. In some cases parents took more careful and contemporaneous notes of events than did the social workers. In other cases, although there was agreement about the facts of what had occurred, social workers and parents interpreted the facts differently. A social worker might have thought that she had explained fully that a meeting was to occur, or that this was an abuse investigation, but the family member had interpreted the communication differently. As we shall note later in the chapter on working in partnership, this difficulty for us as researchers reinforces the importance of communicating with family members using different methods, and repeating key information at different times.

In this chapter we describe the **process** and **nature** of social work involvement, and in Chapters 7 and 8 we consider whether the practice was associated with the participation of the different family members.

Registration and case closure

Although 38 per cent of the conferences did not lead to the placing of a child's name on the child protection register, almost all of the families continued to experience some involvement of a social worker. Twenty-seven of the cases (12 per cent) were closed after the conference, and a further three were closed within six weeks of the conference. Twenty were closed between six weeks and three months, and 21 between four months and six months after the conference. One hundred and forty-two (67 per cent) were still open to a social worker at the six month stage.

Six cases where the decision of the conference had been deferred were the subject of further conferences which decided not to place the child's name on the register, and reconvened conferences decided to register two children. The major reason for deferring a decision was that inadequate information was available during the first conference. However, deferment was used by some workers as a means of control and in order to enforce greater compliance on a parent, usually in cases already known to the department, where the allegation was neglect, a series of minor injuries, over chastisement, or emotional abuse.

> *The actual conference formalises it. An adjournment makes them more aware it is very serious. Chairpersons are very serious. They don't crack*

> *jokes. A chair might nod but it is usually very formal. It was about a chance for improvement. You can register any child, but I don't see any point in registering unnecessarily. Deferment gave her [the parent] a chance to avoid registration. The disadvantage of registration is that it raises expectations in other agencies. Also it can take a lot of confidence away from a parent. Or a parent may say, 'The child is on the register so you've got to provide'.*

In four cases where a child's name had been placed on the register it was removed within eight weeks, and in a further two cases the child's name was removed from the register between two and four months after the conference. In a further 18 cases the child's name was removed from the register between four and six months after the initial conference. Thus in 113 cases (53 per cent of the cohort and 82 per cent of the registered cases) the child's name was still on the child protection register six months after the first conference. (This information was not available to the researchers in respect of seven cases.)

The early stages of the case and previous social work involvement

Although 33 per cent of the families were not known to the social services department before this particular referral, there had been social work involvement which had ended at some time prior to the referral in 35 per cent of cases, and 70 cases (32 per cent) were either receiving a service or being monitored at the time of the referral. Forty per cent of the families had not previously requested help from social services, 56 per cent had requested help and it had been received at least to some extent, and nine had requested some form of service from the social services department which was not provided.

We had information about the degree of satisfaction with the service offered prior to the child protection referral from 62 families. Eighteen (29 per cent) were dissatisfied with the service offered prior to the child protection referral. Seventeen (27 per cent) were fairly satisfied, and 19 (20 per cent) were satisfied or very satisfied although nine of these considered that the service had not lasted for long enough.

Sufficient information was available to categorise the previous work with 140 of the cases according to the 'Hardiker' categories listed earlier in this chapter. Ten came in the 'Backs to the Wall' category, 42 were purely child protection cases (and in three of these the worker was hoping to find additional evidence in order to move the case into the child protection arena). The largest group (41 per cent) came into the 'preventive packages' group. This category was used for cases where the main form of assistance was the provision of services, unsupported by more systematic family casework. Twenty cases came into the 'De-labelling' or 'Down Tariffing' category. Thus only 27 (19 per cent) were offered a service which included both a supportive relationship and the provision of appropriate services. A more usual pattern was for brief interventions around the crisis, or the request for practical help, often on a crisis basis and delivered by the duty worker or intake team.

> *For example, a single mother with three children aged 12, 8 and 1 was referred anonymously three times to social services and the NSPCC during the two months before the child protection conference. These had been followed up and no further action taken. The allegations were of neglect and of leaving the children alone. The fourth anonymous referral alleged bruising to the baby as a result of him being tipped out of his pram whilst his mother was drunk. A planning meeting was held by social services and a home visit made. The duty social worker found no-one at home, but whilst there the eldest child returned from school and demonstrated how he gained entry to the home by shinning up the drainpipe! At the child protection conference it was decided to register the three children in the category of grave concern and decided that the mother's 'life-style and ability to protect' were to be assessed by the key worker. This was carried out during four home visits and two interviews at the office following the conference. Assistance was offered with the payment of gas and electricity bills. The mother was also referred to an alcohol advisory group. Core group minutes four months later stated that the mother had 'co-operated well with what was planned'. She 'finds no real difficulty with the children' and 'she did an awful lot with the children in the summer'. The mother replied in her research questionnaire, 'they just said that if I didn't get myself together and they had any more phone calls about the children, they would go straight into care. There should be a more friendlier way about things and offer some kind of help.' She said she was not 'allowed to go in the conference but was there for when they had finished.' She wrote, 'there were only two conferences about my children, one which put them on the child protection list, which I would have liked to have had a say in, and the one which took my children off, which I was allowed to attend in full.' She said her social worker was appointed to her case, 'after the first conference and just before the last one' and she regretted that she could not have seen him earlier and without the threats.*

This was a 'de-labelling' case prior to the child protection registration, briefly moved into the 'packages of care' group, and then back to 'de-labelling'.

> *A second example is of a mother and her partner who were having problems with her daughter of five. The mother had asked on three earlier*

occasions for help with her and also for help to decorate the house and for clothing. She was redirected each time by the duty social worker to the housing department or the DSS. Her third request for a full-time nursery place for the child was also redirected to the education department. She eventually hit the child with a hairbrush causing bruises which led to the child protection procedures. The police were involved to take photographs of the injuries and in their report to the social services wrote, 'this is a mother crying out for help with a difficult child.' It appeared to have been a classic example of a mother seeking help in advance of the injuries but her request not being given due consideration because of a crisis-oriented duty system. She found the child protection conference 'very distressing. I do not feel as though they really put you at ease' but once she was allocated a social worker the situation improved and she liked her social worker. 'She was always very honest and open about what was going on and always kept me informed.'

In the opinion of the researchers, the use of child protection procedures in this case could have been avoided and a less costly and more effective family casework service offered at an earlier stage.

A third example was of a daughter aged 15-years who was being rebellious. She was punched and bruised by her father on an access visit. Her mother thought she was out of hand and called in social services. The duty system referred to the Child Guidance Clinic and the information given to the mother and daughter was adequate and clear. However, the mother was very upset - 'I had no help from no-one'. She felt that having different social workers labelled her a failure as a 'mum'. She wanted more support after the case conference but felt that the social workers were pressing her to do things that each of them recommended differently, and she did not like them telling her what to do with her children. It might have been easier for her to accept such advice had she had one regular social worker over a period of time. She wanted to be treated as 'a human being, not an animal'. She felt they took over her children by telling her what to do.

In Chapter 3 it was noted that a large proportion of the families had experienced quite severe difficulties in the year leading up to the conference, and 52 of them (87 per cent) said they had told a social worker about their difficulties.

The referral and investigation stage of the work

Table 6.1 shows the source of the referral or allegation of abuse or neglect. Although 47 cases were open to a social worker at the time of the referral, only in 19 cases were the social workers themselves responsible for changing the status of the case from a general child care case to a child protection case. The largest source of referrals was a parent (24 per cent of cases), with referrals from the child (15 per cent of cases) being the next highest group. Most of these were passed through to social services via an intermediary professional such as a health worker or more often a teacher. Teachers and day care workers played a major part in the referral of these children, closely followed by health care professionals.

Table 6.1   Source of child protection referral

SOURCE OF REFERRAL OF ALLEGATION OF ABUSE OR NEGLECT (n = 207)

Source	Number	%
Child	33	15
Mother	42	19
Father	6	3
Both parents	5	2
Relative	10	5
Teacher/day carer	32	15
Foster parent	3	1
Health professional	27	12
Neighbour	9	4
Social worker	19	9
Police officer	13	6
Other professional worker	8	4
Not clear	13	6

Once the referral had been received or allegation made, the initial investigation took place on the same day in 41 per cent of cases, and within a week in 74 per cent of cases. It was more likely that, when the case was already open to social services departments, the investigation would be conducted more slowly in the period before the initial conference. Other circumstances in which the initial investigation proceeded more slowly were those involving sexual abuse where an older child asked that her parents should not be contacted immediately.

Was the conference necessary?

Using the guidance in the 1988 version of *Working Together* which was operative at the time, expanded upon by SSI Reports such as those on Rochdale (1990) and Manchester (1990), and inspection schedules of the Social Services Inspectorate (1993)), we used a rating scheme to consider whether the convening of a child protection conference was justified in the light of Department of Health guidelines (see Appendix for rating protocols). We considered that it was not in 18 cases (8 per cent), and probably not in 17 cases (16 per cent in total).

In 19 cases we considered that it was probably necessary but that the timing was inappropriate. These cases were often those already known to the department, and concerned allegations of emotional abuse or neglect which was not life-threatening and thus there was a possibility of choice about timing. In some cases it was an increase of practical problems which pushed the family over the dividing line between child care and child protection. The stress of acute practical and emotional difficulties combined with poverty led to deteriorating circumstances for the children. However, in the absence of the danger of serious injury it would probably have been more appropriate to work to resolve some of these practical difficulties, particularly around housing and day care, and decide at that stage whether the situation still required child protection procedures. To initiate procedures in those circumstances confused the parents in that child protection concerns became mixed up in their minds with the need for practical help. In all such cases a package of practical assistance was put in place after the conference, and these were most likely to be the ones where a decision was deferred, or the child was very quickly de-registered. We also had doubts about the appropriateness of initiating child protection procedures at a time when a normally caring and competent parent suffered a deterioration in mental health which led to hospital admission. It was very hard to engage these parents with the child protection procedures, and all the work which was undertaken to help the children could usually have been undertaken without the requirement or formal child protection procedures. Action to provide care for the children, sometimes by calling upon relatives, or by the use of voluntary care, or even place of safety orders, could have been initiated in the emergency circumstances of the parent's admission to hospital. The need for formal child protection procedures could have been reviewed in the light of the parent's response to treatment.

Parental permission to interview child

We enquired whether the child was first interviewed in the presence of a parent, or with the permission of at least one parent. When an allegation of abuse was made by a child, often to a teacher or youth worker, it was difficult to be clear when a conversation turned into an investigative interview. For purposes of the study we assumed that a second more formal interview with a headteacher or child protection specialist within the school, or social worker, was the first investigatory interview with the child. In over one-third of the cases the child was interviewed without the parents' permission or knowledge. This interview was usually conducted by a social worker in the school. It is generally agreed that it is not always a good idea for parents to be actually present when a child is being interviewed, especially about sexual abuse. However, to formally interview a child without gaining a parent's consent, or at least telling a parent that an investigative interview is to take place, should only happen if it is considered that there will be serious risk of harm to the child, or prejudice to future enquiries if the parent is informed. In 23 cases it was not clear whether or not the parents' permission had been given, and in five cases there was conflicting evidence. In only 59 per cent of the cases where the child was considered to be old enough for a formal interview, and we had sufficient evidence, was a parent either present when the child was interviewed, or gave permission for the interview, or was told that it was to take place but was not present.

Several of the social workers interviewed seemed unclear about agency policy in respect of seeking parents' permission to formally interview a child, and did not seem concerned about proceeding some way into an investigation before contacting them. The guidance in both versions of *Working Together* is less clear about this than on other aspects of practice. One agency was very clear that a parent **should** be contacted before a child was formally interviewed, and its workers were clear about why they very occasionally did not follow the guidelines.

> *Although it was against the agency policy, in this case I did agree to her [teenage girl] request to interview her without her parents' permission. I did insist, though, that the parents had a right to know.*

We looked more closely at the cases where parental permission was not sought before the first investigatory interview with the child. We anticipated that this would be more likely to occur in sexual abuse cases and indeed parental permission for the child to be formally interviewed was not sought in 37 per cent of cases where sexual abuse was alleged. However, this was also the case in 33 per cent of cases where physical abuse was alleged, in four of the 11 cases where neglect was the allegation, and in three of the seven cases where emotional abuse was alleged. When we considered the severity of abuse, we found that interviewing the child without parental permission was most likely to occur in cases where excessive or repeated physical punishment was alleged. In 47 per cent of these cases (9 out of 19) the child was first interviewed without the permission of a parent. There appeared to be no other difference in terms of the severity of abuse as to whether the child was interviewed with or without the parents' permission in the first instance. In 39 per cent of cases where the child's major placement was with an alleged abuser, the child was initially interviewed without the consent of a parent, as compared with 34 per cent of the cases where the child's major placement was not with the alleged abuser. Thirty-one per cent of the cases where no order was eventually made came into this grouping of children being interviewed without parental permission, compared with 45 per cent of those where a court order of some sort was subsequently made. Our general conclusion was that it was agency policy and/or social work practice rather than (with a few exceptions) the nature of the case which determined whether the child would be formally interviewed about abuse without prior contact with a parent. This is an important issue since, as we shall see, it had an impact on the later willingness or otherwise of the parents to become engaged in the work to protect the child.

Voluntary care

We ascertained whether voluntary or respite care might have been appropriate at the time of the first interview and whether it was offered. It might have been appropriate in 93 of the 216 cases about which we had sufficient information, and was in fact offered in 21 cases. It was requested but not offered in 22 cases, but on the evidence available to the researchers could have been discussed (but wasn't) as possibly helpful in a further 50 cases.

First contact between professionals and family members

We were interested to learn from parents, the older children, and the social workers how the first visit was accomplished, and who was present when abuse was first discussed with the different family members.

They were also asked if they knew that this first investigatory interview this was about abuse or neglect. This was a more complicated question in those cases where a social worker was already visiting since it was sometimes not clear, especially with allegations of neglect or emotional abuse, exactly when the case turned into a child protection case rather than a general family support case. Of the 60 families who replied to this question, 70 per cent said they knew that this was an investigation of abuse or neglect during the first interview, whilst 17 (28 per cent) said that they had not been made aware of the allegation during this first interview. Our conclusions from the records or social worker interviews on the full cohort of 220 cases were similar in that we considered that in 71 per cent of the cases it was made clear at the first investigatory interview that was an investigation of abuse or neglect was taking place, in 25 per cent this was not made clear, and in 3 per cent of cases we were unsure, or had inadequate information.

It was more difficult to be clear about how the explanation to **the child** was given since this was not always clearly explained on the record. Seventy of the children were, we considered, too young for anything other than a very practical explanation of what was happening. Of the 122 children where it was considered that a child was old enough to play some part in the decisions about how the investigation should be handled, and where we had sufficient evidence to come to a conclusion about the extent to which an adequate explanation was given, we concluded that the child was given a partial explanation in 95 cases (78 per cent), and that no explanation or an inadequate explanation was given in a further 21 cases (17 per cent). We considered that the social worker and others involved in the investigation (mainly police and teachers) worked in partnership with the young person at the investigation stage in 6 of these 122 cases (5 per cent).

In view of the emphasis placed on joint working at the referral stage, we were interested to know who took part in the first interviews with the parents and the 166 children who were beyond infancy following the allegation. Table 6.2 gives the responses. It can be seen from this table that, although around a third of the first interviews with children were joint ones with police and social workers, in 26 per cent it was one or two social workers, and in 12 per cent of cases it was police officer(s) without another professional. One or two social workers undertook half of the initial interviews with the **parent who was the main carer**, and around a third were joint social worker and police interviews. A social worker alone was involved in the first interview with a third of fathers allegedly abusing or neglecting the child and this interview was most likely to be conducted by a police officer or officers on their own. Teachers were involved either alone or jointly in a substantial minority of first interviews with the child (13 per cent). Social workers were most likely to conduct the first interview when the allegation was against the mother or parenting pair. The amount of investigation undertaken by doctors is underestimated because infants were left out of this question, and they constitute a larger proportion of those cases where a doctor alone is likely to be involved in the initial investigation process.

In the 122 cases where it was known that a medical examination took place, no parent or relative was present in 23 cases (19 per cent); the mother, sometimes accompanied by the father or another relative, accompanied the child in 82 cases (67 per cent); the father was there in 12 cases (10 per cent), and a relative went with the child in 5 cases (4 per cent). We had information about whether the main carer felt that the investigation stage had been satisfactorily carried out in 76 cases. Twelve (16 per cent) of these were very satisfied and 20 (26 per cent) considered that it was satisfactory. The remaining 44 (well over half) considered that the investigation was not satisfactorily carried out, with 22 of these (29 per cent) being definitely dissatisfied.

We shall return to discuss the nature of the **social work** practice during this investigation and pre-conference stage when discussing the social work process as a whole, but call attention here to the substantial amount of social work time which was given over to the investigation stage of these cases.

Table 6.2 Professionals present at first interview about abuse or neglect with different family members

Professional	With child		With parents/ carer		With alleged abuser (mother or parenting pair)		With alleged abuser (father)	
	No.	%	No.	%	No.	%	No.	%
One social worker	41	20.0	90	43.0	45	43.0	32	26.0
Two social workers	2	1.0	12	6.0	6	6.0	8	7.0
Police officer(s)	20	10.0	25	12.0	16	15.0	49	40.0
GP or other doctor	12	6.0	13	6.0	9	9.0	0	0
Nurse/Health visitor	1	0.5	2	1.0	2	2.0	0	0
Teacher(s)	19	9.0	0	0	1	1.0	0	0
Social worker and police officer	43	21.0	56	27.0	22	21.0	30	25.0
Social worker and teacher	7	3.0	1	0.5	0	0	0	0
Social worker, teacher and police officer	2	1.0	1	0.5	0	0	1	1
Social worker, doctor and police officer	4	2.0	3	1.0	2	2.0	0	0
Unborn child/child too young	54	26.0	0	0	0	0	0	0
Other combination	0	0	4	2.0	2	2.0	1	1.0
Total	205	100.0	207	100.0	105	100.0	121	100.0
Not relevant/not known/not clear	15		13		115		92	

The initial child protection conference stage

Parents

In half of the cases at least one parent or carer was **invited** to the initial conference although only a quarter were invited to attend the whole of it. Thirty-one per cent were invited to attend the end or a small part of the conference, and 18 per cent were not invited at all to this first conference. Thirty-six per cent of main carers **attended** most or all of the conference, and 38 per cent did not attend. Thus 20 per cent who were invited did not attend. Sixty-five of those attending most or all of the initial conferences were known or alleged to have been involved in the abuse or neglect (30 per cent of these parents) as were 32 (35 per cent) of the parents who were not thought to be implicated in the maltreatment of the child. A mother and father or male partner attended together in 28 conferences; a father on his own came to four; and a mother with her own mother to three. In the other cases the mother attended, sometimes with a supporter. This rate of attendance for fathers is an interesting finding in view of the often voiced criticism that social workers rarely succeed in engaging men in their child protection and child care practice.

Children

There were 72 cases where we considered that older children might have been involved in the process. (We took as a rough guide children aged 10 or over unless there were specific reasons why this was not appropriate, such as a serious learning disability). Three of these young people attended the whole of the conference (4 per cent), and six were invited to most of it (8 per cent), although only two of these actually went. Three were invited to and attended the end or a small part of the conference (4 per cent), making a total of 8 who played some part in the conference.

Relatives

There were 13 cases where a relative played an important part in supporting the family even though not as a full-time carer. Six of these attended the whole conference, two went to most of it, one took a small part, and four (31 per cent) were not invited.

Parents not living at home

Thirteen of the 38 parents who were not living at home at the time of the incident and were not implicated in it were not invited to the initial case conference. Nine were invited to the end, and 15 were invited to all or most of it. Nine implicated in the abuse or neglect attended the whole of the initial conference, and three attended most of it. Seven attended at the end and a half (19) did not attend at all. The often expressed anxiety as to whether alleged abusers should attend conferences seemed not to present major problems in practice, in those conferences they attended.

Figure 6.1 gives details about the attendance of the main carers, the children, and non-resident parents at the initial conference. Twenty-two relatives and 13 friends attended at least part of the initial conference in a supporting role. In 78 per cent of the cases where a parent or parenting pair attended they were not accompanied by a supporter. In six cases an interpreter also acted as a supporter, although this practice was not encouraged by those experienced in working with clients whose first language was not English. In two cases a solicitor, and in one case another professional worker attended in a supporting role. Figure 6.2 shows the attendance rates in

Figure 6.1 **Attendance of family members at initial child protection conference**

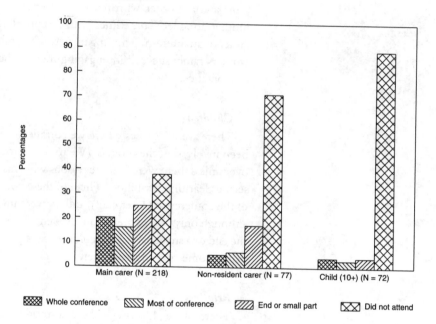

Figure 6.2 **Attendance of main parent(s) at initial conference by involvement in alleged abuse (n = 216)**

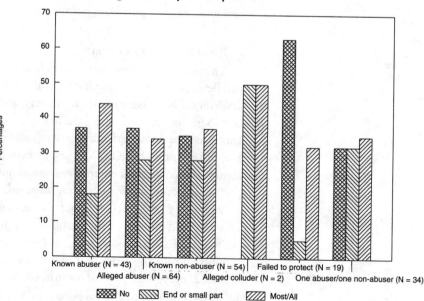

terms of alleged culpability for the abuse. It is interesting to note that those known **not** to be implicated in the maltreatment were not significantly more likely to attend than those who were alleged or known to be implicated.

Preparation for the conference

We asked parents and social workers, and scrutinised the file for indications of how the parents and children were prepared for the initial conference, whether or not they attended, and reached a researcher rating in the light of the evidence available. In six cases the parents were not told that an initial conference was being held, but in 85 per cent of cases we considered that they were well or quite well prepared for the conference, leaving only 16 cases where they were not well prepared. However, a more negative picture emerges from the 74 family members who responded to the questionnaire. Of the 67 who answered the question about whether they considered that the conference was adequately explained to them, almost a third said that it had not been, and a third similarly said that the register had not been adequately explained to them. Forty-two per cent said that they had not been given sufficient information about the child protection process by the social worker before the conference. We have already noted that amongst the small sample and the respondents to the questionnaires, those who attended conferences are over-represented compared with the sample as a whole. It is, therefore, interesting to note that after the conference, despite the general lack of adequate information beforehand, 57 per cent stated that they understood the decisions and recommendations of the conference, whilst only 6 per cent said that they did not, and 37 per cent said they did to some extent. Twenty-four of those who did not attend or attended only at the end responded to the question as to whether their views had been represented at the conference. Half said their views had been represented by the social worker or another attender, and half said that they did not know but thought not, since nobody had specifically asked them what their views were prior to the conference.

We also rated the extent to which the **child** was well prepared for the initial conference. In 87 cases the child was too young for information about the conference to be necessary, and in 39 cases we had insufficient information about the extent of preparation of the child. In 24 of the remaining 94 cases (26 per cent), the child was not told about the conference before it happened, but in 48 cases we considered that the child was at least quite well prepared, including 23 cases where the child was very well prepared. There were three cases where the social worker said that the child had not been prepared for the conference happening because it was not in the child's interests for such a discussion to take place.

Time from referral to conference

We have already noted that in most cases the investigation started on the same day as the allegation was received. However, there was more variation in the length of time between the allegation and the conference taking place. At the time of the research the recommendation from the Department of Health was that conferences should take place within eight days. However, managers and workers told us that, having taken action to ensure that the child was safe at the investigation stage, they found it difficult to complete the work necessary in preparing family members for the conference in the eight or so days recommended. Some stated that they thought it was inappropriate to rush the process, since it was important for the investigation to be completed so that conference members could make decisions based on as much information as possible. Figure 6.3 shows that in less than half of the cases was the initial conference held within 14 days of the allegation being received, and in 36 per cent of cases more than three weeks elapsed. In 47 cases either the information was not available, or it was unclear when the actual allegation leading to a child protection investigation was made. This was most likely when the case was already open to a social worker, or a series of episodes which could denote cause for concern were dealt with by the duty system.

Figure 6.3 **Time between allegation and initial conference**

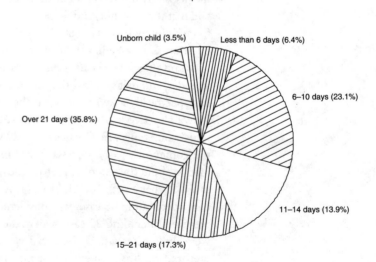

Sample = 173

Unborn child (3.5%)   Less than 6 days (6.4%)

6–10 days (23.1%)

Over 21 days (35.8%)

11–14 days (13.9%)

15–21 days (17.3%)

Size of conference

Several research studies have commented on the difficulty for parents attending large child protection conferences, and the 1991 guidance in *Working Together* (Para. 4.24) states that:

> *Meetings that are unnecessarily large inhibit discussion and do not use valuable resources to the best advantage. Large numbers of professionals, some of whom make no apparent contribution, are particularly inhibiting to parents and children and will in any event probably find the conference a difficult occasion.*

Leaving out the chair, the minute-taker, and the parents or children themselves, in 18 per cent of cases there were five or fewer attenders, and in 29 per cent of cases there were six or seven attenders. In the majority (a third) there were between eight and ten attenders, and in 19 per cent of cases (40 conferences) there were eleven or more attenders.

Conference recommendations

We have already noted that the initial conference resulted in registration in 62 per cent of cases. In 18 cases the recommendation of the conferences was that no further action should be taken. In 127 cases the social services department or another department was to offer help to the family or the child. In six cases the decision was that further assessment should be undertaken, prior to the provision of services. In 46 cases (19 per cent) the conference recommended that court action should either be initiated or continued in those cases where legal action had already been initiated through a place of safety order. In 13 of these police action was also recommended in respect of the alleged abuser, and this was the case also in six cases where legal action to protect the child was not thought necessary making a total of 19 (9 per cent of the cohort) where action in the criminal courts was suggested or taken.

In 23 cases mainly when the child was not registered, (11 per cent) it was not thought necessary to appoint a keyworker; in 33 cases (16 per cent) the social worker involved in the investigation was appointed as keyworker; in 58 per cent of cases a new worker was named as keyworker, and in 8 per cent of cases the decision was taken later about who would be the keyworker. It is interesting to note that the term 'keyworker' was used, and the worker appointed to this role, in several cases which did not result in registration of the child. In our observation of conferences we noted that in some cases, despite the fact that a decision was taken that the child should not be registered, the conference continued to discuss a protection plan and to appoint a keyworker as if a decision had been taken that registration was necessary. Lack of clarity in this respect may lead to confusion on the part of family members about whether they are free or not free to accept the services of the worker thus named by the conference. Some parents greatly welcomed the offer of services even though the child's name was not placed on the register.

> *The first conference I was petrified because I didn't know what the conference was, and I thought they'd put the children's names on the register. This one was brilliant. I didn't know the outcome but I wasn't so scared. I thought protection was that they would take my kids away. They had nothing on me. If anyone had gone through what I've gone through they'd be superwoman. I never know if my ex-husband would be coming up behind me with a knife. My social worker went through all her notes with me and I felt comfortable now. It's weird. She helped me afterwards.*

> *My social worker has, I believe, been very good with me and the children. She was very patient and understanding. She's been just as concerned as myself about how the children are coping with everything.*

In other cases where registration did not happen parents felt obliged to accept the visit of a worker against their will or better judgement.

One mother whose problems diminished shortly after the conference when she was rehoused to more suitable accommodation felt that the conference, which did not register the child, required her to accept social work visits.

> *I had to go to this conference as if I was on trial. If Paul gets beaten up, I certainly wouldn't tell them [social workers]. I'd go to the police before I went to them. They are a waste of time. I think social workers are rubbish. This one who comes is hopeless. I've told her I don't need your help any more but she keeps coming.*

Practice on the way in which family members were informed about the conference decisions varied from agency to agency and team to team. Those parents who attended throughout the conference, or were there at the end, were told of the decisions at that stage. Those who did not attend, or who had attended at an earlier part of the meeting but did not remain until the end of the conference, were dependent on communication from someone who had been at the conference to let them know what had happened. Our discussions with the family members involved in the intensive study made us aware that even when family members are actually at the conference, written information and further discussions are often necessary to ensure that they are clear about the conclusions, and their implications. Some workers were at pains to ensure that the parent, who was not at the conference when the other parent was, received a verbal or written account. This was important with non-resident parents but happened only in a minority of such cases. We saw some very sensitive practice with those Asian families where the father attended the conference to ensure that the mother who remained at home fully understood what had happened. Interpreters were used by some workers, whereas others assumed that the family members who spoke English would communicate with those who did not. A third of the main carers only had a verbal account of the decisions of the conference, whilst just under half were informed verbally and also in writing, either by letter or by receiving copies of the minutes or the recommendations. A quarter were only informed in writing, either by letter or on receipt of the minutes or recommendations. In only a small number of cases were the full minutes received, but in three agencies it was normal practice for the conference decisions to be written on a separate sheet and produced quickly after the meeting and circulated to all those in attendance including the parents. In that way even if the full minutes were delayed, the recommendations were quickly available. In only one case were the decisions of the conference not given verbally or in writing, and this was the case where the parents were not told that a conference was being held.

Just over a half of the family members who responded to our request for their views said that they had received a letter telling them about the results of the conference. It should be remembered that a higher proportion of these than in the sample as a whole attended the conference or were there at the end. It was our impression that workers sometimes considered that they would therefore be adequately informed without the need for written confirmation. Three-quarters of those who did have a letter or other written confirmation thought that its contents told them what they needed to know. Twenty-eight (47 per cent of those who answered this question) said they received the minutes of the conference. However, in some cases they showed us these minutes when we interviewed them, and it was clear that what they had actually received was only a small part of the minutes dealing with the recommendations.

Was registration necessary?

We have already noted that when we considered the conferences alongside the guidance in *Working Together*, the conferences either were not or probably were not necessary in about a quarter of the cases.

We also used the guidance to reach a 'researcher rating' about whether registration was necessary in the 62 per cent of registered cases. Here we found less discrepancy between areas and concluded that in 10 per cent of the registered cases registration either was not, or probably was not, necessary.

After the conference

In 18 cases there was no further action or social work service after the conference. For the remaining cases the social work service started at the investigation stage, or already being provided, continued, usually with a fuller assessment; a full assessment was embarked upon and the case then closed or a full assessment was embarked upon either accompanied by or followed by a social work service. When children were placed away from home, in some cases there was heavy involvement of a social worker with the parents as well as the children. In other cases there was little contact with parents, sometimes because parents refused contact and only saw the worker at formal occasions such as court, but with other parents the social worker made little effort to keep them involved.

In most cases social work help and support, assessment and the provision of services, sometimes including therapy for the different family members, started before the conference and continued until case closure. Sometimes the service was offered throughout by the same worker, but more often the initial investigation was undertaken by one worker, and the case was transferred to a long-term worker after the conference. Whilst family centre and other resource workers were often involved in the assessment, this was less likely to be the case with long-term work. In 30 cases a family centre worker or other resource worker worked jointly with the key worker either during the assessment or afterwards, and in a further 12 cases two field workers worked jointly after the conference. In the majority of cases one social worker doubled as key worker, assessor, helper and therapist.

Assessment and reassessment

In all continuing cases there was some form of assessment or reassessment. A comprehensive assessment based on Department of Health guidelines (1988) was undertaken in 20 per cent of the cases. A different model was used in a further 31 cases so that in a third of the cases there was a full assessment after the conference. A partial family assessment was undertaken in a further 50 cases. In 67 cases the assessment was confined to the abuse and protection aspect of the case, and in 12 cases the assessment focused mainly on the child who was alleged to have been abused. We also noted whether a full family history was included in the records. By the six month stage in about half of the cases a comprehensive family history was available from the file, and a partial family history, usually provided for the initial conference, was on the file in 48 per cent of the cases. In only 16 cases was no family history at all to be found in the file. However, in many cases the researcher had to glean the family histories from a number of entries because they were not written as one report. Increasingly, as the research study proceeded, it became a requirement from the conferences to have a written summary of the investigation findings and the family background. There was evidence on file or from the social worker that a full or partial assessment of risk was undertaken in most cases. Only in 17 cases (8 per cent of the files we saw) was there no partial or full risk assessment on the file.

It is important to note here that in the examination of the files, the researchers counted a mention of finances, conditions of the house, how family members were described (ill or well, etc) what they had done or what had happened to them, as evidence of an assessment. It has to be said, however, that facts were rarely commented on or the opinions substantiated in terms of a professional judgement. There were hardly any social or family histories on the file which were written **specifically** as family histories. The majority were written for the child protection conference or for the court. The pressure of other work, of lack of time, or no expectation to produce such histories may account for their absence. As a tool of the social work trade for getting and weighing up information and providing an opportunity for the social worker to reflect upon the information in relation to the family, the lack seems a regrettable gap. For example –

> *A 15-year old accused her father of sexual abuse. The assessment of the immediate situation was the questioning carried out by the police and social worker. There was no record on file of how that was done nor the details of what was said on which the information given at the case conference was based. The information that an assessment had taken place was evident only from the child protection conference minutes, and a reference in the contact sheet that the social worker had taken the child for the interview. The father was arrested, interviewed and bailed to live elsewhere, but it never came to court. It could be that the whole of the information was given at the child protection conference but not recorded, and that it was a method agreed to preserve confidentiality. However, there was nothing on file as a summary or social history relating to what had happened, the family circumstances, the child's behaviour, or state of mind.*

Similarly, there was a wide spectrum in the files of what constituted a risk assessment. A few, particularly from family centre workers, were detailed family histories of which the risk assessment was a part, carried out over a period of six or ten sessions with the family, and written in consultation with the family. Others were descriptions and comments on the contact sheets and it was possible to deduce from later decisions and actions that they had formed the basis of the assessment of possible risk to the child.

The assessments usually covered the attachment of the children with their parents, but less frequently with siblings and other relatives. Material circumstances were usually included but in almost half of the cases there was little or no reference to the health of the parents. There was a greater likelihood that

problems would be recorded than **positive** features of the family, but nevertheless in most cases reference was made to family strengths as well as weaknesses.

Our conclusion from the file scrutiny and our discussions was that the Department of Health (1988) guidance on undertaking a comprehensive assessment had had a significant impact on **practice** in these agencies although **recording** often left much to be desired. We hypothesised that because of the Access to Files legislation social workers were recording mainly the facts of the assessment, and that, professional judgements which were written and substantiated on file were diminishing. The routine compiling of a family history at a point when a case moved from a response to a simple request for a service to one where the child's welfare was causing concern seems to have gone out of the social work repertoire. This particular lesson, which was emphasised by Wolff in a series of papers written after the Maria Colwell Inquiry (DHSS, 1974 and CCETSW, 1978) appears not to have been learned. Had such a history been on file at the time when a support case tripped over into a child protection cases, it seems likely to the researchers that a more appropriate response might have been made in some cases.

As these responses from social workers show, assessment was usually combined with helping:

> *It's the continuous assessment really. It's also keeping them together. Mum will ring up and say "I can't get him to school" so I just get down there and take him to school, and then he gets the message and he'll go. The baby is a handful and she fell down the stairs and had a big lump on her head. I got a stairgate from Argos. I go with mum to hospital for her appointment but a lot of it is about money. It's so frustrating. Social security are not being competent. They won't send her money without the green form, and the Mum often forgets she has to fill the green form in. I've asked them to send it to me or her mother and they won't, but now we've got her on sickness benefit with a 3-monthly doctor's note so I hope it will be better, but I've spent so much time chasing round, phoning, going with her, sitting for hours, I could tear my hair out.*

> *In my assessment I was looking at the general condition of the house, at the child, at what food there was, at the upstairs rooms. I always asked if I might do that and then I'd make comments on it, and I do praise very much. She is always pleased to show me.*

On the other hand, assessment was sometimes pressed by the worker or the conference on reluctant parents, and seen by both as something to be got over as quickly as possible.

> *When I started the assessment I stood on the doorstep and I smiled! I tried to be as nice as possible about a rotten thing.*

They [the family] still are a bit resentful of me coming. It was really difficult to start with — with Julie because she said she keeps her house clean and feeds her baby, and she couldn't accept why we were involved. It wasn't until after the review conference that things began to change when the Chair really laid it on the line to her about Samantha who was registered then. It took a long time to get them involved, but they've worked very well especially since the review conference. They were fighting me up till then. I kept saying to Julie, "I don't really have to be here, but it's because of the children, and it's to help you help them. I'm sorry but this is all part of it, and it must get done and the quicker it's done the quicker we can be off."

The parents declined to be involved in the assessment and they set restrictions on what work we could undertake with the child. The time with the parents varied according to how long mother would tolerate us.

The parents didn't see the need to have any outside intervention or assessment or help or resources. I wasn't seen as relevant enough to be home for when I had arranged home visits. The children were not interested in any participation in what I proposed. John preferred to watch the television. He was polite and responded when spoken to. Jill liked to go on with her homework, and Jenny preferred to go and play out with her friends.

The following quotations show how teamwork, including interagency work, was combined to help all family members and assess the situation.

The nursery has been very helpful in the assessment. Finding a place for Danny was important and they were worried about him too. I harassed them and the Under-Fives officer about a place! When they gave me the place it was like manna from heaven, and it's when something like that happens that you realise how worried you are.

Our team has a separate assessment team within our child care team. If families are referred for assessment, they have a written time-limited contract involving attendance at the resource centre and including a psychiatric or psychological interview, plus time for play sessions with the children on their own, plus interviews with any other professionals or family involved. The report turns out to be like a guardian ad litem report and is shared with the family and sometimes includes at the end their views if they disagree with what's in it.

The work I undertook for assessment was in three parts, as co-operation was vital between the foster family, the natural mother and the separated putative father and his extended family. Each aspect needed specific support and work around planning for the future of the child. Being open and honest from the beginning and involving all parties in the planning was important. We tried to make an agreement between the participants and myself which was worked out in partnership. There were anxiety provoking aspects of the work; there was concern about what I would find and how the family would respond. Would I make the correct assessment of the situation and would there be an element of violence?

Multi-disciplinary and inter-agency work

Before the conference the investigating team was usually a combination of police, paediatrician and social worker. After the conference the team responsible for working together to carry out the recommendations usually consisted of one or more social workers, the GP, a health visitor or school nurse, and teachers if the child was at school.

We were interested to discover the extent to which work after the conference was in fact multi-disciplinary. A social worker was involved in all cases where work continued. Leaving aside those cases where no work was undertaken after the conference, in just over half there was no indication of multi-disciplinary work. In 50 cases (26 per cent) one or more social workers worked with one other professional worker, and in 31 cases (16 per cent) two other professional workers were routinely involved in the work as well as the social worker. In only four cases was the bulk of the work undertaken by another professional with the social worker carrying the case management/ key worker role. This finding is consistent with the conclusion of Hallett (1993) that there is much rhetoric in the commitment to multi-agency **work** but that **joint work** in the main means joint **investigation**.

We did not explore the work of the other professionals in any detail, but these comments give an idea of the very mixed reactions of family members, and the social workers. There were some very positive comments about the work of the specialist child protection police officers and about teachers. A father said:

> *The police gave me most of the information as I dealt with them first. Social services just gave me the same information but in more detail.*
>
> *A Mother of sexually abused teenager said: 'Jan [police officer] gave me a birthday present. The caring, that's a great help. They weren't just treating you as another case. Another job-lot, so to speak. They do the job very well, the forensic and all that.*

Comments about teachers were mainly positive, despite resentment on the part of children about being interviewed at school. A mother said:

> *The schools have been wonderful. They really have. They've always said, if there are any problems don't hesitate to contact us. We'd rather know*

about problems than have them blow up out of proportion. They said we
are here to help children as well as educate them.

Even those parents accused of maltreatment tended to be positive or
neutral about the specialist police. On the other hand, comments about
police making criminal investigations who were not specialists in child
protection work were almost always negative. Negative feelings sometimes
spilled over on to the social workers who were present at the time when
parents felt themselves to be badly treated by the police. Another mother said:

The police treated me like a pig. They were going in my cupboards and in
my freezer and pulling out the frozen cabbage and took the mickey out of
me about the cabbage.

This father, who was accused of sexually abusing his daughter of four
during an access visit said:

Total shock, knock on the door, I had my house coat on, and they asked
me to get dressed. I didn't have anything on underneath because I don't
wear pyjamas. When I got to the police station they asked me why I didn't
wear pyjamas which I thought was irrelevant. I felt like a woman who'd
been raped and then being interrogated afterwards. I felt totally disgusted.
I never stopped puking up for days. No food, just acid and blood. I don't
mind being asked questions but there were two police officers and they were
trying to compete and you're feeling numb anyway and you find it fairly
hard to comprehend what's going on. They put me back in the cell for 3–4
minutes and then they came and said they weren't arresting me and I
could go. They did ask me if I wanted a solicitor and I had no reason to
need one so I didn't.

Parents were equally divided about the role of the small numbers of
guardians ad litem involved in these cases. One mother clearly thought the
guardian was on her side:

The court guardian was very helpful and supportive. He explained what
my chances are in getting my daughter back and he knew that it was all
framed up and the social services didn't handle the case in the best manner.

Others were equally clear that the guardian ad litem was part of the social
services department and told us that they were not willing to be totally honest
with them.

Our respondents had very little to say about nurses and doctors. Generally
their comments were positive or neutral, but we did not gain an impression
from family members that they strongly associated with a well worked out

protection plan. There was some resentment about the role played by doctors or nurses at the investigation stage, at least one mother asking to change her health visitor after the conference.

> *Over all of them is Dr [paediatrician]. They are all going back with their bits of information and telling him.*

> *I had trouble with the school nurse shouting out in the street at me. I hadn't kept Donald's appointment for weighing at the hospital. She stopped the car and said it out of the window, all the other mothers were listening. She could have spoken to me privately or sent a letter.*

These comments by social workers represent the range of more negative experiences.

> *Errors were made at the hospital. A child abuse referral was not made initially, merely a child concern referral and Kevin was discharged home without a full investigation or medical. The consultant paediatrician advised his staff when he came on duty the next day that an injury of this nature should always be treated as a possible case of abuse. It was then referred to us as possible child abuse. The parents had been told that the hospital were satisfied with the explanation given and there would therefore be no further enquiries made. This obviously made our work far more difficult and it was very stressful for the parents.*

> *It's difficult with other professionals. They're seeing the family differently about the care of the children. It felt as though you were working at odds with them. The health visitor was anxious about the children feeling that these children would be better off in care for a while but it's social services responsibility so she can say it without taking responsibility. It was one person undermining us that made life difficult saying different things to the client.*

These are some of the more positive comments about inter–agency work.

> *I had weekly telephone liaison with the health visitor for the assessment and the care of the new baby and I and the health visitor and the baby's mum and the baby's grandma wrote the plan of action together. The baby's grandma thought it was very harsh. The health visitor and I maintained very intensive monitoring at first to prevent the mum backsliding.*

> *The education welfare officer and I explained to Tommy about our meeting with his mother and her anger and uncooperativeness. He said she was always like that. I explained to his mother in hospital that I would be seeing the children at school.*

> *A family of five children had received help since 1981. It included: three previous social workers who visited weekly; the current social worker who*

visited weekly; regular appointments with a psychiatrist; a 'Homestart' volunteer; a health visitor visiting weekly; the family GP on regular visits to the health centre by the mother; a family aide; foster carers when the children were in voluntary care; child-minding; and family therapy at the Child and Family Centre. This huge commitment to the family did not become obvious until the child protection conference was called when the protection plan formalised what was happening and required the key-worker to coordinate it. It also changed the focus from the mother and her needs to the children and their needs.

Despite the exhortations in all the literature and guidance to work together, these examples of joint work are found in only a minority of cases.

Family members were asked who had been most helpful to them. Twenty-one of the 63 who responded mentioned relatives or friends. Those who named a professional worker as the person who helped them most responded as follows:

- Key social worker   20
- Health visitor   5
- Other social worker   4
- GP   3
- Solicitor   3
- Advice worker   2
- Police officer   2
- Probation officer   1
- Foster parent   1

No service

Following the assessment, the level of social work service frequently dropped or the service was discontinued. This quotation shows how an assessment period was used to confirm the acceptability of a 'de-labelling' plan prior to case closure.

What I did was minimum intervention, mainly to save us being drawn into a protracted matrimonial dispute over access. The more we got to know about the case, the less clear were mother's motives for referring the case, but to act precipitously and remove or ward the child because both sides were probably telling lies was also unwarranted.

In 52 cases there was no social work service for the parents after the **assessment** was completed, although in some of these cases the child in care continued to receive a service in his or her own right. In 17 of these cases it was not known whether or not the parents would have wished to have some form of continuing social work involvement; in 25 cases a service was neither wanted nor offered, and in 10 cases a service was wanted but was not offered.

The protection service

In 52 cases where the child remained with a parent (a quarter of the total sample) the social worker continued to visit the parents who were reluctant recipients of social work attention, and in 111 cases (just over half) social work help to parents and child continued and was welcomed by the parents. There was some indication from the file that in 96 of these continuing cases (45 per cent) the parents were offered some choice about the nature of the social work service, and in a further 38 cases they were offered some choice about some aspects of the service. It was rare for them to be offered a degree of choice about the social worker who would be allocated to the case, although this did happen in 37 cases (17 per cent of the 220 main parents). Sometimes the choice was made in terms of sex or race of worker, and sometimes there was a discussion with parent(s) about whether the investigating worker should continue to be the key worker.

Written agreements

In 70 cases (35 per cent of the 200 where we had sufficient information) there was a clear written plan on file about the assessment or services to be offered and there were usually indications that the plan had been discussed with the carers and occasionally their signature was included. This sort of clear plan most often followed an assessment at a family centre or by a specialist team. In a further 75 cases there was evidence from interviews and from the file that there was a plan which had been discussed with family members but which was not set out in written form. There was evidence of a partially worked out plan in 32 cases, and in only 23 cases (11 per cent) was there no evidence of a plan for the work. Only in 15 cases (8 per cent of those where work continued and enough information was available) was there a lack of clear information for the family about any changes which were expected, and in 146 cases (three-quarters) the purpose of the work and any requirements for change were clearly spelled out.

Review conferences

Although more family members were invited to review conferences, Figure 6.4 shows that similar proportions actually attended as attended initial conferences. Figure 6.5 shows attendance at review conferences in terms of whether the parent was implicated in the abuse or neglect. It can be seen that those who were alleged to have abused the child were as likely to attend the

Figure 6.4 **Attendance of family members at review conference (n = 137 Conferences)**

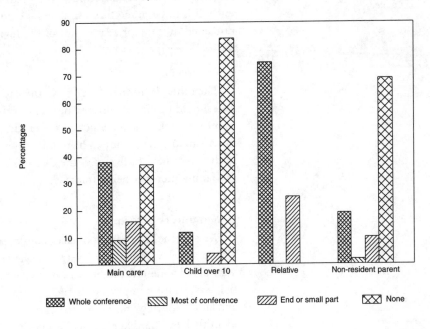

Figure 6.5 **Attendance of main parent(s) at review conference by involvement in alleged abuse**

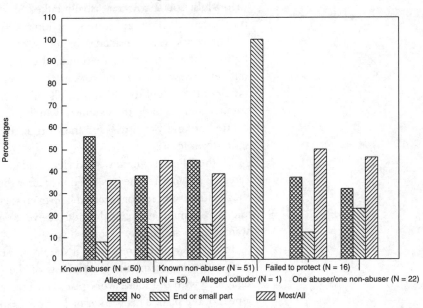

whole or most of the review conference as known non-abusers. However, more known abusers than non-abusers attended **none** of the review conference. It is to be noted that a sizable minority of known non-abusing parents remained outside for a large part of the review conference

Case closure

The other decision to be taken in the later phase of work was whether the case should be closed. Seventy per cent of the cases were still open at the six month stage. Of the 56 which had been closed, the main carer was informed in writing of case closure in half of the cases, but was only informed verbally in the other half. In five cases the case was closed but there was no record of the family member being informed.

Social work practice

We approached the task of analysing social work practice in several ways. Those social workers who were interviewed or completed questionnaires were asked to describe their main approach to helping the family, and asked to tick a checklist comprising the major approaches in use in child protection and family social work. They were also asked to fit the case into the categories identified by Hardiker and colleagues in their study of preventive work (1991). The researchers also allocated the case, in the light of the evidence available, to one of these categories. In this section the terms 'help' and 'helping' are used as more global terms which may include therapy. We found that whilst social workers usually talked about 'therapy', family members usually talked about and were more interested in being helped.

The work was considered in terms of the nature of the relationship between the main carer, the child, and the worker; the extent to which different casework or groupwork methods were used. There was a researcher rating of the extent to which the bulk of the work was with the child or the parents, and similarly the extent to which the aims of the work were child-centred or family-centred, and the work had a long-term, medium-term or short-term focus.

Of the 74 cases where we had clear evidence about the views of the main carers as to whether they received help after the conference, 30 per cent said they neither wanted nor received help from social workers. Fourteen per cent said they wanted help but did not receive it, and 56 per cent said that they wanted help and received some help.

In considering the responses it should be noted that around one-third of the parents were unwilling recipients of the social worker's attention and disagreed with the social work plan, and a further third disagreed with some aspect of the plan. This worker had a clear strategy for attempting to involve family members in such a case.

There was a real theme about agreeing to differ. I was trying to listen to what she had to say and feed back to her what she said had gone wrong. Not trying to instruct her. Trying to get some idea about how it had got to here, so that I could understand her. I acknowledged that they were ambivalent about me, but made myself available to them to use as best they could.

Table 6.3 **Components of the social work service to parents/main carers**

Service Components	Number of times this was part of service (n = 210)	Percentage of cases
Supportive relationship	123	59
Therapeutic relationship	38	18
Advice	146	69
Practical help	113	*53
Group work	13	6
Social skills/parenting skills training	59	28

*Includes 21 per cent where a great deal of practical help given

Table 6.3 summarises the different components of the social work service offered, though not always accepted by, the families at some stage during the case for the 210 cases where we had sufficient information. From this it can be seen that advice giving was a major component, followed by the provision of a supportive relationship and practical help. Work which had a clear therapeutic component aiming at changing family interaction or behaviour was less in evidence. A list of the various ways of describing practice was compiled after the pilot stage of the study and Table 6.3 gives the number of times each of these was mentioned by a social worker or was clearly indicated in the file. Like many researchers in this field, we found that models or methods of social work practice were rarely clearly described on file. When interviewed some workers were able to give either a clear description or a recognisable method, whilst others found it difficult to describe their way of working. Even when workers had a preferred model of practice, most area team workers said they used a range of methods. Those working from specialist settings were more likely to use specific methods, or so it appeared from a small number of records.

It's systemic family work, together with specific individual programmes for some family members. I like paradox. But you have to be flexible to use different approaches with different clients.

In 29 cases we were unable to identify any particular method or style of working. The list is a combination of clearly identifiable methods and more general approaches, and includes the ways in which workers described their work. The approach most frequently used was family casework, but it is also noticeable that even after the conference in one in five cases the key worker was not primarily aiming to help or achieve change, but rather to investigate and evaluate. This is perhaps not as surprising as it may seem when one remembers that around one in three of the main parents said they did not want a social work service after the conference. In view of the lack of clarity about methods used, we also asked the social workers to describe their work in terms of categories developed by Hardiker et al. (1991) when describing the different styles of practice in preventive work referred to earlier in this chapter. Figure 6.6 gives the number of times that these categories were mentioned. Some examples of the main groupings were:

Backs-to-the-wall

> *Mum was extremely angry and not understanding what it was about and hotly denying it. I tried to look at the bits and pieces that made sense to her and I tried to support them both [mother and child] because neither would have anything to do with each other. Mum didn't want to have anything to do with the conference at all. She said Social Services hadn't done her any favours. She thought it was a cut and dried affair in which they were found guilty. It was difficult to involve her. I respected her need for a space*

Figure 6.6 **Overview of work in the 220 cases**

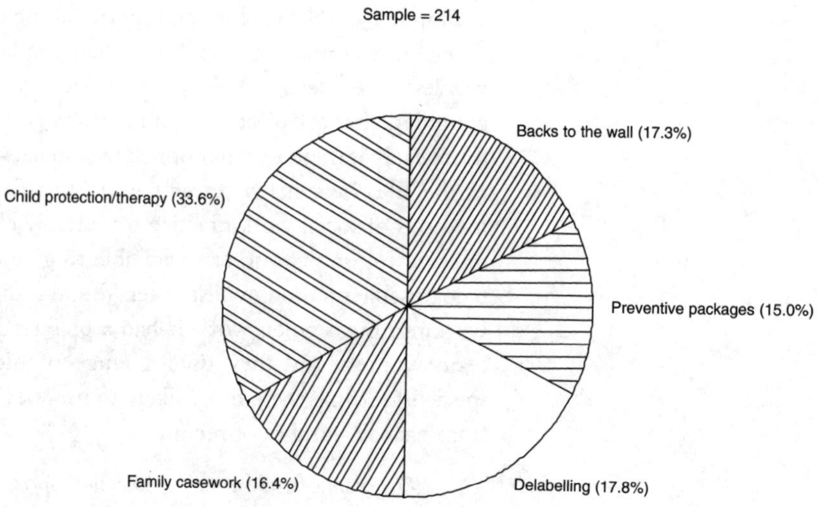

Sample = 214

Backs to the wall (17.3%)

Child protection/therapy (33.6%)

Preventive packages (15.0%)

Family casework (16.4%)

Delabelling (17.8%)

for a while but said "Could I let her know the important things" She said she'd like me to do that.' (The mother responded to the fact that social worker had kept her informed and had been quite helpful.)

They were both equally difficult because they were suspicious. They presented a united front. No, it's not been plain sailing. They don't welcome me with open arms.

Preventive packages

The family were quite reluctant to make use of the help offered. They refused the support of a Family Care worker and the father didn't take up on the offer of help with his alcohol problem. However, they accepted the financial and practical help offered, plus the playgroup for "special needs" children and holidays for the children, and so far they've attended one appointment at Child Guidance.

De-labelling

I think we were trying to defuse the hype which had grown up around this family.

Family casework

I accepted that things weren't going well for her. She was depressed and I felt it was more to do with her depression than being untidy. I explained this to her. We had to provide some practical things for the family after the conference. We had discussions and made a deal. Part of it was that I'd give things and she would maybe give something back.' [The social worker wrote to seventeen charities in this case and obtained £500 from the DSS as a community care grant. She organised the borough's clean-up squad, the local church's decorating team, a family aide, and Section 1 (Children Act 1980) money for bedding and furnishings.]

Labelling/Up-Tariffing

Social services received a phone call from a social worker in the armed services in Europe to say that a young wife was extremely concerned about the fact that her father had moved in with a younger woman in Great Britain who had three children, the oldest of whom was ten and the youngest three, because he had consistently sexually abused her and her sisters throughout their childhood. She did not want these children to be at risk of being abused in the same way. She and her sisters went on to prefer charges in retrospect, but the case had not yet come to court. Social services called a child protection conference and decided to talk to the mother of the children, her co-habitee (the father of the young woman who made the allegation) and the children in the family. The dilemma for social services was that the co-habitee was not a past Schedule 1 offender nor had his case as yet been heard in court; therefore there were no grounds for asking him to leave nor for removing the children. Their only option was to assess what was happening at home by interviewing the family members separately, which they did. School was also asked to monitor the children carefully. The mother was very angry at the allegation and refused to consider her co-habitee moving out and nor did she wish for further contact with social services. No evidence that the children were at risk arose from the interviews, nor from school.

Child protection/Child therapy

The parents were defensive and the child confused and fearful. It was the importance of balancing the need to satisfy the requirements of the investigating agency — you know the leading questions etc, whilst at the same time trying to achieve what was best for this particular child in these specific circumstances.

The priority is protecting the child. It supersedes the initial partnership of working with the family.

There was a difference of focus. The child must be protected at all costs so the care and control hats are always on. In general cases there is more focus on enabling parents but in this case the care hat had priority.

A 14-year old had made an allegation of sexual abuse against her father. The social worker said — 'I was open and honest with her. I didn't make any false promises. I believed her and I was not shocked. I used the same words as she did. Sophie wanted to try remaining at home, though she knew it would be difficult. Her father agreed to continue sleeping elsewhere for the time being, and I was going to work with them all in an attempt to maintain the family unit whilst ensuring Sophie's safety. I wanted to do feelings work with her and loss counselling. I told her that adults are supposed to be responsible and caring and trustworthy and that it was not her fault. I said it didn't matter if she enjoyed the sensation of being special to her dad. He was in the wrong, not her. We planned to do a "Secrets" book. The police officer didn't believe her. He said he caught her out on lies. However after approximately 3–4 weeks she couldn't stand the pressure put on her by her mother and she ran away from home. I'm left with the strong feeling that this department let Sophie down. The outcome is that she's abandoned by her family, she doesn't ever want to return home, they don't want her home and she is insecure and rejected and unhappy.'

Length and place of interviews

There were many contacts with the family members other than focused visits, such as phone calls or brief visits to convey messages. When these are omitted, for the 163 cases from which we could form a reliable view about the length of interviews, in 61 per cent of cases the average interview was an hour or less, but in 63 cases (39 per cent) the average interview or contact with the family was for an hour and a half, or more. These cases were usually those where family centre or resource team workers were involved, including those where a family would attend for a half or whole day. The location for the contact between the social worker and the parents varied but was mostly in the family home (133 cases, 71 per cent). In a further 20 cases work was sometimes undertaken in the family home and sometimes in a resource centre. In only 7 cases was most of the work undertaken in the social services office, and in 24 cases the main location for the work was in a child or family centre or child or family guidance clinic (13 per cent).

The work with the child was more likely to be undertaken outside the family home, but in 77 cases (43 per cent), most of the work was still carried on in the family home. In 44 cases (30 per cent) the work was undertaken mainly in a child or family centre or a child guidance clinic, or equally in one of these settings and the family home; and in 20 cases (16 per cent) most of the work with the child was undertaken in the foster home. There was no consensus from family members about which they preferred, although children strongly disliked being interviewed at school. This appeared rarely to happen on a regular basis, but when it did it stuck in the memories as inappropriate.

The focus of the work

There is debate in the child protection literature about whether child protection work is or should be mainly child focused. In those cases where our information was adequate the researchers rated the cases in terms of whether the main focus of the work was the parent, the whole family, or the child. We concluded that the aim of the work concerned change or support for the whole family in a quarter of the cases; the main carer and the child in 45 per cent of the cases; and either exclusively or mainly the child in 24 per cent of cases. In 11 cases (5 per cent) the work was considered to be totally parent centred.

The aims of the work might be child focused, but with the major recipient of social work attention being the parent. This was particularly likely to be the case with an infant where the concern was neglect, or a conference was held on an unborn child and the plan was to ensure that the parent was able to give good enough care when the child was born. For the 206 cases where we had sufficient information, the work was mainly directed at a parent in 41 cases (20 per cent of cases where we had adequate information) and at the whole family in 34 cases (16 per cent). The work was directed at the parents and child equally in 82 cases (40 per cent) and the child alone in 18 cases (9 per cent). In 31 cases (15 per cent) there was no attempt to help or change the situation in the family, and the work was directed totally at investigation and evaluation of risk.

Success and adequacy of social work process

The social workers were asked to rate the success of their work in the particular case. There were 155 responses to this question. Three said they found it impossible to say; 30 (19 per cent) said that they had been unable to engage the family, and two said that their work was definitely unsuccessful. Twenty-two (14 per cent) thought their work was not very successful, leaving a quarter who thought that their work was successful in obtaining information and 59 (38 per cent) who thought that their work was successful in bringing about change.

In the light of all the evidence available the researchers were able to rate the adequacy of the work, bearing in mind the degree of difficulty, in 211 of the cases (see Appendix 1 for protocol used). This rating was based on the extent to which the work appeared to have a focus and be competently carried out in the light of generally agreed guidelines about good practice. We considered that the work was very adequate in 93 cases (44 per cent) and adequate in 64 cases (30 per cent). However, there were clear weaknesses in 37 cases (17 per cent) and we considered the service to be poor in 17 cases (8 per cent). The responses from the 68 families from whom we have direct information about their views about the social work service suggest that the researchers might have been overly positive in our middle ratings. Twenty-nine of the 68 felt they were definitely supported by the social worker (43 per cent) and a further nine (13 per cent) thought they were supported to some extent, whereas 30 (44 per cent) considered that they had not been supported overall by the social worker. Thirty-six (54 per cent) felt that they had received help from the social services department, whilst 46 per cent felt they had not received any help, or had been harmed by the contact.

Social work with alleged abusers who had left home

It has already been noted that alleged abusers who were not living in the family home during the six months following the allegation were in two groups – those non-resident parents who had been accused of abuse during an access visit, and those who were accused of mainly sexual abuse and left the home when the allegation was investigated, often going into custody at least for a limited period. The low level of involvement of these family members was usually related to the low level of social work activity. In some cases they were in custody. There were few examples of social workers making a concerted attempt to keep alleged abusers outside the household informed, and very little evidence that they went further than this in their attempts to keep them involved. In a few cases where an alleged abuser was either in custody or away from the home awaiting trial, a social work service was provided by a probation officer. However, there was one case where the social worker took the mother to visit the father in prison to discuss together their parental responsibilities for their child currently in fostercare. One long interview with a prison probation officer was extremely helpful to us in understanding the position of the alleged abuser and the social workers within the penal system. This officer considered that it would be desirable for the probation service to be routinely alerted by social services of these situations so that the alleged abuser could be interviewed early in the process. Little attention has been paid in the literature to the role of the probation service in the early stages of sexual or physical abuse cases when the alleged abuser is in custody or when criminal charges are pending. More attention has been paid to therapeutic and corrective work with convicted abusers in the later stages after conviction. However, our conversations with probation workers suggest that early involvement of a mainly practical nature, including liaising between the social worker for the child, and the alleged abusing parent, could lead to more positive outcomes for all concerned, including the child.

Case cameos illustrating these cases of fathers being away from home but alleged to have abused the child during contact visits have been included in Chapter 3. Generally the social work response was to have minimal contact with these fathers and to support the mother in discontinuing access. This practice left us feeling that there was a risk of social workers colluding with the exclusion of the father from the life of the family (which often included a new stepfather). There was rarely a full assessment of the attachment of the child to the father and the impact of this abrupt loss of contact.

In a significant minority of cases, however, social workers did go to considerable lengths to offer help, advice and support to non-resident parents, whether or not they were implicated in the abuse.

> *The father in an Asian family had left home after physically abusing his child and because of his own mental health problems. He had left home on previous occasions but could not manage money. When he had returned previously he had mismanaged the family's money. The social worker helped the mother to get her own Income Support whilst he was away. The mother then took the father back into the home, but the social worker persuaded the mother to keep the separate income arrangements, and arranged for the father to maintain himself financially even though living with the family again.*

The worker offered a long-term casework service to each family member separately, and to the family as a whole which incorporated a skilled mental health service for the father as well as child protection and family support work.

Another father said:

> *I look at things in an old fashioned way – either you've done it or you haven't and I hadn't. When the social worker came she was very nice, she was very polite. Well, she would be wouldn't she. She wouldn't be likely to come with all guns blazing would she. We had a good conversation about what I thought happened and she advised me when I got to the conference if I had anything to say, to say it – just come out with it. We all know that this sexual abuse goes on, and I knew why she'd come and it's a terrible thing. But it's also terrible when you know you haven't done it.*

No charges were made, and the social worker believed that it was not likely that he had abused the child, but he had not seen his daughter two months later when he was interviewed. The social worker said:

> *I didn't meet the father until after he'd been arrested and interviewed by the police. He obviously found it uncomfortable that I took what his daughter was saying seriously and was not prepared to immediately believe his denials. I too felt awkward in his presence and was rather relieved when he was not around later.*

> Father – *'It was fairly apparent from my son's mother that her attitude to everyone was giving cause for concern to everyone, not just social services and that's why I'm here at the conference. I was visited by the social worker. She brought a letter my son's mother had written to her, making allegations about me physically abusing and sexually abusing him and not being his father. It's all part of her mental illness. The social worker opened the letter in my flat and said she wanted to read it to me. It was quite appalling – there were twenty or thirty things the letter accused me of. It was the first time I'd met the social worker and I thought it was a good way of starting off. In the past I've had to qualify myself and stick up for myself and explain things and defend myself. But this social worker seemed to know what my son's mother was like.'*

> Social worker – *'The father wanted to bring his new partner to the interview I arranged and he did and we talked to him about things that had upset Stacey. She'd seen some adult videos and heard the noise of his lovemaking at night with his new partner and they'd visited a nudist beach and we talked about all these concerns. It was very hard to get his new partner to see that Stacey had been brought up in a different family where her parents' sexuality was a different matter. The new partner thought*

*sexual matters should be out in the open and up front. They were both
very defensive. I didn't talk about the touching because I was so unclear
about it myself and I thought if anything further came out in Stacey's
session I could take it up later.'*

The social work service to the children

It was less easy to identify in detail the components of the service to the
children, in part because of the wide age range. However, in the light of our
knowledge of guidelines about social work practice to children in child
protection cases, it was concluded that the work in 100 cases (49 per cent) was
very adequate, and in a further 70 cases (34 per cent) the work with the child
was adequate (83 per cent in total rated as very adequate or adequate). In 19
cases we considered that there were some clearly identifiable weaknesses and
in 15 cases (7 per cent) we considered that the service to the child was poor.
These ratings are supported by the direct evidence from the ten young people
who returned questionnaires, and the 14 who were interviewed, where
around three-quarters were satisfied by the service offered by the social
worker, and around a quarter expressed serious reservations. There was a
strong relationship between the young peoples' satisfaction with the service,
and the extent to which they considered that their social workers had listened
to their opinions and wishes and given them serious consideration.

Work with the child

One social worker described the following work that she undertook with
the children. The children had lived all their lives with their mother's episodes
of mental illness and going into voluntary care with the same foster carers – a
package which appears to have worked satisfactorily for everyone. The
children then disclosed serious sexual abuse by their mother and her friends,
and a Care Order was applied for and eventually a long-term plan of adoption
made. The social worker did life-story work, new family-finding work, work
about their mother's illness, and work about moving. She also did a dream-
book. The children had had frightening and upsetting dreams which the
social worker encouraged the fostermother to help the children to write
about and draw.

Other social workers wrote:

*I used specific books with Tina, colouring, drawing and activity books,
and they dealt with aspects of your own body, touching and feeling. I made
her aware that the police officer and myself saw loads of children and how
important children are, and I told her about a few naughty things I did as
a child to help her relax and laugh. She joined in with the other activities
and physically relaxed and talked quite freely too, but in the end I was*

unable to undertake further sessions with her at the family home because of her mother's presence. Her mother insisted on being present and Tina was inhibited by that. It was difficult to engage her as her mother constantly spoke for her. The school was identified and agreed as a good venue but Tina vetoed this when it was arranged for fear of other children becoming aware of the sessions.

Yes he [the 2-year old] does know who I am. I always play with him, and he's always there, and he gets a lot of my attention. I visited him at the fostercarers. I called on Pete [dad] and he was there once, and when I was going he cried, he didn't want me to go, he was really upset and sobbed and sobbed. He probably thought I was going to take him to see his mother.

I've really felt like piggy-in-the-middle. There was a difficult time when I supported Melanie [child] without necessarily believing her, and I was saying less to the parents than I might have done. I suspect they thought I'd gone quite tight-lipped really. It was very difficult. My difficulty was not knowing how I felt about the abuse and whether it had happened. In a sense having to believe, because one has to, having to believe the child, I felt sort of wobbly about it. So much so that I didn't want to do the therapeutic work with Melanie. I didn't like her and I don't like her very much now, and I felt I had to try the hardest with her.

Whereas older children were able to articulate their wishes with regard to where they wished to live, there were ways in which younger children also expressed themselves clearly if the social worker was able to observe their behaviour. For example –

A 4-year old made it as plain as she knew how by her non-verbal behaviour that she was not going to be in any kind of contact with her mother's co-habitee after he had smacked her so hard that he left hand marks on her [the incident which caused the initial case conference]. The social worker noticed that when he came into the room she went out, and that when she came into the room and he was there she skirted him warily. Her behaviour made it clear that she preferred to live with her aunt and grandmother in preference to her mother and co-habitee. When she was 'forced' to go home to her mother she behaved so badly that the mother was glad to send her back to aunt and grandmother where she behaved well! She told her mother that she did not like the co-habitee being there. She was a positive, forceful child with a clear mind of her own. Her behaviour made it easy for the social worker to see what her feelings were with regard to the situation. The 'participation' of the child in the process was there for an observant eye to see.

Another worker described her work with young children:

The children were too young to be directly involved in this case, but I had regular contact with them and helped establish myself as a familiar trusted adult, especially once they were rehabilitated home to their mother. I was seen as a friendly adult with their mother and accepted by her as a welcome visitor. I used informal play and chatted to the 4-year old during the contact visits in the fosterhome and at home.

In the next two Chapters we shall consider whether the nature of the practice, and the attempts to involve family members did in fact result in their participation.

Summary

- The protection process and social work practice at the different stages of the 220 cases and with the different family members were described in the words of the parents, children and social workers.

- Attention was particularly given in the analysis to whether the practice was likely to involve the family members.

- 67 per cent of the cases were still open to a social worker at the six month stage and only 13 per cent were closed immediately after the conference.

- 53 per cent of the cohort and 82 per cent of registered cases were still on the child protection register at the 6 month stage.

- Using the Department of Health guidelines the researchers concluded that 60 per cent of the conferences were necessary and that it would have been appropriate to have registered 50 per cent of the children (compared with the 61 per cent which were registered).

- Children were more likely than parents to have a say about how the **investigation** was handled. The practice of proceeding some way into the investigation, and in particular of interviewing children without first telling their parents was resented by the parents and made it more difficult to engage them in the work. This happened in just under half of the cases where the child was old enough to be formally interviewed. Well over half of the parents from whom we had information considered that the investigation was not satisfactorily carried out, but some (usually mothers of sexually abused children where the alleged abuser wasn't or was no longer in the family home) were full of praise, especially for specialist police officers. The work of CID police came in for heavy criticism.

- There was considerable variation as to which professionals were present when the parents, the child and the alleged abusers were interviewed.

- In less than half of the cases was the initial conference held within 14 days of the allegation being received. However emergency action was taken in all cases where the child was at serious risk prior to the conference.

- In just over a third of cases the main parent(s) attended for most or the whole of the conference. Although a small minority of those who attended wished they had not done so, the majority were pleased they had gone and some found it a very positive experience. Almost a third of those who attended considered that the conference had not been adequately explained to them. In over half of the cases where parents attended, a mother and father or male partner came together.

- Comprehensive family assessments were undertaken on about half of the cases, including a majority of those which were registered, but in a substantial minority only child protection aspects were assessed.

- It was rare to see a full family history on file, even in those cases when a comprehensive assessment had been undertaken. Agreements about the work to be undertaken were rarely on file and even more rarely signed by parents. Social histories and agreements were more likely to be in evidence if a specialist children's services team or family centre was involved in the assessment.

- Work after the conference was multi-disciplinary in only a minority of cases.

- Just under a third of the families from whom we had information did not ask for help after the conference and were resistant to the attentions of the social workers and other professional workers. Others who wanted help considered that they did not receive it, or it wasn't the sort of help they considered that they needed.

- Family casework involving a supportive or therapeutic relationship and the provision of a range of services was the main method of helping the families. Within this broad approach a range of theoretical approaches was used. In a substantial minority of cases the work was directed at child protection or therapy only and no service was offered to parents. This was most likely to be the case when children were in statutory care, although some workers strove hard to provide a service to parents in these cases.

- In just under half of the cases where there was an ongoing service the parents were offered some choice about the nature of the help to be offered, and in 17 per cent of cases the main parents had some choice about who the social worker should be.

- About two thirds of the workers thought their work was at least fairly successful. The researchers rated the work overall as either adequate or very adequate in three quarters of the cases but poor in 8 per cent of the cases.

- Just over a half of the parents from whom we have direct information thought they were helped and supported by the social worker, but 46 per cent said they had not received any help or been harmed by the contact.

- The service to the parents who were no longer in the family home, whether or not they were alleged to be involved in the abuse was, with a few notable exceptions either poor or non-existent.

- Once significant relatives had been identified as having a role to play they were likely to receive a good service and be involved in the work.

- Our data on work with the children is less complete, but from the evidence available we concluded that in 83 per cent of the cases the work with the child was at least adequate.

Chapter 7

The Nature and Extent of Family Involvement

In Chapter 6 we considered whether practice and agency policy appeared likely to lead to the family members being engaged as partners in the work to be done to protect the child. In this chapter we follow through the protection process and indicate the extent to which family members were **actually** involved, participated, or were partners in the process, decision-making and practice. In Chapter 8 we shall attempt to tease out any variables in procedures and practice which appear to be associated with greater or lesser involvement of family members. We also need to remind the reader that the issues around involvement and the extent of involvement may be different for the different family members, and that the nature of the problems within the family, and the nature of the abuse or neglect will also have an impact on the extent to which partnership is a realistic goal.

In the previous sections we have concentrated on the service to the main carers at the time of the child protection conference, since most of the information was available about this group. In this chapter we consider the extent to which all those who might have participated in the process were in fact involved, a total of 385 persons, including main parenting figures, children aged ten or over, parents not living in the family home, three siblings accused of abusing a brother or sister, and 13 relatives who were heavily involved. These included parents who were **known** abusers, others who were **alleged** to be involved, and parents who were known **not** to be involved in the abuse or neglect. (See Chapter 2 for the proportions in each group).

We have previously referred to the allocation of family members to a 'best', 'middle' or 'worst' scenario in terms of whether we considered that there would be obstacles to working in partnership. One hundred and seven came into our 'best' scenario group; 170 in the 'middle' group and 103 in the 'worst' scenario group. Insufficient information was available from the remaining five. In part this was based on whether there was agreement about the nature of the problem. We have already noted that, whilst there was agreement in about a third of cases and partial agreement in another third, there was disagreement about either whether abuse had happened, its severity or who was responsible in the remaining third of the cases.

At the time of the data collection there were few guidelines about the involvement of parents who were not the direct carers of the children in child protection procedures. The research studies referred to in Chapter 1 all concentrated on the primary carers' involvement, occasionally mentioned the involvement of children and young people, but had little to say about the involvement of a parent not living in the family home at the time of the abuse, whether or not he or she was implicated in the alleged maltreatment. Relatives were almost always referred to as supporters of the parents, rather than as people who might need to be involved in their own right because of their concern for the welfare of the child.

The investigation stage and strategy discussions

The practice of social workers at the investigation stage has been described in Chapter 6. In this chapter we consider the extent to which family members were involved in this practice and the procedures such as strategy meetings or discussions. The key indicators as to whether family members were involved in the work at this stage were:

- the giving of information about the allegation, and the protection process;
- the extent to which family members were involved in the detailed decisions about how the investigation should proceed;
- whether or not they were invited to the initial child protection conference;
- how their views were canvassed and how they were prepared for the meeting, whether or not they were to attend.

We have already noted in Chapter 6 that it was not unusual for workers to have interviewed children formally before contacting a parent. Not surprisingly, parents were often angry when this happened and were less likely to consider that they had been involved in the investigation stage. Their anger at interviews taking place without their being consulted made it more difficult to build an atmosphere of trust, and engage them in the work.

This mother was alienated by how far things had gone before she was informed:

> *We should have known first about the case conference. Everyone else knew. They should have said, "Do you think we should have one?" I wouldn't have minded then—if they'd asked me first. It cheesed me off—all talking about my kid.*

This father considered that he was not given a clear picture of the investigation, and that his views were not appropriately placed before the conference.

> *My wife attended the conference. I was told I was not allowed to go. I would've liked to have gone. They didn't even want to know my wife's views at all let alone mine. We'd have liked to have known exactly who was going to be present at the conference – you know various solicitors and the NSPCC. The conferences were very one sided as far as my wife and I were concerned. We had the impression that we were being tolerated rather*

than included in the meetings. This prevented the social workers and all the other helpers from seeing the real problems which were afflicting our daughter.

This mother, who was not implicated in the abuse, did not consider that she was involved until much later in the process.

If someone had come round first to make sure if there was anything wrong about what had happened, I would have been less traumatised. It makes you very defensive about the situation. You felt you were walked over rough-shod. We felt we were on trial and I hadn't done anything wrong. But I couldn't say that in case it was misconstrued. That it might be seen as though I concurred. The bruises on my daughter were consistent with being punched, and I couldn't understand why her face was so swollen. It didn't add up to me, and I was in a state of shock.

A mother and her partner also felt that valuable time was lost in confrontation. They also drew attention to the fact that 'co-operation is a two-way process.'

We feel that social services should be less blinkered and more open to the views of the parents in the first weeks, and taken more seriously. We did eventually gain co-operation but we felt it was too long in coming. They tried to sweep us under the carpet.

On the other hand, this mother was greatly helped by being involved in the investigation process:

My social worker told me what she could do and we went for an interview and my daughter was videoed and she had the police involved. It was lovely, it really was. My social worker involved me in everything they done. She explained everything they were going to do before it happened. She came round and told me and explained it all to me and she phoned to say when the appointment was and it was OK and whether I could get transport. I can't condemn it at all. My daughter's been a lot better since the interview.

Figure 7.1 shows the researchers' rating of the extent to which different family members were involved in the investigation stage of the work. (See Chapter 2 and Appendix 1 for a fuller discussion of the rating categories). Only 7 (2 per cent) of the 368 individuals on whom we had adequate information were treated as partners, and a further 37 (10 per cent) were kept fully informed and participated. Children and concerned relatives were more likely to participate than the main carers, and non-resident parents were least likely to be fully involved. Only 7 per cent of the main carers, but 40 per cent of the non-resident parents were rated as not involved or were rated as being placated or manipulated at this stage of the case.

Figure 7.1   **Involvement of family members at investigation stage (researcher rating)**

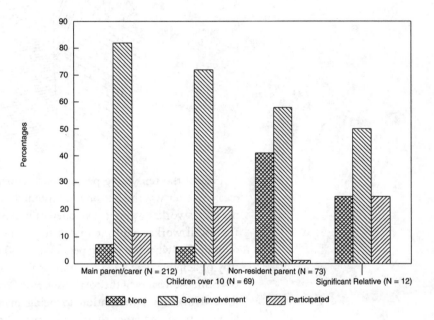

The involvement of the children at the investigation and conference stages

We paid particular attention to the extent to which the social work practice with the child was participatory. (Figure 7.2). The factors contributing towards the rating were:

- was the child seen on his or her own?
- was information given specifically to the child in an age appropriate way?
- did the social worker check that the child knew what was happening and invite the child's views about how the investigation should proceed?
- was the child or young person invited to give their views to the conference and consulted about how these views should be put across in the conference?
- if attending the conference, was the young person adequately prepared for this?

Figure 7.2 **Involvement of 122 older children in investigation stage**

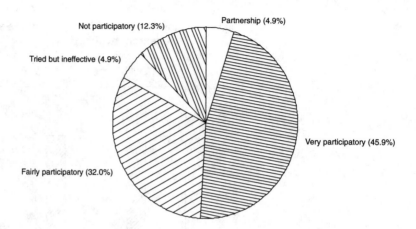

Sample = 122

Not participatory (12.3%)

Partnership (4.9%)

Tried but ineffective (4.9%)

Very participatory (45.9%)

Fairly participatory (32.0%)

Five of the ten young people who returned questionnaires said that the social worker was the person who listened most to them. Only one said that the social worker was not at all open or honest. The questions about whether the social worker explained what he or she was doing; whether they paid attention to what the young person said and whether they discussed the best way of helping all yielded far more positive answers than negative, with well over three-quarters of the total answering 'Yes' or 'To some extent', and only four saying 'No'. In relation to being invited to the meeting and being allowed to say whether their views carried any weight, the responses were more circumscribed with an even balance between 'Yes', 'No' and 'To some extent'. Most of the young people knew their social workers wrote things down and that they could see what was written, and six of them had actually seen it. Only three would have liked to complain or change their social worker, but none of the ten young people said they had been told how it was possible to do this. These replies even though from a small number give a picture of most of the young people being fairly well involved and consulted. Six of these ten were in care at some stage either prior to the conference or during the six months which followed. The other four were all supported by their families. Two of these found the social workers were very helpful but two were at odds with them. The questionnaires were supplemented by the comments of the young people we interviewed. Ten year old Anna expressed relief at being able to talk openly and this was experienced by several of these young people:

> You're allowed to say anything. I could say I don't like that 'cos it's boring and it would be alright.

Peter, aged 13, was pleased that he was kept informed of what was going on, and that he was able to attend the conference and other meetings:

> *They were talking about me and mum and everyone else so I wanted to hear what they were talking about. What they were saying and whether it was correct or not. It was the meeting that my mum and I went to so that they could decide whether or not she was good enough to keep me.*

It was not clear who had explained to Pam, aged 10, about the register, but clearly someone had:

> *The register's there so you don't get hurt.*

Pat, aged 16, had been dissatisfied with her first social worker, but managed to get a change of worker:

> *When my dad had gone my mum kept putting all the blame on to me for what had happened and saying "It's all your fault, you shouldn't have let him touch you." My mum started treating me bad and then my brother did, and she got my sister to treat me bad as well. What I've been telling my social worker I was sure she'd been going behind my back and telling my dad, and I was sure she had, and I couldn't hack it, so I asked to change my social worker. My nan suggested it because I was so worried about it, and my nan phoned up and said so. Janet [the new social worker] contacted me. Since I had Janet, I was talking to her and it was more helpful. She was more understanding then the first social worker.'*

The first worker had let Pam down by not picking up early enough that it was inappropriate for her to be working with Pam as well as with the father who had abused her, but to her credit when she did learn of this she did not delay in arranging for a different worker for Pam, whilst she continued to work with the mother and father.

Some young people were less satisfied for a range of reasons. Natasha, aged 12, said:

> *All they do is ask you question after question after question. They did ask me if I wanted to answer the questions. I didn't say no because they'd think I was rude. I just hoped it would finish soon.*

She clearly did not feel safe enough to express her views about the process. Another 11-year old does not appear to think that what she said was listened to:

> *My mum and dad listen to me — our nan listens to me. The other lot [social workers] they just give us sweets, something to do — give us papers*

to draw on. Then it was alright but now I'm looking back, now you're getting us to look back, they weren't listening.

Those children who went into care were more likely to say they were listened to, but this was not invariably the case. Rashida said:

> *The first time they wanted me to go into care I said I didn't want to go into care because I had lots of support from my boyfriend's dad and his sister. She was my best friend. Then we broke up and I did want to go into care. The social worker said "It's Saturday and your parents are very nice people." I said, "I don't want to go home." He said, "Give me a good reason, it's a Saturday and there aren't very many places." He didn't listen to me at all.*

These young people were critical about how meetings and conferences were conducted:

> *When I didn't want to do something quite a few times they persuaded me otherwise, and in a few meetings my words were twisted and I was patronised sometimes especially by the teamleader.*

> *I ended up telling the teacher. I was very upset. She said she wouldn't phone anyone 'til next day, but she phoned as soon as I left and the social worker came. The school secretary came to my class and dragged me out of my lesson and said, "Social services are here". She could have told me she had phoned.*

> *I went to the case conference, the only one I had. No, I didn't know who would be there till I got there. It was pretty nerve-racking. I went in there and they told me my mum was coming and she didn't turn up. She'd probably been told I'd be there. I didn't say much. I'd have liked to say more. I don't know what would have helped me. They said I could write some notes down, but I didn't bother. If I could have thought of things to say, I would have said them, but they were saying "Do you understand?" and I thought I don't know and it made me feel more nervous.*

The children's more general comments about social work practice have already been included in Chapter 6. However, it is worth re-emphasising here the extent to which the children disliked being interviewed in school and yet were unable to prevent this happening. However, many positive comments were made by the children and young people about the social workers, police officers and teachers in the early stages of the investigation, and the time leading up to the first conference.

Giving information – written and verbal

We also ascertained what leaflets and other information were given about such issues as the provision of services including accommodation, the possibility of care proceedings, emergency protection orders or other court procedures; the nature of recording and the information about access to records, and complaints procedures.

Nearly 5 per cent of the 345 family members about whom we had adequate information received none of the necessary leaflets and only 12 (3 per cent) received all the necessary leaflets. At the start of the research we had enquired of each agency which leaflets were available. We found that many social workers who were interviewed were unaware of which leaflets were available, and even if they were aware of them they did not have ready access to stocks of them.

Each of our sample agencies had a leaflet for parents about **child protection procedures**, and about **care and court procedures**. These were the ones most likely to be available and given to parents, although they were rarely given to family members who were not part of the household. None had information about their procedures which was specifically aimed at **children and young people**, although some workers were resourceful in using more generally available booklets about child protection couched in language appropriate for children.

We were aware that information might be given in verbal as well as leaflet form and that a letter might substitute for a leaflet. We therefore asked more detailed questions about the different sorts of information which we considered ought to be given during this period. Seventy-seven per cent of the main carers, and 81 per cent of the total number of respondents about whom we had information received no written or verbal information about recording and access to records at this stage, and only 32 (16 per cent) of the main carers and six (2 per cent) of the total number of family members received both a leaflet and verbal information about recording procedures. These responses were typical:

> We've never been shown any records or offered the chance to look at any such thing. But if allowed, you can bet that we'll be doing just that.

> We should have been told we could see them. We only knew from the questionnaire [from the research] that we could. I was quite amazed actually.

> I wasn't told anything about looking at the case records. I was told it was private to them only.

It was only towards the end of the study that complaints leaflets were available in most of the study areas so, not surprisingly, the situation on complaints was even less adequate, with 86 per cent of the main carers and 90 per cent of the total number of family members receiving no information on complaints at this stage. Only five of the main carers and seven of the total sample (3 per cent and 2 per cent respectively) had both verbal and written information about complaints. This father gave a typical response:

> We didn't complain because we had no-one to complain to that we thought would listen and be able to do something about our unsatisfactory situation. We didn't ask for the social worker to be changed because we didn't think it would have made any difference. She was constrained by social services' policy.

A more positive situation is found in relation to information on abuse procedures where only 6 per cent of the main carers and 12 per cent of the total sample received no information about the abuse procedures in the period leading up to the initial conference. Fifty-five per cent of the main carers and 53 per cent of the total group received verbal information only, and 39 per cent of the main carers and 35 per cent of the total group received both verbal information and a leaflet or written information. Information on care or accommodation was not considered relevant in almost 60 per cent of the cases. Where it might have been relevant, no information on accommodation or care was received in 15 per cent of cases, verbal information only was available in 69 per cent of cases, and verbal information together with a leaflet or other written information was available in 20 cases (just over a quarter).

These proportions are in respect of the parents. We had insufficient information about the availability of written information for the children.

The initial child protection conference

Whether parents' views were given and listened to

The 73 family members who completed questionnaires or were interviewed were asked if they were able to give their views at the first child protection conference, either directly or indirectly. Twenty-two per cent were unable to complete the question since they had not been present and did not know whether their views had been represented. Twenty-three per cent said they had been unable to give their views to the conference, but 33 (45 per cent) considered that they had been able to give their views to the conference either directly or through the social worker or another attender. A further 12 per cent said that they had been able to put their views across to the conference members to some extent. On the other hand, only 50 per cent considered that their views had been social worker or another attender. A further 12 per cent said that they had been able to put their views across to the conference members to some extent. On the other hand, only 50 per cent considered that their views had been listened to, and 33 per cent felt that their views had definitely not been listened to.

There were a number of examples of the way in which parents were listened to in the conferences. One social worker described the way in which she enabled the mother to present her views:

> *She was asked to prepare what she would like to say, and to bring someone along with her. Paper and pen were provided during the conference. Time was given to them to speak at the conference.*

At a conference observed by a researcher, the police report criticised the mother for having no food in the house, not enough beds and bedding, and that it was a dirty house. The mother was very annoyed and upset about the criticisms. When the chairperson asked for her comments she went into great detail about 'two turkey steaks, frozen cabbage, potatoes, peas and carrots, cake and custard' and said 'The kids never go hungry'. She explained that she bought food every day. Her indignation was evident and seemed to confirm her truthfulness to the conference, as well as presenting an explanation of her cultural difference in the way she shopped.

At another conference we observed at a hospital, after the main allegations of abuse and neglect were presented, the social worker reported that the 3-year old's index fingernail was missing and the other one bruised. The father said 'She was born without one', and suggested it could be verified by the hospital as the 3-year old was born there. The hospital social worker checked into it and found it to be correct. The senior registrar went on to state that the baby was below the 3rd centile in weight which he said was serious, but the mother pointed out that the baby had been 'premature', so the senior registrar quickly revised what he had said because his calculations were a month out, and the baby's weight was normal.

This father, who did not attend the conference, seems to have been very unclear about what went on in the conference:

> *I'd like to know what was talked about. We didn't know what was said, what we were accused of, and there were other things in reports I'd been accused of. They don't say nothing. They don't come out with nothing. They tried to get me to tell them so they could take action legally. They just hinted at things. I always got the feeling because Gina is quiet and withdrawn that I'm being accused of sexually abusing her. That's always at the back of my mind. No-one really said anything about it. It's sometimes the way they talk, it's hard to pinpoint it. I don't think they were open and honest.*

A mother, who had a long history of involvement with social workers, was so pleased to be invited this time when she had previously been left out that she was prepared to put up with a short exclusion:

> *They said they had to have a talk between them. You seem more involved*

than before — well, I was never asked before. I was out for about 10 minutes. I did ask but I wasn't told.

These two mothers who attended throughout were very positive. The first was given some choice about which room would help her to feel most comfortable.

I'm glad I came. If I'd been at home, I'd be thinking about them all talking behind my back. I'd have been worried more. Being here, I knew exactly what's gone one, even though Jenny [social worker] tells me everything any way.

That's what I like. I feel part of it. I don't feel pushed out of the way. Normally, if I'm in a crowd, I clam up, if I don't know people.

A small proportion of parents had positive feelings or were neutral about registration. Most were deeply upset at hearing their child's name was to be placed on the register. This mother speaks for the majority:

We say just leave us alone. She [social worker] told us to do this, do that. It made me feel that no-one trusted me. I kept trying to fight my tears back. The registration makes me feel I'm not trusted, that I'll finish up battering her [the child].

Whether parents' views carried weight

Thirty-one per cent of those who answered this question felt their views had definitely carried weight about whether the child had been abused or neglected, while 49 per cent considered that their views on this had carried no weight at all. The remaining 20 per cent thought that their views had carried some weight. A larger proportion (59 per cent) considered that their views had carried no weight on the question of whether registration and a protection plan was needed, with only a quarter believing that their views had definitely carried weight on this issue.

There was a question of care for the child in 27 of the cases where we had direct information from family members, and 15 (56 per cent) of these considered that their views had carried no weight on whether the child should be accommodated or in care. A quarter considered that their views definitely carried some weight when this decision was taken, and one in five felt that their views had had **some** influence on the decision.

Parents were more likely to consider that their views carried weight about the kind of help which would be provided but even here only 41 per cent felt that they definitely influenced the decision about the help to be made available, whilst almost a quarter felt they had some influence on this decision and over a third said that they had no influence at all. This mother considered that she had influenced the type of service available:

> *I've been treated very well. They've helped me out decorating the house; a new bed and bed linen, so they helped really well. Yes, my social worker kept coming round making sure everything was all right. She came every week at the beginning. Now I don't see her so often. She thinks I'm managing on my own. She arranged a holiday for us. We chose it and booked it, and she gave us the money. It was very nice. They did all they could for us. I was very happy with my social worker. She spoke to you straight how she found us. I like people like that. It was all to do with her getting things sorted out and the way she treated me.*

Twenty-four of those who did not attend were asked if they thought that their views had been represented at the conference and half said that they believed that they had, whilst a half said that they did not believe that their views had been represented. Of those who did not attend, only a quarter believed that their views had had any impact in the meeting, whilst 69 per cent felt that their views had carried no weight at all. A father whose child remained at home said:

> *No, we didn't really contribute to the plans. We were told what was going to happen – not consulted. The ball was in the social worker's court. I wanted to co-operate with her but had I not wanted to, I'd felt I'd have had to because of having my name on the register. We didn't have the option to tell them to go away. We never knew what our rights were.*

Communications before and after the conference

Family members responding to the questionnaires or the interviews were more likely than not to be satisfied with the amount of information they were given prior to the conference. Fifty-eight per cent felt that they had been given good information by the social worker before the meeting, whilst 42 per cent felt that they had not received adequate information before the meeting.

It has already been noted that it was fairly unusual for the full minutes of the conference to be made available, but that other methods were almost always used to give the results of the conference fairly quickly afterwards to those main carers who had not attended. Communication of the results of the conference to family members who were not currently living in the household was much less thorough, and it is not clear how the children themselves were informed in the majority of the cases. Twenty-five per cent of the parents or carers not living in the home at the time of the conference were not told the decisions by the social services department and were left to find out as best they could. Thirty-four per cent had only a verbal explanation, often several weeks after the conference; ten, however, received either the full minutes or a large part of the minutes; 12 received verbal information about what happened as well as a letter, and 13 received only a letter telling them about the decisions of the conference. Of the 62 children aged over ten where we had sufficient information, four (7 per cent) either were not informed that there was a conference, or were not specifically told the results, whilst the majority (63 per cent) were only told verbally. Seventeen of the young people (29 per cent) were told verbally and also received the information in writing, four of them receiving a copy of the minutes.

The family members who were interviewed or responded to the questionnaires were more likely to have been at the conference, since that is where we mostly came in contact with them, and were also more likely than the sample as a whole to receive a copy of at least part of the minutes. Forty-seven per cent of those who answered this question said that they had received the minutes of the conference, although we are aware that in most cases this was only the final recommendations of the conference. There was inconsistency about whether parents or significant relatives who did not attend were informed other than through the parent who was there. These parents, who were in a residential family unit at the time of the research interview, said:

> Mother *'No, we didn't have any choice about anything – they decided. We wanted to be as a family but they were treating us as a separate thing. We told them we were trying to get a house to be a family but it didn't seem to sink in. As far as they were concerned I was on my own with the two of them [children].'* Father *'I was never told anything. All I knew what they told her [children's mother] and she told me. There's a problem of communication. What we're trying to get him [social worker] to do and what he's actually doing are two different things. He's not trying. He says he's got the children's welfare at heart. I don't think he actually wants us to move out of here [the residential placement]. He ain't been doing his job properly.'*

A mother who had attended a part of the conference and was then asked to leave said:

> *'The people involved just talked over me and said they would decide and let me know – which they didn't.'*

On the other end of the continuum, one team working in an area where many mothers did not speak English as a first language had a policy of ensuring that any parent not at the conference was given a personal explanation, where appropriately through an interpreter, of the process and conclusions.

Despite this somewhat patchy approach to communication about the conference, 57 per cent of the 54 who completed this part of the questionnaire or were interviewed said that they had fully understood the decisions and recommendations made at the conference; 37 per cent said that they had understood them to some extent and only three (6 per cent) said that they had not understood the decision and recommendation of the conference.

Figure 7.3 gives the researchers' ratings for the extent to which family members were involved at the initial conference stage. Figures 7.4 and 7.5 and Table 7.3 give the researchers' ratings for the extent to which family members were involved in the key decisions made at the conference stage of the protection process. From these it can be seen that the majority of family members were involved to some extent, but that few participated or were partners at this early stage. Few were fully involved in the decision about the degree of risk, and even fewer in the decision about registration. Indeed, even when parents attended conferences throughout, it was common for the chairperson to explicitly tell them that they must play no part in the discussion about whether registration was necessary. Parents knew that they were unlikely to be allowed a vote on registration, but definitely wanted their views about any positive and negative consequences of registration to be listened to. They were more likely to participate or be partners in decisions about the protection plan (18 per cent) and about the help to be offered (18 per cent). Although children were more likely than parents to be involved in decisions about how the **investigation** was conducted, their position was reversed at the conference stage and none were considered to participate or be partners. Figure 7.6 shows that children aged 10 or over were as likely as their parents to be involved in the making of a protection plan and that non-resident parents were least likely to be involved.

Figure 7.3   **Involvement of family members at initial child protection conference stage (researcher rating)**

Sample = 377

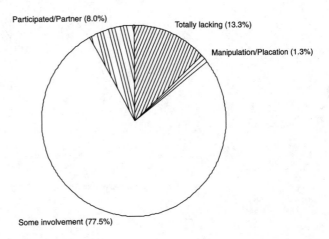

Participated/Partner (8.0%)   Totally lacking (13.3%)

Manipulation/Placation (1.3%)

Some involvement (77.5%)

Table 7.3 **Summary of involvement of different family members in main decisions**

Decision	Main parent(s)/carer(s) PP		NI*		Child over ten PP		NI*		Non-resident parent(s) PP		NI*		Significant relatives PP		NI*	
	N.	%	N.	%	N.	%	N.	%	N.	%	N.	%	N.	%	N.	%
About how investigation should be carried out	25	11	14	7	15	21	4	6	1	1	30	40	3	25	3	25
About risk of abuse or neglect	16	8	17	8	3	4	17	24	1	1	31	40	2	17	2	17
About registration	5	2	23	11	0	0	17	26	0	0	27	36	0	0	1	8
About care or accommodation	2	3	6	8	7	27	2	8	0	0	10	35	2	25	1	12
About protection plan	42	21	6	3	14	20	6	8	4	6	19	27	3	23	0	0
About help or services offered	39	21	9	5	15	24	8	13	4	6	22	35	4	33	1	8

NOTE:
PP=Participated/were partners
NI*=Not involved – (includes categories involvement totally lacking, manipulation, placation).

Figure 7.4 **Involvement of family members in decision about whether child at risk of harm (researcher rating)**

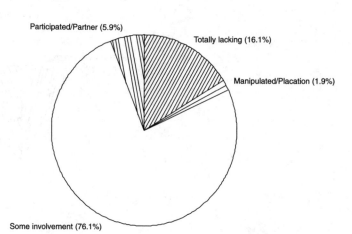

Sample = 372

Participated/Partner (5.9%)
Totally lacking (16.1%)
Manipulated/Placation (1.9%)
Some involvement (76.1%)

Figure 7.5   **Involvement of family members in decision about registration (researcher rating)**

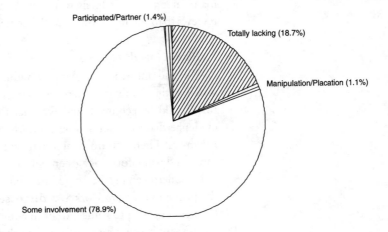

Sample = 369

Participated/Partner (1.4%)

Totally lacking (18.7%)

Manipulation/Placation (1.1%)

Some involvement (78.9%)

Figure 7.6   **Involvement of family members in decision about protection plan (researcher rating)**

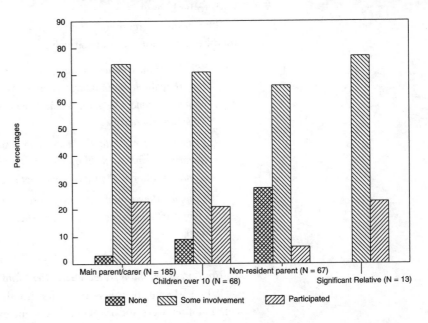

Percentages

Main parent/carer (N = 185)

Children over 10 (N = 68)

Non-resident parent (N = 67)

Significant Relative (N = 13)

None   Some involvement   Participated

The social work service after the initial conference

We have discussed in Chapter 6 the social work process after the conference. It was less easy to identify the extent to which family members were involved in the later stage, other than in any review conferences. The main carer was more likely to be invited to attend subsequent conferences or reviews than the initial one, but the actual attendance rate was little different.

Plans of work

We had information about whether there was a clear plan of work, whether the family members were consulted about change needed and how this should be achieved, and whether there was any written agreement or evidence that the plan had been clearly explained and discussed with family members. There was **no written agreement** on the record in 69 per cent of cases, and some form of agreement on the changes needed and/or the work to be undertaken in 63 cases (30 per cent). There was evidence, however, that the plan about future work was **discussed** with the main carer in 129 cases (61 per cent) and to some extent in a further 33 per cent of cases. There is a greater emphasis on **explaining** plans that had been made than on **negotiating** with the family members about what these plans should consist of. Although 75 per cent of the cases remained open, 46 per cent of the main carers interviewed or who completed the questionnaire stated that they had not received any help after the conference; 45 per cent thought that there was important information which was kept from them, and 23 per cent said that they were not asked after the conference by the social worker how they would wish to be helped.

The words 'agreement' and 'contract' were often mentioned by family members, but not always positively:

> We should have drawn up an agreement together, but due to shortage of time **they** did it. I didn't agree with it. They just said this is what we've been doing and we've put it down. They said at the meeting, "Have they signed the contract?"

> I did not get on with the male social worker and said I did not feel confident or open with him. He said he disliked me and yet the social services would not change him for another.

> I suppose **they** would call it help or support, but all they were doing was coming with their programme. It was **their** agenda of what **they** wanted to cover.

Frankness and honesty between client and social worker

When asked if they were frank and honest with the social worker, 62 per cent said they were and 19 per cent to some extent, although 12 (19 per cent) said they were not. A mother who had physically assaulted her 10 year old daughter said:

> *I found the social worker and others involved to be treating me as if I was a criminal. Therefore, why should I be honest? I held back a lot of information which I would not have done if they had allocated an appropriate social worker at the time.'*

Only 62 per cent thought that the social worker was frank and honest with them, and 19 per cent thought that he or she was definitely not frank and honest. A father who did feel able to be honest said:

> *They were always very open. At that stage I began to realise they were not just social workers. They were people.*

The proportions of other professionals involved in these cases who were considered to be frank and honest were: 71 per cent of doctors; 54 per cent of fostercarers; 68 per cent of health visitors; 63 per cent of police; and 62 per cent of teachers. Although the numbers are very small (only 12 commented about the guardian ad litem), fewer than half thought the guardian ad litem was frank and honest with them, and 36 per cent thought that the guardian was definitely not frank and honest with them.

Involvement if the child went into voluntary care

The other area of work after the conference involved practice and procedures when children were accommodated or in care. Twenty-nine per cent of the parents from whom we had a response said that voluntary care was offered at some stage, and 12 said care proceedings were used as a threat at some stage. For the 23 of our respondents who had a child in care at some point, 56 per cent considered that they were consulted about what should happen to the child in care, but one in five said they were definitely not consulted. Of the 78 main carers whose children were away from home at any point, the researchers concluded that 61 per cent were consulted about the arrangements for care, and that 24 per cent were consulted to some extent, with 11 (14 per cent) not being consulted at all on the care arrangements.

When the researcher asked 14-year old Mandy and her two sisters for their reactions about not being offered help until after the court case (since numerous notes on file had commented about it not being possible to start therapy until after the trial), she looked blank. She then went on to list all the help and support the girls and their mother had received, which included a short and very well organised period with a foster mother when her mother had to go into hospital. The foster mother continued to give support, including looking after the children when they were not needed in court because their mother wanted to be there, throughout the trial.

There appears to have been little involvement of family members in most cases when children went into care via the courts. In some of cases the workers made strenuous attempts to involve family members, even in the face of threats of violence, but in others the researchers concluded that there was very little attempt to engage parents when the children left home. This mother's comments were typical:

> *I wasn't allocated any social worker until the end of the case. So many different social workers comes to the court at each sitting. I was not involved in any of their work. I was treated like a guilty one and they tried to make me lie against my husband in order to get my daughter released.*

These two quotes show how the anxiety about whether they would lose their children dominated the thought processes of some parents at the time of the conference and for some time after:

> *They are saying we are taking them off you and the next week they are alright, and then "we are thinking of taking them off you again", and they were thinking of putting them on an at risk register. You're on a knife-edge all the time.*

> *I was worried. But at the back of it all, they are talking about taking my kids away. I will go for them one by one. It's like a threat hanging over us all the time.*

Conclusions about the extent to which family members were involved overall with the procedures and the practice

Social workers also were asked if they considered that they had successfully involved family members in the process, and Figure 7.7 gives the answers in respect of the main carer and the child. The response rate to this question in respect of the other family members was not sufficiently high to produce in table form, but their comments are reported below. It can be seen that they concluded that they were more successful in involving the children in their work than the parents. Some considered that they were able to involve parents at later stages when their early attempts had been unsuccessful, and in that sense their views were similar to those of the parents. In some cases, however, the involvement of the parent at the earlier stage did not continue after care proceedings were initiated.

Social work practice, agency policy and participation

In Chapter 6 we have described in general terms the extent to which social

Figure 7.7   **Social worker rating of success in involving main parent and older children in work**

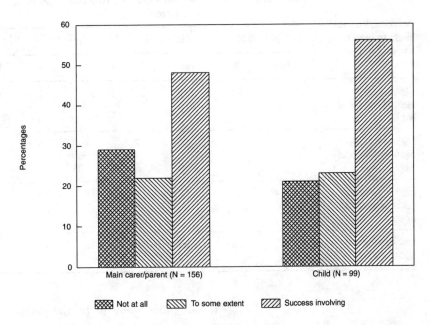

work practice and agency policy appeared likely to facilitate family participation. It has already been noted that it was more difficult to involve family members in some cases than in others. The researchers therefore rated the practice of the social workers and the agency policy in these cases insofar as it appeared to follow guidelines about good practice in helping these particular family members to be involved in the work. Table 7.4 shows the extent to which the agency policy and social work practice as implemented in these particular cases were rated by the researchers as likely to lead to working in partnership.

We noted in Chapter 2 that the agencies or area teams were chosen because of their wish to make a serious attempt to involve family members in their child protection work. We have already noted in this chapter that, while there were few cases where both the policy and practice throughout the case led to family members and agency working in **partnership**, in the cases studied, over 50 per cent were rated as 'medium' or 'high' in the extent to which both social work practice and agency policy were likely to facilitate the involvement of the main carers. At the other end of the continuum, in 29 cases (13 per cent) the agency and social work practice was rated as 'low' in their attempts to involve the main carers in the work. There was a similar pattern with the relatives and children, but practice with the parent not living in the home was rated as likely to result in their involvement in only about a third of the cases.

Table 7.4 **Researcher rating of agency procedures and social work practice in the case**

Practice/Policies likely to lead to working in part-nership	With total sample (n = 381)		With main carer/ parent (n = 217)		With child over ten (n = 72)		With relative (n = 13)		With non-resident parent (n = 76)	
	No.	%	No.	%	No.	%	No.	%	No.	%
High/medium agency and social worker	193	51	115	53	37	51	9	69	30	39
High or medium agency/low social worker	23	6	16	7	4	6	2	15	1	1
High or medium social worker/low agency	104	27	57	26	18	25	2	15	26	34
Low agency and social worker	61	16	29	13	13	18	0	0	19	25

It was more likely to be the case that the social work practice was participatory but agency procedures were not, than the other way round, and this was particularly marked with the non-resident parent where in some cases social workers went to considerable lengths, even when there were no agency policies about the involvement of a non-resident parent, to make sure that they were fully informed and were enabled to attend child protection and other meetings.

Parents' views of participation overall

We have already noted that there were serious obstacles to working in partnership in a third of the cases (our 'worst scenario' group), and that around a half of the family members did not agree with the social workers about the degree of risk or the sort of service that was appropriate. It is therefore not surprising that even when strenuous attempts to work in partnership with family members were made, this was not always achieved. There were, however, other cases where it ought to have been easy to work in partnership with family members (our 27 per cent 'best scenario' cases), but this did not happen, due to either agency procedures or social work practice. The parents or carers who responded to questionnaires or were interviewed were asked a series of questions about whether, on looking back over the period since the first interview, they felt they had been kept informed about what was happening; whether overall they understood what had been happening in the course of the child protection procedures; whether overall they contributed to the plans and whether they actually took part in the decision-making. Fifty-seven per cent said that they understood what was happening, but only 43 per cent said that they contributed to the plans and only 35 per cent said that they took part in the decision-making. When asked whether overall they considered that they had been included and involved, just under a half said that they had, and just over a half said that they had not. They were also asked whether they felt that they had been more involved by the social services department in what had happened than, for example, in their routine contacts with professionals such as teachers, or health personnel. Thirty-two did not answer this question, but those who did said that they felt less involved during the child protection investigation than with other contacts with professionals.

This mother saw how the issue of power and anxiety made it inevitable that there would be a difference:

> *When you're involved with something like social services you're nervous because they've got that power to take your child away from you, and really all you're trying to do is please them, give them the right answers as they want to hear, and hope that it's to their satisfaction. So you're on your best behaviour, with your best suit on. But if you go to them at school, you're just hearing about their work and you're more relaxed about it.*

For parents and children alike, being involved, and receiving a competent and caring service, were intertwined:

> *She still keeps in contact with us. She is a lovely lady. They kept us aware of the situation [police and social worker, jointly]. Their caring attitude was the thing. They weren't official. They came as normal caring people. They did their job efficiently, but in a caring way.*

In contrast, efficiency without caring was not conducive to involving parents or children:

> *The social worker was only concerned about her own benefits and doing her job correctly. Likewise the health visitor. No-one really cares about the parents in these situations. I also felt as if they were laughing behind my back.*

Researchers' ratings of the extent of family member involvement

In the light of all the evidence, the researchers rated the extent to which the different family members contributed to the overall planning about how the case was handled and about the services to be made available, and – more specifically – the extent to which they were involved in the making of key decisions. Finally, there were two researcher ratings (using the more and the less stringent definitions of involvement) of the extent to which the family member was involved in the process overall, and this was compared with the rating of family members from whom there was direct evidence (see Figures 7.8 to 7.11). The conclusions of the researchers are more positive than those of the smaller number of family members from whom we had direct responses. This is probably explained by a tendency for the researchers to compensate for the degree of difficulty of the case. This rating also looks at the case as a whole, and takes into consideration the fact that earlier difficulties were often resolved so that in the later stages of the case the family member was more fully involved in the decision-making process and practice.

Using the more differentiated definitions of participation listed in Chapter 2, we concluded that 13 per cent of the 378 family members about whom we had sufficient information were not involved, were manipulated or placated; 71 per cent were involved or consulted to some extent; and 16 per cent participated or were partners. (Figures 7.12). If only the main parents were included the picture is slightly more positive in that, of the 217 for whom we had adequate information, 7 per cent were rated as not at all involved, manipulated or placated; 75 per cent as fairly well involved and consulted; and 17 per cent as participants or partners. (Figure 7.13). The most positive picture is to be seen if the children considered old enough to participate are considered, with over a quarter being rated as participating or being partners in a way which was appropriate to their age (Figure 7.14)

Figure 7.8   **Researcher rating of involvement of main parent in work and decisions**

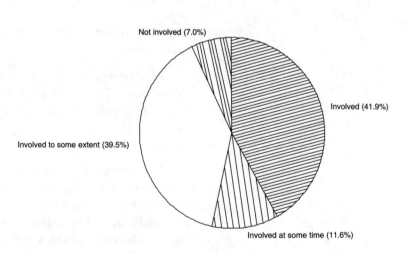

Sample = 215

Not involved (7.0%)

Involved (41.9%)

Involved to some extent (39.5%)

Involved at some time (11.6%)

Figure 7.9   **Parents' views of their involvement in the work and decisions**

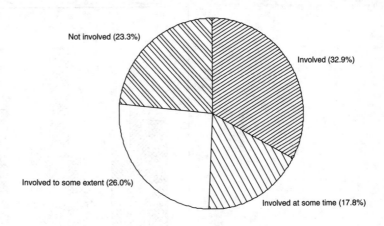

Figure 7.10   **Researcher rating of involvement of children aged 10+ in the work and decisions**

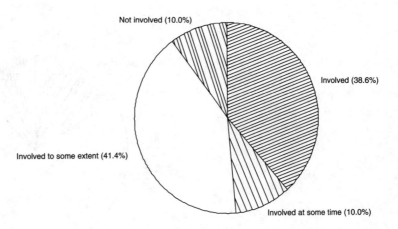

Figure 7.11 **Researcher rating of the involvement of 378 family members in the work and decisions together with views of 112 family members**

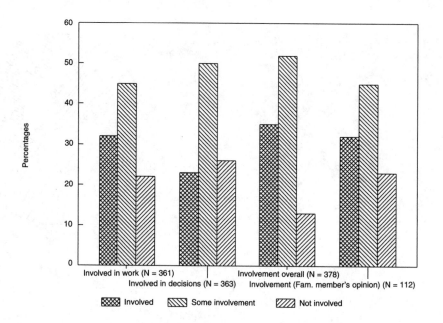

Involved in work (N = 361)   Involvement overall (N = 378)
       Involved in decisions (N = 363)   Involvement (Fam. member's opinion) (N = 112)

Involved   Some involvement   Not involved

Figure 7.12 **Researcher rating of extent to which 378 family members participated**

Sample = 378

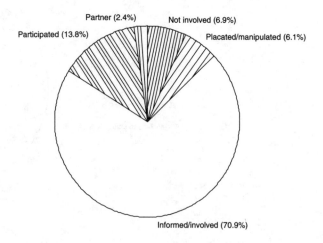

Figure 7.13   **Researcher rating of whether main parent participated**

Sample = 217

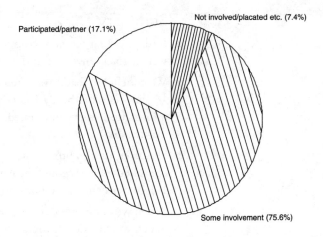

Not involved/placated etc. (7.4%)

Participated/partner (17.1%)

Some involvement (75.6%)

Figure 7.14   **Researcher rating of involvement of children considered old enough to be involved**

Sample = 128

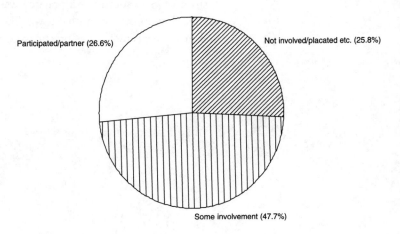

Participated/partner (26.6%)

Not involved/placated etc. (25.8%)

Some involvement (47.7%)

In the following chapter we consider whether certain characteristics of the family, the abuse, the social worker, or the agency were associated with greater or lesser degrees of participation.

Summary

- In this chapter we have considered the extent to which family members were actually involved in the work.

- We concluded that it was rare for them to participate or be partners (only 16 per cent of the 378 family members on whom we had adequate information were thus rated, and less than 3 per cent were in the 'partnership' group).

- However, using a broader definition of involvement (being informed, and consulted) 42 per cent of the main parents; 39 per cent of the children over 10) 10 per cent of the non-resident parents were rated as involved.

- When we considered the involvement of family members in the decisions which were made, we found that children were more likely to be involved in decisions about how the investigation should be conducted than were parents; it was rare for any family member to be involved in the decisions about risk and registration, but that the main parents were more likely to be involved in decisions about the protection plan (21 per cent participated or were partners) and the help offered (again 21 per cent participated or were partners. Children over 10 were more likely than parents to participate in decisions about whether care or accommodation was appropriate and about the services to be offered.

- Agency procedures and practice were rated as likely to lead to the involvement of family members in just over half of the cases, in just over a quarter of cases social work practice was highly rated but agency policy rated as low in the extent that it was likely to lead to family involvement and in 16 per cent of cases practice and policy were rate.

Chapter 8

Characteristics Associated with Working in Partnership

In the preceding chapters we have described a complex picture of the child protection service in 220 cases. A total of 385 individuals (parents, children or close relatives) might potentially have been involved as partners at least in some aspects of the service. In this chapter we attempt to tease out the characteristics of the families, the types of abuse, the agency policy, and the social work practice which were more or less in evidence in those cases where family members participated or were partners in the process, or were excluded from it.

We must stress that variables overlapped and that the number of variables, and the lack of precision in some of them, as well as the 'soft' nature of our researcher rating outcome measures, made it inappropriate to use the statistical tests which would have allowed us to suggest causal relationship between variables and outcome. However, *chi square* tests are used to indicate whether any associations between variables and outcome were unlikely to have occurred by chance. We have already seen that the main parents, the child, and that group of relatives whose significance was recognised by social workers, were more likely to be involved than parents who were **not** living in the same household as the child at the time of the conference.

Figure 8.1 lists those variables which were significantly associated with researcher ratings of the involvement of the main parent(s) in the protection process and the work. This analysis uses a less specific researcher rating of involvement than the more detailed degrees of partnership used in Chapter 7. This is because only small numbers came into the 'participated or were partners' group, leaving many cells with small numbers. The figure gives the researcher rating of whether the main parent(s) were involved using the categories 'no', 'to some extent or at some time' and 'yes'. Characteristics are grouped in terms of family or abuse related variables, variables about the children, and agency or social worker related variables.

Figure 8.1 **Variables significantly associated with main carer(s) being involved in the protection process overall (researcher rating) (N = 220). [Overall 42 per cent were rated as involved; 51 per cent as sometimes or to some extent; and 7 per cent not at all involved].**

Variable	χ^2	df	Sig. p =	Comment
				Variables about the family, or the nature of the abuse
Whether involved in abuse/neglect	9.350	4	< .05	57% of the non-abusers; 40% of the alleged abusers; and 33% of the known abusers were involved.

Figure 8.1   *Continued*

Variable	χ^2	df	Sig. p =	Comment
Parent admitted abuse/ neglect	19.857	4	< .001	Only 1 in 5 of the parents who did not admit that they played a part in the abuse but were believed to be implicated was involved; 49% of those who admitted being at least partially implicated, and 56% of those who were not implicated were involved in the work.
Agree about degree of abuse	37.1	4	< .0001	Only 19% were involved if they disagreed with the social worker about whether abuse had happened or its seriousness; 43% who partially agreed, and 63% who agreed were involved.
Agreed who responsible	23.2	4	< .001	Only 19% of those who disagreed with social worker about who was responsible and 37% who partially disagreed were involved compared with 55% who agreed.
Agreed parent implicated	15.84	6	< .05	If parent not implicated 53% were involved. Where it was alleged the parent was implicated only 23% of those who denied being implicated were involved; compared with 40% of those who partially agreed they were implicated and 50% of those who agreed they were implicated.
Parent committed to child	14.6	2	< .001	If parent always committed to child's welfare or always committed but own problems sometimes dominate, there is more likely to be involvement with the protection process.
Outcome for parent(s)	52.8	4	< .0001	Good outcome for parents associated with greater involvement. 62% of those parents who had a good outcome were involved compared with 22% where there was no change, and 21% where there was a poor outcome.
Parent agreed with assessment	31.11	6	< .0001	Only 17% of those who did not agree with the assessment were involved in the process, compared with 69% who did agree.
Parent understood what was happening	14.65	6	< .05	Parents who understood what was happening and how procedures worked were more likely to be involved.
Variables about the child and any period in care				
Legal status six months later	18.088	6	< .01	Less involvement if the child went into care on a care order or voluntary care some time after the allegation.
Siblings not in care	10.36	4	< .05	If the child in care, and a sibling at home, there was less likelihood of parents being involved (28%) than if all children in care (44% involved) or no child in care (45% involved).
Child's major placement is not with parent(s) who is/are alleged abuser	6.38	2	< .05	If alleged abuser not at home, 58% of parents involved compared with 37% when alleged abuser in home where child had major placement.
Outcome for child	25.3	4	< .0001	Outcome for child rated as good associated with involvement. 53% of those parents whose child had a good outcome were involved compared with 22% where there was no change and 24% where the outcome for child was poor.

Figure 8.1 *Continued*

Variable	χ^2	df	Sig. p =	Comment
Rating of child's involvement	32.1	4	< .0001	More parents rated as involved (59%) if child rated as involved. In 59% of the cases where the child participated, the parents were involved.
Child had few problems	8.11	2	< .05	Parents more involved if child rated as having no serious behaviour or health problems.
Variables about the agency policy and/or social work practice				
Agency	50.277	12	< .001	20% involved in Greenshire; 61% in Midborough; 20% in Innerborough; 52% in Outerborough; 65% in Northtown; 57% in Westshire; 16% in Eastshire.
Parents attended most or all of initial conference	49.07	6	< .0001	76% of those who attended most, and 66% of those who attended all the initial conference were involved in the protection process and none of these were not involved at all. Only 26% who did not attend and 25% who only attended a small part or the end only were involved. 10% of these were not involved at all.
Child interviewed without parents' permission	13.69	2	< .01	Only 23% were involved if a formal interview with child took place without parents' permission, compared with 55% who were involved when their permission for interview of child was sought.
Parents knew at first interview that it was an allegation of abuse	21.32	6	< .01	Only 25% were involved of those who did not know at first interview that there was an allegation of abuse/neglect.
Parents attended review conference	20.78	2	< .0001	More involved if parents attended review conference (if one was held) (59% involved if attended, compared with 24% of those who did not attend).
Adequacy of social work with child	56.82	6	< .0001	Rating of very adequate service to child associated with involvement of parents (60% involved), compared with 33% involved when service rated as adequate, and 11% when service rated as poor.
Adequacy of service to parents	105.5	6	< .0001	If service to parents rated as very adequate 71% were involved in process, compared with 35% if service rated as adequate, and 3% if service rated as poor.
Agency policy participatory	57.7	4	< .0001	If agency procedures and practice were rated as participatory in the case, 61% of the parents were involved; if agency policy and procedures were rated as not participatory, only 7% of the parents were involved.
Nature of work	14.88	6	< .05	More parents were involved (52% involved) if work was categorised 'preventive packages', 'de-labelling' or 'family casework' than 'backs to the wall' or 'child protection/up-tariff'.
There was a clear plan of work	63.35	2	< .0001	Where there was a clear plan of work, 59% of parents were involved compared with only 6% where there was no clear plan of work to be undertaken.

Figure 8.1 *Continued*

Variable	χ^2	df	Sig. p =	Comment
Parent received help	33.93	4	< .0001	66% of those who received help or services were involved compared with 10% of those who wanted help but did not get it, and 31% of those who did not receive help or services and did not want it.
Parent consulted about change needed	31.61	4	< .0001	
Choice of help offered	47.63	6	< .0001	
Information given on change needed	25.69	6	< .001	
A supportive relationship was provided	48.4	4	< .0001	
Advice was given by social worker	37.19	4	< .0001	
Skills training was part of the service	13.94	4	< .01	
Practical help given to family after conference	30.85	4	< .0001	
Help given to whole household	25.21	8	< .01	
Main method was described as family casework or client centred therapy	19.08	4	< .001	54% who received a family casework service were involved compared with 42% who received more tightly defined methods of therapy including family therapy, behavioural work, task centred work; and 8% who received only brief crisis intervention or child protection/child therapy only.
Worker had a long or medium-term focus	10.6	4	< .05	
Type of assessment	16.43	4	< .01	If assessment based on 'Protecting Children', 47% were involved; if a full family assessment used another assessment model, 52% were involved, but only 33% were involved if only child protection aspects of the case were assessed.
Race of social worker	9.9	2	< .01	78% of parents were involved if the main social worker was black or Asian, compared with 41 per cent if the main social worker was white.
Worker is strongly participatory in attitude	23.07	4	< .0001	High likelihood of involvement

Figure 8.1   *Continued*

Variable	χ^2	df	Sig. p =	Comment
Social worker thinks participation is low priority if child protection an issue	9.56	2	< .01	Less likelihood of involvement

The reader should bear in mind when reading the tables that 42 per cent of main carers were rated as involved, 51 per cent involved at some time or to some extent, and 7 per cent were rated as not involved at all. When the full cohort of 385 families members is included, 35 per cent were considered to be involved, 52 per cent at some time or to some extent, and 13 per cent not at all.

Although the broader categorisation of involvement is used for most of the analysis since so few could be allocated to the participation or partnership group, a tighter definition of partnership is used for some of the variables. When these tighter definitions are used the reader should note that 13 per cent were rated as not involved, manipulated or placated, 71 per cent were informed or involved to some extent, and 16 per cent participated or were partners. For the main part of the analysis the cohort of 385 family members was considered, but for some variables the cohort of 220 main parents was more appropriate.

Variables about the family or the nature of the allegation

The only variable about family composition which was associated with either more or less involvement was whether the family member was male or female, or whether a parenting pair were considered jointly. Lone female parents were significantly more likely to participate or work in partnership than either a parenting pair or a father (Figure 8.2). This accords with many studies of social work practice which find that social workers are more able to engage women in their work than men. However, there is qualitative data which suggests that fathers do value being invited to child protection and other meetings, and a more open style of working may be a more appropriate one for improving the extent to which they are engaged in the work. Although only half as many men as women participated or were partners, a majority did become involved to some extent.

None of the other variables about the parents or family composition was significantly associated with the degree of involvement. There was a tendency

Figure 8.2   **Sex of family members by researcher rating of involvement**

n = 378 (P<.001)

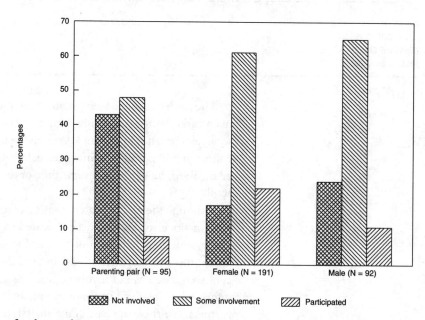

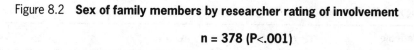

for those who were described as middle class or upper class to be either **more** or **less** involved and not fall into the middle group.

Somewhat surprisingly none of the variables we considered about the problems of the parents was associated with the extent of involvement. There was a trend towards parents described as having immature personalities being less involved, but this was not statistically significant and there was no such trend with parents who had a history of violence, mental illness, substance abuse or marital conflict. Linked with this, it did not appear to make a difference if the family had previously requested a social work service or had previous involvement with the department.

The nature of the allegation and attitudes of family members to the allegation and the investigation **were** associated with whether it was possible to work in partnership. Fifty-seven per cent of the non-abusers but only 33 per cent of the known abusers were rated as being involved. An even stronger association was found between involvement and whether the parent who was alleged to have been implicated in the abuse accepted a degree of responsibility. A similar pattern is found when there was agreement about the **severity** of abuse and about who was responsible for the abuse. Parents who agreed with the conclusions of the **assessment** which followed the conference were also more likely to be involved. We had predicted that there would be an association between agreement between worker and client and the likelihood of them being able to work in partnership, and as expected agreement about what had happened, and its significance for the child, was associated with some degree of involvement. However, although they tended to be involved to some extent, only 20 per cent of those who were not implicated in the abuse participated or were partners, not a significantly larger proportion than the 16 per cent of those who **were** known to be implicated. Those who were alleged to have maltreated the child but where the culpability never became clear were, not surprisingly, least likely to participate or be partners, but here again it is interesting to note that 11 per cent of them did become involved in working with the social worker (Figure 8.3). There was not a statistically significant association between the identity of the alleged abuser and the extent of involvement (Figure 8.4).

It is interesting to note that there was a trend towards fewer family members being involved in the work if the alleged abuser was not a parent. This fits with other studies which indicate a level of dissatisfaction with the service given after the investigation in such cases.

Turning to the nature of the allegation and the severity of the abuse. Figure 8.5 shows that neglect cases, and to a lesser extent cases arousing grave concern, were more likely to bunch in the middle group, whilst more emotional abuse cases fell into the participation group, and sexual abuse cases were more likely to be in the 'not involved at all' category. When only the main parents are considered more of the emotional abuse cases which are actually registered are likely to be in the not involved group (Table 8.1). It

Figure 8.3 **Family member implicated in abuse by involvement in work**

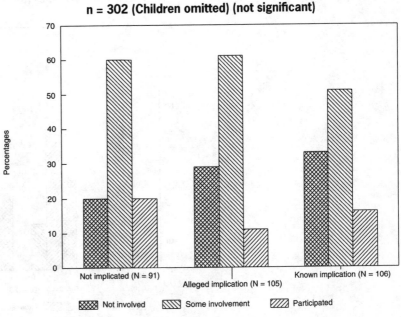

n = 302 (Children omitted) (not significant)

Not involved   Some involvement   Participated

Figure 8.4 **Identity of alleged abuser by researcher rating of involvement of family members**

(n = 377) (not significant)

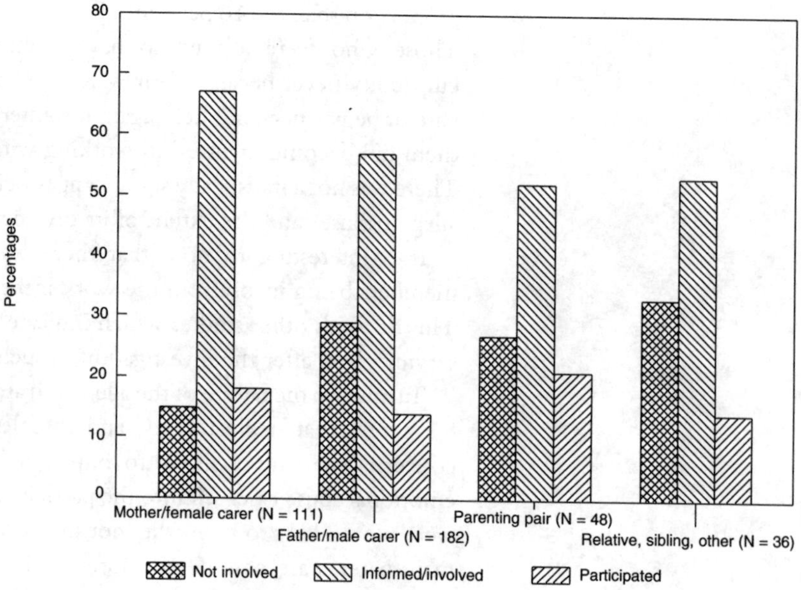

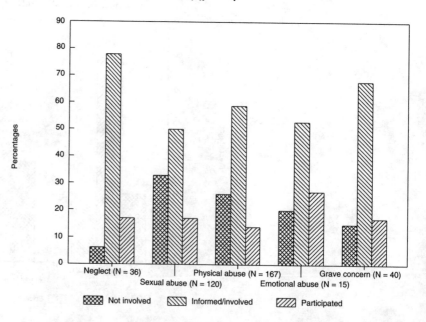

Figure 8.5 **Type of abuse by involvement of family member**

(n = 378) (p<.05)

Table 8.1 **Category of Registration by Researcher Rating of Involvement of Family Members (Main Parent(s) only)**

Category	Not involved/ placated/ manipulated		Informed and involved to some extent		Participated or was a partner		Total	
	No.	%	No.	%	No.	%	No.	%
Neglect	0	0	10	99	1	9	11	100
Sexual abuse	10	34	16	55	3	10	29	100
Physical abuse	16	27	34	57	10	17	60	100
Emotional abuse	3	33	5	56	1	11	9	100
Grave concern	5	9	16	61	5	19	26	100
Total	34	25	81	60	20	15	135	100

(P<.01)

should be noted, however, that numbers are very small in this category since only nine children were registered in the emotional abuse category.

Whether or not the child's name was placed on the register was not significantly associated with involvement but Figure 8.6 shows a trend towards greater involvement if the child's name was **not** placed on the register.

The severity of abuse was not significantly associated with whether or not the family member was involved, and indeed there was a trend (20 per cent compared with 16 per cent for the group as a whole) for family members to be more involved if the allegation was of serious injury or serious neglect. The explanation for this, as we shall see in the next section, is likely to be that workers invested more time and effort where the child appeared to be more seriously at risk (Figure 8.7).

There was no statistically significant association between the source of referral and the extent of participation, although there was a trend towards less involvement if referral was made by a professional other than a social worker, and greater involvement if the referral was made by a parent (54 per cent were involved) or the social worker (63 per cent were involved). This latter trend is somewhat surprising in that one might have expected some resentment on the part of the parent if the social worker already working with the case set the child protection .process in motion. There is no obvious explanation other than that the worker was able to build on an already existing relationship to explain why the child protection referral and case conference were necessary. Alternatively, registration led to a more comprehensive service to parents who were already asking for help. Again, somewhat surprisingly, there was no association between the extent of the involvement

Figure 8.6 **Registration by involvement of family member
(n = 377) (not significant)**

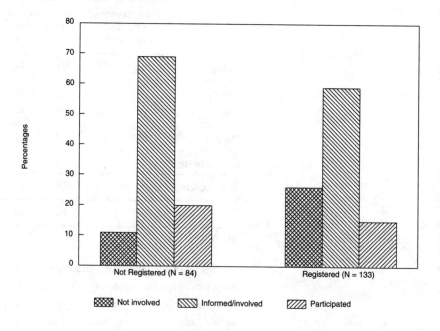

Figure 8.7 **Severity of abuse by involvement of family member
(n = 375) (not significant)**

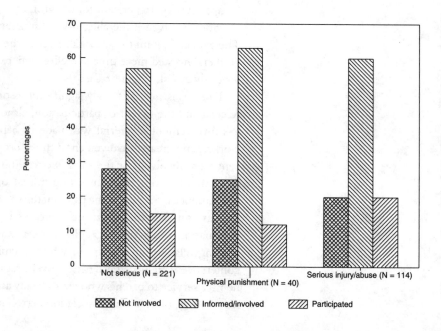

Figure 8.8 **Scenario by involvement of family member (responses of family members) (n = 112) (not significant)**

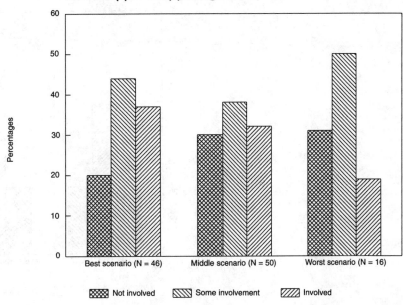

and whether or not the conference recommended that legal proceedings either in the criminal courts or to protect the child should be taken. It should be noted that the **recommendation** for legal action did not always result in such action being taken. Also, when the allegation was of sexual abuse against a non-resident parent or other male figure, the mother and child were likely to **want** a criminal prosecution to be initiated.

Our allocation of cases to the 'best', 'middle' and 'worst' scenario groups was based on the information we had about the families, their attitudes to the allegation, and the nature of the abuse. We anticipated that this variable would be significantly associated with whether or not the parents were involved. On the broader outcome measure this did not prove to be the case, indicating that the hypothesis that some family members will be more difficult to engage than others was not totally borne out, except for a small number of cases at each end of the continuum (Figure 8.8) When the total sample is considered and the tighter definition of partnership is used, there is a significant association between allocation to 'best', 'middle' or 'worst' scenario groups, with 22 per cent of those in the 'best' scenario group participating or being a partner (Figure 8.9). However, it should also be noted that 29 per cent in this group were rated as not involved, placated or manipulated. At the other end of the scale 9 per cent of those in the 'worst' scenario group participated or were partners, and fewer in the 'worst' scenario group were not involved at all than was the case for the 'best' scenario group. This suggests that we must look elsewhere for the reasons

Figure 8.9 **Scenario by researcher rating of involvement of family members (n = 375) (p<.01)**

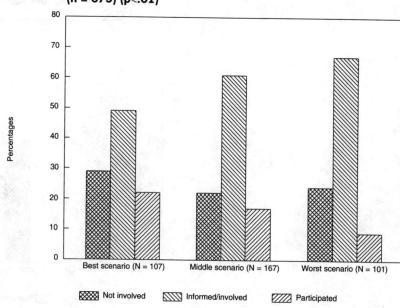

why some families work in partnership with the professional workers and others do not than simply to the characteristics of the family members or the nature of the abuse.

Variables about the children and their placements

There was no association between working in partnership and the sex of the child. There is both quantitive and qualitative evidence to suggest that outcomes were worse, whether measured in terms of the outcome for the children, or the extent to which working in partnership was achieved, if the children themselves had serious behaviour or health problems. With some of the young people, the behaviour problems appeared to result from family problems and relationship difficulties which had built up over the years. One social worker tried valiantly to work in partnership with a young woman who moved from home through four different placements within a six month period, and was rarely to be found at the address where she was supposed to be. In another case the allegation was of serious physical abuse by the mother. However, the attempt to engage her in the work was made more difficult because she believed herself to have acted in the child's interests in chastising her. This was because she found herself 'at the end of her tether' because her fourteen year old daughter was frequently brought home by the police, and was in serious physical danger as well as being emotionally and sexually harmed through her activities as a prostitute. It is interesting to note that no child protection conference was called when it was known that she was being sexually harmed and in physical danger on the streets, and only when her mother physically harmed her did a conference take place. The mother was not surprisingly angry that she received, as she saw it, little help prior to her having taken things into her own hands and physically punished her daughter. This was a 'worst' scenario case, and is rated as having a poor outcome for the child as well as there being minimal involvement of either mother or child.

Turning to the placement of the child, brief periods away from home at the investigation or the assessment stage were not associated with family members being more or less involved in the process. However, when the child's major placement was in care or accommodation there was a trend towards less involvement of the parents. There was a statistically significant association between the parents not being involved and the child being in care or accommodated at the end of the six month period of the study. Somewhat surprisingly a place of safety order or wardship following the allegation was not associated with the extent of involvement of the parents, although in some cases in the qualitative study the taking of compulsory action clearly did impede the willingness of a parent to become involved. It may be that for those workers who are striving to work co-operatively, the taking of an order to protect the child involves considerably more contact with family members which can be used to work through the difficulties and move towards working in partnership. In contrast, when the case does not require this high level of activity, a less purposive pattern of work may result in the families feeling that their concerns are not being properly addressed. This finding is consistent with the work of Fisher at al. (1986) on older children coming into care, but conflicts with the findings of Millham et al. (1989) and Packman (1986) who found that parents were less likely to work with social workers if compulsory removal was used to protect the child.

If the child was in care or accommodation and siblings remained at home, there was an association with a lower level of involvement of the parents. These cases usually concerned an allegation of sexual abuse or over-chastisement made by a teenager against a parent. In such cases a rift was sometimes opened up between the young person and the parents. The social worker found him or herself having to choose between the version of the truth presented by the young person and that presented by the parents, and in such cases it was likely that either the parent or the young person participated, but not both. However, the allocation of different workers did lead to the possibility of both parents and young person becoming involved in the work. These cases of serious conflict between a young person and the rest of the family were a small minority, and did not therefore affect the association between the child being rated as involved in the work, and the parents themselves participating.

Variables associated with race and culture

At this point it seems appropriate to comment on the issue of the race and culture of the family members and its relationship to working in partnership. We have not specifically highlighted issues of race and culture in earlier chapters, although reference has been made to the race of the child in some of the case examples where this has been appropriate. Parents and children from minority ethnic groups were neither more nor less likely to be involved in the work than white families, even though the situations which brought them into the child protection arena were often more complex and difficult to handle (Figure 8.10). Disagreements about the appropriateness of physical punishment featured in a disproportionate numbers of cases involving black families. The social work teams providing services for the majority of the

Figure 8.10 **Involvement of family member by race of child (n = 378) (not significant)**

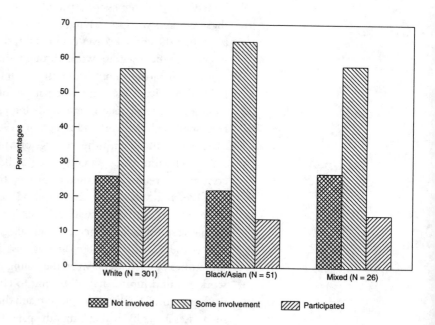

black families in our sample were backed by well-established policies for involving family members, and had much to tell us about their attempts to engage parents and children in their work. Where a social work team had a high proportion of workers from minority ethnic groups both they and their white colleagues had given much thought to policies to increase family involvement. Regrettably we were not able to interview many families from minority ethnic groups to back up our impression that their attempts were generally as successful as possible given the circumstances of the families. The researcher's notes about one family read:

> *The family was of Asian origin and because the social worker was Asian she was able to persuade the father's psychiatrist to modify his approach by producing a full family history for him, which stressed the ethnic background and relevance to their experiences. She was able to empathise with all the family members.*

On the other hand, a white worker was not able to engage a father in another case which involved heavy chastisement:

> *The family's attitudes to authority were counter-productive. They have some learning difficulties and thus change was difficult to effect. I was feeling threatened and experienced high levels of stress because of the risk. The attitude of Asian fathers can seriously block our ability to involve them in the work with the family. Race is a factor in enabling parental participation.*

The researcher's comments on another family of Indian origin show that attempts to involve the family members and understand the cultural aspects of sexual abuse were only partly successful:

> *The family were of Indian ethnic origin. The uncle of the child, the current head of the family, was the alleged abuser in a case of sexual abuse in another social services area. The child in the case from the other area had said that the child in our sample was involved. The mother and maternal grand-mother were shocked and horrified and refused to see the social worker after the first visit made to explain the allegation. The family moved out of the area to relatives in a nearby district and their solicitor wrote on their behalf to say he would prosecute social services for trespass if they visited the family again. The team manager consulted with the social services legal department and organised a warrant to gain access to the child, but in the event it was not used because the maternal grandmother came to the social services office to try and sort things out. The initial child protection conference asked for a report to be made by the social worker via the Asian Women's Resource Centre on the attitudes of that community to child sexual abuse and cultural differences. This was presented at the deferred conference. Contact with the family was still being negotiated six months later, but the maternal grandmother was still involved in talking to the team manager.*

An African-Caribbean mother who did take part in the study certainly felt that she would have preferred to have a black worker who would have been better able to understand her views about what would be helpful to her and her son.

> *I found the social worker and others involved to be treating me as if I was a criminal—therefore why should I be honest? I held back a lot of information which I wouldn't have done had they allocated me a black worker.*

This is another example of a case where failure to involve the mother led to decisions being made on the basis of less than adequate information. This mother was a deeply caring woman who was depressed by her inability to go out to work because of the lack of day care. The child's father was accused of overchastising him and indeed she had left him because of his heavy-handedness. However, she and her son were both insistent that continued contact between father and son was essential to his emotional well-being. This lack of confidence in the social worker might mean that she will not seek help in protecting her son if further problems arise.

Variables about the social work practice and agency policy

The qualitative material suggests that there were, indeed, some cases where the extent of family problems, the difficult behaviour of a young person, and the lack of agreement about what exactly had happened and its seriousness, meant that even highly skilled conscientious and caring social workers with a strong commitment to working in partnership were unable to engage family members. However, our finding that some family members were involved when they had very serious problems and were initially located in our 'worst' scenario group, whilst others with few problems and in the

Table 8.2 **Researcher rating of agency policy for this case by researcher rating of involvement of family member(s)**

	Not involved/ placated/ manipulated		Involved to some extent		Participated or was a partner		Total	
Policy	No.	%	No.	%	No.	%	No.	%
Not participatory	64	59	42	39	2	2	108	100
Variable or moderately participatory	20	15	87	67	23	18	130	100
Participatory	10	7	93	67	36	26	139	100
Total	94	25	222	59	61	16	377	100

Missing = 14   [$\chi^2 = 107.10$ df = 4   p < .0001]

'best' scenario group were not involved, suggests that it is to social work practice and agency policy that we should look in order to understand why some families were more involved than others. In Chapters 5 and 6 we described the social work practice and agency policy. From our discussions with workers and managers, and analysis of the records, we identified some variables in social work practice which we hypothesised might be associated with a greater or lesser degree of family member involvement.

Agency policy

There was a statistically significant association between the involvement of family members and the agency providing the service, with considerably higher rates of involvement in the three London boroughs, Northtown and Westshire than in Greenshire and Eastshire (Figures 8.11 and 8.12). These workers were very clear about the importance of the backing they received from the agency:

> *I feel the policy of the borough for participation and clear procedures makes actions and approach easier to manage.*

> *What's needed for participation is preparation and training prior to implementing it. It's vital to help ourselves, the parents, and other agencies to overcome our fears and worries about how it will work or what may be difficult about it. Generally clear cut procedures leaflets, pro forma letters, etc are very helpful as aides-memoire when the social worker is advising parents. One is less likely to forget something. It also helps parents feel we are serious about it rather than it's a half-hearted token gesture approach.*

Table 8.3 **Social worker's attitude towards working in partnership (researcher rating) by researcher rating of involvement of family member**

Attitude	Not involved/ placated/ manipulated		Involved to some extent		Participated or was a partner		Total	
	No.	%	No.	%	No.	%	No.	%
Strongly in favour of working in partnership	21	18	61	53	34	29	116	100
In favour of full involvement of family members	47	24	126	65	22	11	195	100
Favours informing but ambivalent about partnership	8	31	17	65	1	4	26	100
Total	76	23	204	60	57	17	337	100

Missing = 48   [χ^2 = 31.72   df = 4   p < .0001]

Figure 8.11   **Researcher rating of involvement of family members by agency (n = 376) (p<.001)**

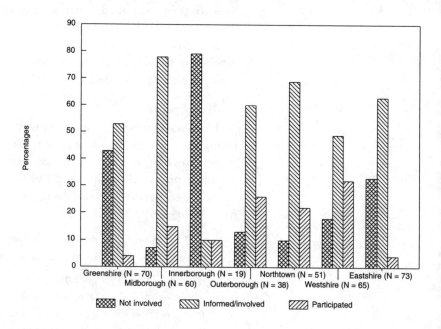

Figure 8.12   **Family members' views of their involvement by agency (n = 111)**

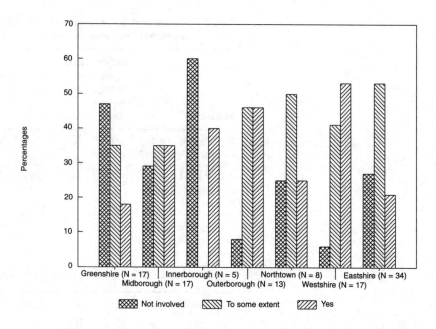

There was also a significant relationship between family member involvement and parents attending most or all of the initial conference, and this difference in policy is likely to be the main explanation for the lower levels of involvement in Greenshire and Eastshire since those two counties only invited parents to the end or a small part of the conference. (We were unable to consider the impact of attendance of **children** since that happened in a very small number of cases). From our qualitative material it appears that a policy of encouraging parental attendance at all or most of the child protection conference results in more general changes in policy and practice which are independently associated with family involvement.

Contrary to our expectations, in view of the fact that all those family members who were asked to leave the conference said they would have much preferred to be there throughout, there was no statistically significant difference in the rates of participation between those who attended **all** the conference and those who attended most of it (Figure 8.13). In looking to our interview responses, it appears that there was little difference in the overall policy and practice of the agencies and teams where families attended all or most of the conferences. It may be that workers who had to ask family

Figure 8.13   **Family member attended initial conference by researcher rating of involvement (n = 376) (p<.0001)**

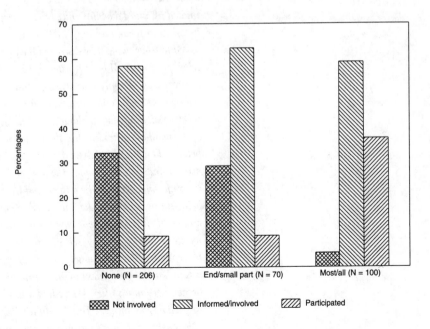

members to leave for a small part had to spend more time explaining and justifying this policy, and telling family members what went on when they were not present. This extra time and effort might have paid off in terms of greater involvement. One social worker said:

> *I find it very difficult. I think it's like the Spanish Inquisition having parents go in and out of conferences. You have to say to them you must endure the first one. The next one, you're a fully fledged member. I find it very difficult for them.*

In view of the strong message from family members that they did resent being excluded for part of the conference, and the extra social work time which was needed to make this policy work, we would still suggest that wherever possible full attendance is desirable. However, this finding does suggest that if it **is** necessary for some family members to be excluded for small parts of the conference, this can be achieved without losing the impetus towards working in partnership provided that careful explanations are given about why it is necessary.

This account by a mother in our 'best scenario' group who was invited to a small part of the conference and rated as only partially involved gives some strong messages about why a policy of inviting family members to only a small part of the conference or only at the end was associated with lack of participation.

> *It was horrendous. I was asked to arrive at 2.30 and at 2.30 I'd be invited in, and I'd be introduced to the people who'd be there, and then I'd be asked to speak and they'd tell me what they thought, and then I'd be asked to leave while they discussed the case, and then at the end I'd know whether or not he'd been registered. Once I got to the waiting room I was aware I was the only one waiting, and I said to my friend "You're not telling me I'm the only one who's turned up. They are all in there and the meeting's taking place without me." I thought the meeting started at 2.30 and I would be introduced to the people who would be discussing my son before. Then my social worker eventually appeared an hour after I'd arrived and that was awful. Coming into the room was really very, very uncomfortable. It was like a them and us situation, and I felt so inhibited being sat next to them. I'd have liked to have been able to sit across a table and see their reactions, but when you sit next to someone, you sense their reactions, but you can't see eye to eye. The way the room was was horrendous. Not big enough for the people, and little things were quite intimidating—being next to the chairman—he was bloody patronising— he was very much like "We've had a nice little talk and we'd like you to say what you think." But he didn't help me to say what I thought. Obviously he couldn't put words into my mouth, but he didn't give me*

*any clues as to what normally you are expected to say, or what was
expected of me to say. I may as well not have spoken for the amount of
interest that was taken.*

*The end of the conference made me extremely angry because I was
sitting in the waiting room and I'd been told I'd be told the results—their
decision as to whether he'd be registered or not at the end of the meeting,
and I don't know why, but everyone had left before I was called back in.
Now I'd have liked to have gone in and then argued the point again
because they had made the wrong decision. It was like being told "Right,
we've registered him – oh, and by the way, we'd best call the mother in and
tell her before she buggers off to tea!" This arrangement of coming in and
out is horrendous.*

The attendance of parents at the review conference was also strongly
associated with family involvement. Most of the teams we studied invited
parents to review conferences and this association for those who actually
came is therefore likely to be explained by the **intervening work** in some
cases having set a pattern of working jointly with the family member but not
in others.

Some variables concerned both agency policy and social work practice,
such as the question discussed in more detail in Chapter 6 about whether or
not the child was interviewed without the parent's permission. When the
child was formally interviewed without the knowledge of at least one parent
there was a trend which did not reach statistical significance, for the parents
not to be involved in the subsequent protection process. (Only 23 per cent
were involved compared with 55 per cent where the parent was present at the
first interview or was at least told that it was taking place). (Figure 8.14).

Table 8.4 **Child interviewed without parent(s)' permission by researcher rating of
involvement of family member(s) (main parent(s) only)**

Interviewed	Not involved/ placated/ manipulated		Involved to some extent		Participated or was a partner		Total	
	No.	%	No.	%	No.	%	No.	%
Without permission	13	28	30	64	4	8	47	100
With permission	13	16	51	62	18	22	82	100
Total	26	20	81	63	22	17	129	100

Missing (including child too young) = 91. [p < .07. Not significant]

Other variables which combined practice and policy were around the
management of the first interview with the parents. Parents who were not

clearly told or failed to understand that the interview concerned an allegation of abuse or neglect were less likely to be involved overall in the process of protecting the child. We had conflicting findings on the question of who conducted the first interview with family members. When the **researcher rating** of the involvement of the main parent(s) is considered, there was no association between who conducted the first interview about abuse and the extent of involvement. However, when the **responses of family members** are considered, there was greater involvement if the family member was first interviewed by the police or another professional alone than by a social worker either alone or with another professional. One possible explanation for this which arises out of the interviews is that a well handled first interview in which the parents are courteously treated and their feelings of shock, worry and guilt acknowledged goes a long way towards establishing a working relationship based on trust. Some of the interviews were undertaken by professionals (mainly the police) out of office hours when no social worker was available. By the time the social worker arrived on the scene the immediate crisis was over and the parents were sometimes less receptive to going over the story again with a new person, especially if they had already made a strong relationship with the police officer as a supportive and caring figure. O'Hagan (1989) has written about the contribution to child protection work which could be made by crisis intervention method and theory, and there was support in our interviews for his argument. Those interviewed by the police alone were more polarised, 41 per cent being involved and 41 per cent definitely not involved compared with those interviewed by social workers who were more likely to be involved to some extent (47 per cent). Six of the nine who were interviewed about the abuse initially by a health professional or a teacher without the presence of another professional were involved and none of these was not involved at all. This lends support to those teachers and health professionals who consider it to be good practice to speak with parents about their concerns before or at the same time as they make the referral to the investigating agency.

Social work practice

Many of the variables about social work practice were obviously influenced by agency policy, most notably the availability of resources. Workers who were able to spend time with family members in order to inform them about the procedures, give them appropriate leaflets, and try to understand the family member's point of view, were more likely to succeed in working in partnership and this is clearly related to agency policy in ensuring that time, resources and leaflets were available. Our qualitative data suggest that some workers were able to engage family members even when the agency policy and resources were not obviously encouraging this, but they had an uphill

Table 8.5 **Professional(s) present at first interview with family member by researcher rating of involvement of family member**

Professional(s) present	Not involved/ placated/ manipulated		Involved to some extent		Participated or was a partner		Total	
	No.	%	No.	%	No.	%	No.	%
Social worker(s) only	27	16	108	66	29	18	164	100
Police only	25	42	28	47	7	12	60	100
Other professional only	5	17	18	60	7	23	30	100
Social worker and other professional	24	25	58	59	16	16	98	100
Total	81	23	212	60	59	17	352	100

Missing = 91. [χ^2 = 16.03 df = 6 p < .05]

struggle when compared with those whose agency fully supported attempts to work in partnership with parents and children.

We considered first the overall adequacy of the service to the child and to the parent, and found that an adequate social work service to the child, the parents, or both, was significantly associated with the involvement of the parents and children (Table 8.6). Our rating of adequacy was based on an assessment of the extent to which the practice followed the generally agreed guidelines to be found in Social Service Inspectorate reports and social work texts. To be rated as adequate, the work needed to combine understanding of and empathy with the family members with practice which appeared to be well planned and competently carried out. Those who did not request help or declined it when it was offered might be rated as receiving an adequate service provided the worker kept them fully informed and behaved with courtesy and respect towards them, and efficiently followed the procedures. However, in the majority of cases family members expected a worker to indicate that he or she cared about them as people, and to offer help over a range of difficulties, and not only those which were associated with the child protection inquiry. For workers to efficiently follow the procedures was not sufficient to be rated by the parents or the researchers as providing a satisfactory service if it failed to provide at least some of the help requested or needed.

Several of those parents who needed and wanted help commented scathingly about workers who were 'only interested in doing their job and following their procedures'. Unsurprisingly, if we consider only those parents who wanted help, those who said they actually received help were more likely

Table 8.6 **Adequacy of social work service to family member (researcher rating) by researcher rating of involvement of family member**

Adequacy	Not involved/ placated/ manipulated		Involved to some extent		Participated or was a partner		Total	
	No.	%	No.	%	No.	%	No.	%
Very adequate	0	0	94	64	53	36	147	100
Adequate	13	12	85	80	8	7	106	100
Some weakness	34	52	31	48	0	0	65	100
Poor service	40	82	9	18	0	0	49	100
Total	87	24	219	60	61	17	367	100

Missing = 18. [$\chi^2 = 233.18$ df = 6 p < .0001]

to be involved or to be partners than those who did not consider that they had been helped.

A problem was sometimes created by agency or team policy when it was the practice not to offer services until a full assessment had been completed after the conference. This approach, which a professional colleague with whom we discussed it referred to as a 'nil by mouth' approach, tended to alienate families and was not conducive to working in partnership. In one case it was two months after the initial referral and at the end of a very labour intensive assessment that the parent with several children, one of whom had a disability, was offered a much needed pushchair by the long-term team worker who took up the case. The practice in this case could not be faulted in terms of following guidelines and the skills and effort expended, but was not perceived by the family member as either adequate or participatory. The new worker was quickly able to redress the balance and at the six month stage was beginning to engage the parent in the work. This parent, like a majority of those interviewed by Farmer *et al* (1995), appreciated a change of worker. However, the majority of those in our study did not wish to change their worker, and some preferred to see the case closed rather than accept someone new coming to visit when a transfer was proposed. This difference may be explained by the fact that more parents in our study attended the whole of the conference and when the investigation and conference stage was well handled, alliances were formed as worker and client came to know each other better in the crisis.

This is not to suggest that a well conducted assessment is not a positive factor in facilitating family involvement. On the contrary, when full assessments were undertaken, the family members were more likely to participate than if only child protection aspects were assessed. By a full assessment we mean one which looks at the family's present situation in the light of past history, considers the positives as well as weaknesses of each family member, the pressures upon them, and the resources which they might be able to call up themselves. Full assessments as opposed to those which only look at child protection aspects and risk are more likely to uncover areas where help is needed, and services can be provided when need is identified under the provisions of Part III and Schedule 2 of the Children Act 1989.

Some variables concerned the style and method of practice (see Chapter 6 for a fuller description). When help was offered to the family as a whole and not only to the child or a sub-group of household members, there was an association with the main carer taking part and this was also the case if the worker had a long or medium-term focus rather than a very short-term focus.

Figure 8.14   **Researcher rating of involvement of main parent(s) by type of work (n = 214) (p<.001)**

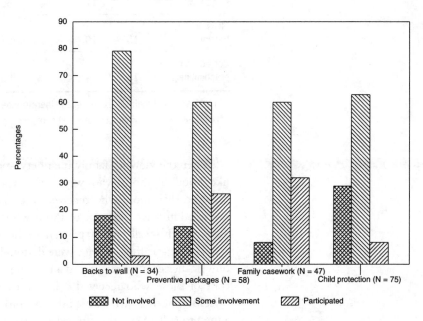

Not surprisingly, work which came into the 'Hardiker' categories of preventive packages, de-labelling, and family casework was more likely to be associated with working in partnership than work which was allocated to the 'backs to the wall' or 'child protection' or 'up-tariff' categories (Figure 8.14). A supportive or therapeutic relationship, the giving of advice and the provision of practical help were associated with family involvement (Table 8.7).

If an attempt was made to provide a therapeutic relationship but the offer was rejected by the parents, they were least likely to be involved.

Table 8.7 **Type of service by researcher rating of involvement by family member**

Type of Service*	Not involved/ placated/ manipulated		Involved to some extent		Participated/ was a partner		Significance
	Number and percentage of cases where this service was provided						
	No.	%	No.	%	No.	%	p =
Therapeutic relationship	7	10	42	62	19	28	< .0001
Supportive relationship	17	9	123	65	50	26	< .0001
Group work or group therapy**	3	12	14	56	8	32	< .05
Advice	39	17	134	60	52	23	< .001
Skills or other training	15	19	45	57	19	24	n.s.
Considerable practical help	18	14	82	63	31	24	< .0001

*These were not mutually exclusive and therefore percentages do not add up to 100 per cent.
**NB Caution needed because of small numbers.

When the views of family members were considered, there was a greater likelihood of those who were offered a family casework service being involved than those who received 'preventive packages' or a 'de-labelling' service. Fifty-five per cent of those who received a service categorised as 'backs-to-the-wall', and 40 per cent of those who received a 'child protection only' or 'up-tariffing' service were definitely not involved, as compared with only 18 per cent who received a preventive packages service and only 6 per cent of those who received a family casework service. However, it **was possible** for those who were offered a protection only service or one which aimed to collect evidence in order to have a clear decision about the nature and extent of abuse, to be involved in the work in that nine of the parents in such cases considered themselves to be involved.

There was a less strong association between the provision of group work or group therapy, but no association between skills training and involvement.

Family casework is an inclusive term for a range of different methods offered in the context of a helping relationship, established either with the aim of achieving change in personal or interpersonal functioning (therapeutic) or to provide support. The small number of cases where it was clear that a specific method such as psychodynamic casework, task centred intervention,

Figure 8.15 **Social workers' description of method by researcher rating of involvement of family members. (N = 191) (p<.01)**

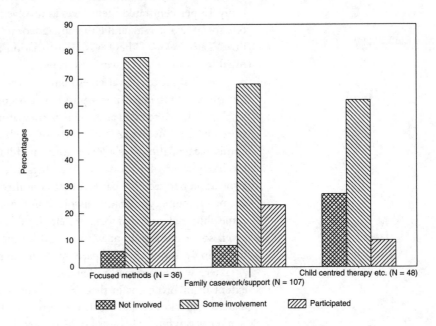

crisis intervention, or family therapy was used meant that we were unable to use these variables in the analysis. However, when grouped together (Figure 8.15) there is a trend towards greater involvement if family casework was the main method, with slightly fewer being involved if more tightly defined methods were used. From the comments of family members it is possible to surmise that any one of these methods, with the proviso that it is offered in the context of a caring relationship and carefully explained to family members, is likely to be associated with working in partnership. Because purposive work which was based on a careful assessment and was negotiated with the family was associated with family member involvement, we concur with Doel and Marsh (1992) that a task centred **approach** and O'Hagan (1989) that work based on crisis intervention theories, are likely to help to achieve family involvement. However, the more narrowly defined task-centred **method**, with its emphasis on brief intervention, is unlikely to be appropriate except for the small proportion of families who were looking for a particular service to help with a specific problem. Time limited and tightly focused casework might have been helpful at an earlier stage, but by the time most of these cases reached child protection conferences, longer-term support and/or therapy was usually needed.

As with the ratings by researchers, family members were also more likely to rate themselves as having been involved if a supportive relationship was offered or advice and practical help were given. There was a less strong association between the provision of a therapeutic relationship and the main method of help being described by the social worker as family casework. Only 15 per cent rated themselves as involved if the work was described by the social worker as child therapy, advocacy for the child, evaluative or investigative work. There was no association between involvement and the usual location of social work interviews.

The final group of variables concerns the attitudes of the social worker towards working in partnership and their attempts to do so. Not surprisingly, workers who were rated as strongly participatory in attitude were more likely to succeed in involving family members whilst those who considered that family participation was a low priority if child protection was an issue were less likely to involve the family members in their work. There was a strong association between the parent being consulted about the change needed and the parent being successfully involved in the work. Parents who were given some choice about what form of help should be offered, and those who were given some choice about who should be the social worker were also, not surprisingly, more likely to participate in the process.

There was an association between the race of the social worker and the extent of involvement in that 78 per cent of parents were involved whose main social worker was black compared to 41 per cent if the main social worker was white. This was borne out by the rating of the family members from whom we had information, although numbers were small and the trend did not reach statistical significance. Six of the 13 who had a black social worker said they were involved compared with 28 (30 per cent) of those who had a white social worker. The age of the social worker did not appear to make any difference nor the years in social work. There was no statistically significant association with qualification although there was a trend towards the parents being less involved in the small group where the social worker was not qualified. When only the family members' responses are considered, there was an association between the length of time that the social worker had been engaged in child care social work and family involvement. Interestingly this was not in the direction one might have anticipated in that more family members considered themselves to be involved if the worker had been in child care work for less than five years, and family members were least involved it the worker had been involved for ten or more years. This association suggests the possibility of social workers who have been engaged in this work for long periods becoming tougher, more distant and less caring in their attitudes, and showing other characteristics associated with 'burn out'. Whether or not the worker was only involved in child care work or spent some time working with other client groups was not associated with either more or less involvement.

When the views of the family members are considered, there is a trend towards the family member being less involved if work after the conference was carried out by a **multi-professional** group of workers than by one or more **social workers**. Farmer *et al* (1994) and Hallett (1994) found, as we did, that the bulk of the work after the conference is actually undertaken by social workers and other professionals only tend to be involved, in the majority of cases, in processes such as review conferences. Cases of consistent, planned multi-disciplinary work were few, and it may be that there was something specific about those cases, such as particularly hostile or violent parents, which made it more difficult to involve the family members. We should not discount the possibility that professional alliances in some way have a negative effect on the quality of alliances with family members. Until more work which is truly multi-disciplinary is undertaken outside clinical settings, it will not be possible to explore how inter-agency and multi-disciplinary work can best achieve the involvement of parents and children.

The characteristics and personalities of social workers and family members

Social workers to some extent, but family members almost invariably, spoke in terms of individual or personal characteristics which were often linked with whether or not they liked each other as people, and in turn with whether they were able to work together. There were three groups of characteristics: the personality and working **style** of the worker, which was separate from the actual methods used; the extent to which the worker believed in the value of and was determined to make strenuous efforts to work in partnership; and the less tangible attributes which we can only put down to 'chemistry' in the relationship between the worker and the parent or child. Questions to the social worker and the family member about whether each liked the other as a person drew instant recognition from family members and support for the contention that liking and being liked was associated with positive outcomes.

> *A ten year old girl said: 'My social worker is so open – she doesn't keep things from you—she's so friendly.'*
>
> *Her mother said: 'Oh yes, she did care about us.'*

Three other mothers said:

> *I like our social worker – it's the way she is – she's not nosey – she's down to earth.*
>
> *The thing that made it easier basically – they were caring. They made me feel they were concerned, that I was a person. She was a similar age to me – a person who cares a lot about children and has children of her own. They told us about their own lives.*

> *Her attitude was very good. She was sympathetic, just a very, very nice person, gentle. The other guy, I refused to let in. He was very aggressive, very accusing. He shouldn't be a social worker. I got cross with him.*

Parents whose two children were in care said:

> *He [the social worker] never seemed willing to help at all. He was more interested in fighting against myself and my husband. He's the nastiest most deceiving person we've ever met, and we don't know how he managed to get into social services. We thought social workers were supposed to help not hinder. We wanted more information on our children's growth and their abilities, what they'd like and dislike and the chance to have them to stay with us over the weekend once in a while. They could've tried not being so two-faced.*

The parents and children described the different ways in which some social workers took the trouble to learn about them and their fears, anxieties, pressures and strengths whilst not appearing to be 'nosey'. The ability to do this was frequently associated by those we interviewed with social workers conveying the message that they really did care about them as individuals. When this happened, the model of practice, or the method of assessment, was less important. Those we interviewed attributed a lack of involvement to a wide range of attributes in the workers. Some were described as too young, some as too old; some as not being adequately trained, and others as being too well qualified.

> *One of them spoke down to me. A lot of them seem to be straight out of university and don't know about life.*

Being patronised was seen by the parents as particularly alienating. Most social workers shied away from this question as to whether liking or disliking the family member helped or hindered working in partnership, although a few were ready to say that they did feel personally more warmth towards some of their clients than others, and that sometimes this made their work easier and sometimes more difficult. Some workers deliberately kept at an emotional distance:

> *My antennae are more on "red alert" for possible danger signals in child protection cases and it creates more distance between myself and parents, especially if parents are alleged abusers and I am more geared up for possible confrontation situations, especially if removal of a child looks like a real possibility.*

These workers did speak of characteristics of the families or their response to their intervention as making it more difficult to involve them:

If you have people who are very slow and unable to read and comprehend complicated matters they become more confused. Their words were only given through me which is a little difficult I suppose considering I'm there to protect the child. But everyone else (i.e. the professionals) was there at the conference. It's part of my social work report to represent the parents' views. I've always tried to be fair. It's difficult. How do you know what is fair? You know what you feel, but is what you feel fair? They [the parents] came to the end of the conference and I and the team manager explained the decisions of the conference and what we intended to do.

If the family is very hostile, my desire to involve them is reduced.

The relationship between outcome and working in partnership

A good outcome for the **parents** was strongly associated with greater involvement in the protection process and social work practice. This tends to support the argument that being involved in the processes which are affecting their lives is therapeutic for parents.

Usually the factors which appeared to be associated with the likelihood of a satisfactory outcome for the child were also associated with a good or moderately good outcome for the parents, except for the small number of cases when purposive practice resulted in a care order and the plan for a very young child to be placed permanently outside the family. It was reasonable to assume at least a moderately good outcome for such a child, whilst for the parent(s) the problems which led to the necessity of permanent separation appeared to preclude the possibility of a satisfactory outcome.

In Chapter 4 we described how we rated the outcome for the child and listed the variables which were associated with better outcomes for the children. Figures 8.16 and 8.17 and Tables 8.8 and 8.9 indicate an association

Table 8.8 **Outcome for child by researcher rating of whether main parent was involved**

Outcome	Not involved		Involved to some extent		Involved		Total	
	No.	%	No.	%	No.	%	No.	%
Good	6	43	59	54	73	81	138	65
No change	8	57	34	31	12	13	54	25
Poor	0	0	16	15	5	6	21	10
Total	14	100	109	100	90	100	213	100

$\chi^2 = 25.31$ df = 4   p < .0001

between better outcomes for the child and greater involvement of the child and the parents. Eighty-one per cent of the main parents whose child had a good outcome were involved compared to 13 per cent where there was no change, and 6 per cent where the outcome for the child was poor.

Figure 8.16   **Researcher rating of outcome for child by researcher rating of involvement of main parent in the protection process (n = 213) (p<.0001)**

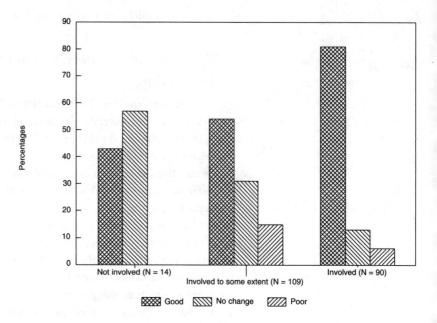

Table 8.9   **Outcome for child by researcher rating of whether child was involved (children aged 10+)**

Outcome	Not involved		Involved to some extent		Involved		Total	
	No.	%	No.	%	No.	%	No.	%
Good	5	42	24	63	15	68	44	61
No change	3	25	7	18	4	18	14	20
Poor	4	33	7	18	3	13	14	19
Total	12	100	38	100	22	100	72	100

Not significant

Figure 8.17 **Researcher rating of outcome for child by researcher rating of involvement of child (children aged 10+ - n = 72) (p<.01)**

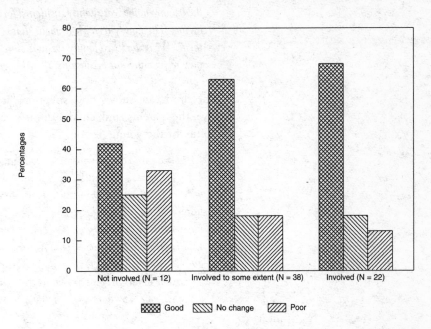

Clearly the involvement of family members is not sufficient to ensure a good outcome in that in 6 per cent of the cases where the outcome for the child was poor, the researchers considered that the parents were involved in the social work and protection process. This may at least in part be explained by the fact that some children and some parents who had very serious problems were engaged in the protection process but that the process itself, however well carried out, was unable to make inroads into the very severe difficulties of the child. Contrast these two cases. In the first, although the social worker tried very hard to involve the parents and indeed gave herself some credit for achieving this to some extent, the good outcome for the child was essentially because of her characteristics and temperament. In the second, the parents and child were involved, but the worker was not optimistic about a positive outcome for the child. The social workers said:

> *I'd give it seven out of ten as to whether the parents participated. It was hard work for me each time I had to start over again and be determined that they would participate. The fact that there was to be another conference helped because it was a focus and there had to be an end to it by then. I think I helped them to see how much of a credit their daughter was to them – she's extremely bright and a lovely girl.*

I think for Becky [the child] it may have been the same outcome as if this had not all happened because she's quite a determined girl, but I hope the leaving home was slightly cushioned for her because of being supported by me. The family were clear about that — that I had supported her and them. We've had two family sessions since she came back home but now they're fizzling out because its all OK again.

The third case shows how strenuous attempts by the social worker to involve the parents and child cannot overcome the barriers to a good outcome for the young person.

Marie was a child of mixed race parentage whose single parent mother struggled against many difficulties to bring her up. Despite her affection for her child, her own problems frequently intervened and there was a long history of social work help, almost from Marie's birth. At 13 she was involved in prostitution and her companions had convictions for violence. Efforts were made to involve both Marie and her mother in the social work process and to some extent they were successful. However, it was impossible to rate the outcome for Marie as anything other than poor when we considered her chances of leading a reasonably satisfactory adult life.

A fourth case indicates that working in partnership may be only partially successful but the outcome for the child may be good.

A pre-birth conference was held on the third child of a young mother who had herself been in care and was known to be engaged in prostitution. The two previous children had been adopted. The mother attended the pre-birth conference and plans were worked out for her to be given support in caring for her new baby. When the child was born the key worker showed creativity and great energy in trying to engage the mother. However, personality difficulties and ambivalence towards social services which had built up through her own childhood thwarted all attempts to provide adequate protection. A place of safety order was taken and care proceedings initiated, still with the hope that a restoration plan could be worked out. At that point the young mother refused any further contact with the worker and refused to visit the child in care. Attempts at partnership broke down, but plans were well underway for the child to be placed for adoption. Thus the expected outcome for the child was reasonably good, whereas that for the mother was poor and the case was rated as one where attempts to work in partnership were not successful.

These cases illustrate the interrelationship between working in partnership and outcomes for the child and other family members. Figure 8.18 is our attempt to show these complex relationships between variables and outcomes

Figure 8.18 **Diagrammatic illustration of the relationship between variables, practice, partnership and outcome**

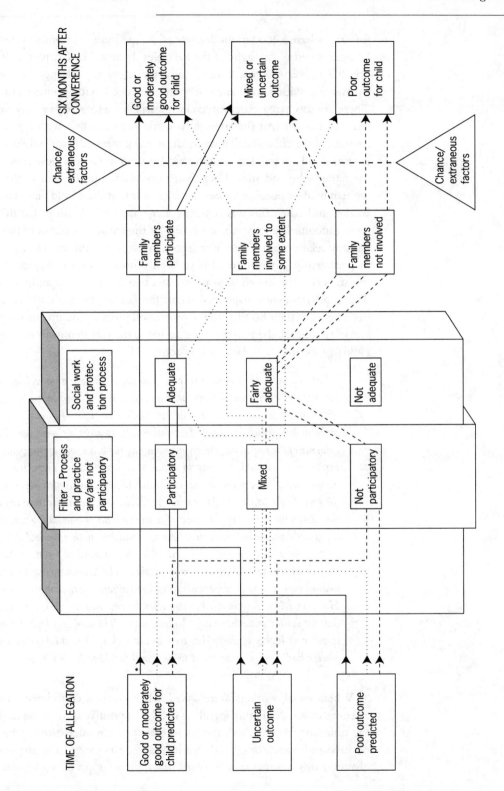

* The lines give just a few possible paths for the process from the allegation to the interim outcome for the child at the 6-month stage for cases where a good or moderately good, medium or poor outcome might be anticipated in the light of the variables discussed in Chapter 4. It is not possible to say to what extent, and precisely how, attempts to work in partnership with family members are associated with positive outcomes. There are too many other intervening variables. However, in only one case did we consider that the attempt to work in partnership with a parent was harmful to the child and that was in the initial stages of the case where a young person could not build up trust in a worker who was also in close contact with the father who had abused her. Fortunately, attempts to involve the young woman made it possible for her to make clear that she would like a change of worker and when this was achieved there was no indication that the long-term outcome was any worse because of the earlier problems in building a trusting relationship. There were more cases where **not** attempting to work in partnership when it could have been possible to do so appeared to the researchers to be linked with poor outcomes for the child and the parents. This most frequently happened when the family and the child clearly did need help but their hostility to the protection process, and the inability of the worker to engage them in that process, led to the case being closed before the child's problems could be properly addressed.

> *Eleven year old Andrea, was placed on the child protection register in the category of emotional abuse after a conference had been called by the school nurse who was alarmed at her small size, lack of growth, and problem behaviour in school. Her father and stepmother were, on the evidence of the conference, clearly mishandling the behaviour of this young person who was still reacting to the loss of her mother. There was a disagreement between the parents and the child protection conference about the sort of help which should be made available, and the family considered that they were coerced by the threat of court proceedings into taking part in a full child protection assessment. Andrea and her mother worked out a strategy for telling the social workers what they wanted to know so that they could get shot of them as soon as possible. The temporary impact was to draw parents and Andrea closer together in alliance against the workers. However, when the researcher visited after the case was closed, it was clear that the family, and particularly Andrea, was still in need of help, but that it was now highly unlikely that they would seek it. The child protection process had acted as a deterrent to the family seeking further help.*

When social workers were asked whether they considered that their attempts to involve family members had had a positive or negative impact on the outcome for the child, most said that they considered that it had been positive and none considered that it had been negative. The major reason given for this was that they believed that their attempts to work with family members had speeded up the process of assessment, planning, and the provision of appropriate services. Thus, even if their attempts to involve the family members were in the end unsuccessful, they considered that they were able to make plans which were in the interests of the children more quickly than if family members had been left on the outside of the whole process. Most of the workers interviewed argued strongly for working in partnership for civil libertarian reasons, but also, when considering the particular case, were likely to say that the outcome for the child as well as the parents was more favourable if they had succeeded in involving each of them at least to some extent. These quotes from social workers illustrate this point.

> *I involve the family in child protection work by respecting them as individuals -both adults and children—by being fair and open and by listening and showing an interest in what they have to say. I try not to be seen as having pre-conceived ideas and I keep the family updated constantly. I reason with them why their presence is essential at case conferences because others are making decisions concerning their children. It gives them an opportunity to get a clearer picture of what goes on.*

> *Parental participation is even more vital in child protection work to engage parents and children, than in other work where social services is merely a service provider or a gate-keeper. However child protection work often starts in a way that immediately brings the department and clients into conflict. This is not exclusive to child protection work but is a significant factor in this work.*

Involvement of the young people

There were 75 children aged 10 or over who we considered might have been involved in a planned way in the protection process. Numbers were small and few variables were significantly associated with greater or lesser degrees of involvement. Those which did indicate differences were:

About the family or the alleged abuse

- **Type of abuse** ($p < .01$) When the allegation was of sexual abuse or emotional abuse, the young person was more likely to be involved.
- **Severity of abuse** ($p < .05$). More young people participated where the abuse was allocated to the 'serious' category, and fewer where it was in the 'physical punishment' group.
- Young people were more likely to be involved if they themselves made the referral or the referral was made by a social worker or other professional, and least likely to be involved if a parent made the referral ($p < .05$).

- There was a trend towards more of those where the child was not registered being in the partnership or being partners group (36 per cent compared with 12 per cent of those who were registered) but this did not reach significance (p .06).

- There was a trend towards more young people from working class backgrounds taking part than those from middle class families (p .059).

Variables about agency and social work practice

- Where the social work with the young person was rated as very adequate, he or she was more likely to take part (p < .01).

- Where agency procedures and social work practice were rated as participatory, the young person was more likely to take part (p < .0001).

- There was a trend towards the young person participating if the type of social work was child protection, up-tariffing (28 per cent participated) which does not reach statistical significance (p < .07).

- Young people who were given a choice of help were more likely to participate (p < .05).

- If a supportive relationship with parents was established, the young person was more likely to participate (p < .001).

- If advice was given, the young person was more likely to participate (p < .01).

- Young people were more likely to be involved if the social worker was aged between 25–30 (p < .05).

- Young people were more likely to take part if the social worker had between two and four years' experience in child care social work (p < .05).

- Only five young people attended all (3) or most (2) of the initial conference, and three came in at the end. There was no difference in the 'participation' group between those who attended or did not attend, but 16 of those who did not, and none of those who did, were rated as not being involved at all, manipulated or placated.

- There was no difference in the proportion of young people who were interviewed initially with or without parental permission who were involved, but 31 per cent of those who were first interviewed without parental permission were definitely not involved, compared with 11 per cent of those who were interviewed with parental permission (p < .08).

- There was a trend towards those young people where the outcome was rated as poor being less likely to participate but this did not reach statistical significance.

The earlier analysis of the 385 family members included the young people and much of the earlier discussion is relevant to them. Nine of the young people who responded had received a child protection only service and three of these said that they had been involved in the work, four to some extent, and two not at all. The seven children who had received a more family centred service were all involved to some extent or definitely involved. This finding is in keeping with that from the study by Farmer *et al* (1994) who found that children were more likely to appreciate a service which treated their parents with respect.

When teenagers disagreed with their parents about what should be done, it was particularly difficult for social workers to engage both in the process. To side with one rather than the other appears not to be associated with good outcomes. If bridges were not maintained, there was a high likelihood that a young person would be alone and isolated in the community. A white social worker used his Asian colleagues as consultants in his attempts to be a bridge between an angry and rebellious girl of Pakistani ethnic origin who was on the receiving end of severe physical punishment and wanted to join her friends in the children's home:

> *I was checking back all the time that I was getting a clear picture of what the family wanted, but also getting across that compromise and negotiation were needed. Yasmin couldn't have it totally as she wanted it. [This social worker suggested working on particular aspects of the problem, and there was a long list on the file of possible aspects. The family declined to work on some of them—for example, marital problems. This was a 'de-labelling' case but in a very active way in trying to stop the family becoming dependent. The social worker was actively facilitating their involvement. It was very difficult because of the language and problems associated with cultural differences.]*

Participation of parents who were not living in the family home at the time of the conference

So few of the 27 parents or step-parents **not implicated in the abuse** were involved in the protection process or the social work task that it is not possible to identify variables associated with greater or less involvement in any systematic way.

Only three of the parents or step-parents **implicated in the abuse** who were not living in the family home at the time of the study were considered to participate and none were described as partners in the process. Two of the children in these cases were under the age of one, and one was over 12. All three were white. One of the parents was a mother and the other two were fathers. One was known to be implicated in the abuse and two were alleged to be. There was one case each of neglect, sexual abuse and emotional abuse, the last two being registered and the first not. Two were in the 'no serious injury' group, and one came in the 'serious abuse' group. Using the more general categorisation of 'involved', 'involved to some extent', and 'not involved at all', 23 were not involved at all (45 per cent), 22 were involved to some extent (43 per cent), and 6 (12 per cent) were allocated to the 'involved' category. One of the five from whom we had direct information said he was involved, three said they were to some extent, and seven said they were definitely not involved.

The following characteristics were associated with the non-resident parents being involved at least to some extent:

About the family or the allegation

- having more than one child (p < .05);
- two or more children being alleged to be maltreated (p < .05);
- child registered in a category other than neglect (p < .05);

About agency policy and social work practice

- living in Westshire (only 25 per cent were not involved at all compared with an average of 46 per cent—numbers too small for statistical test);
- being one of the five who attended most of the initial child protection conference (p < .01);
- being one of the six who attended all or most of the review conference (p < .01);
- the social work service for the case as a whole was rated as adequate (p < .01);
- the combined agency procedures and social work practice were rated as participatory (p < .001);
- receiving some help from a social worker (p < .001);
- being consulted about change needed (p < .001);
- understanding what was happening in the protection process (p < .05);
- help was offered after the conference (p < .01) although 5 were involved to some extent when help was not offered but not wanted after the conference;
- there was a choice about the help offered (p < .05);
- information was given on the change needed (p < .01);
- a supportive relationship was offered (p < .01);
- advice was offered (p < .001);
- help was given to the whole family (p < .05);

- a strategy meeting was held before the initial conference (p < .05);
- the source of income was state benefit (p < .05)

Conclusions on variables associated with working in partnership

We conclude this section by emphasising that some **workers** were more willing than others and some were more skilled than others in engaging family members in their work. Some **agencies** were more determined than others to engage family members, with the result that their workers felt supported in engaging in creative practice, both in terms of resources and the feeling that they would receive agency backing if they needed it for this method of practice. In broad outline, no amount of skill, energy and resources could have resulted in the involvement of some parents and some young people in the work. Even in such cases, however, attempts to engage family members sometimes resulted in their becoming more involved in the later stages of the work. On the other hand, it must be a disappointment that some family members who were not implicated in the abuse and were only too willing to work in partnership with social workers to help their children were not enabled to do so. In looking in more detail at those cases where working in partnership would not be easy to achieve, but was achieved, we conclude that the key factors are the attitudes, skill and efforts of the social workers backed by agency policies and procedures which encourage them to find creative ways to inform, involve, and eventually work in partnership with parents and children.

Chapter 9

Conclusion

Implications for the protection service and social work practice

We undertook this study at the time when the Children Act 1989 was about to become law, with its requirement that social workers attempt to work in partnership with parents and children even when the protection of the children was at issue. Doubts were being expressed about whether attempts to work in partnership with parents might be at the expense of the safety and wellbeing of their children. Our study is complex because it seemed important to look at a total cohort of children who might be in need of protection and not simply at the cases of a few volunteers. Our data is inevitably incomplete for some of the 220 cases where parents were unwilling to give us permission to look at the case file, and the reader has therefore had to bear with us as our analysis has involved differing totals depending on the reliability of the data for the different variables and ratings. Many of the variables and the intermediate and final outcome measures are 'soft' and based on researcher ratings. For this reason, as well as the small numbers in some cells and the numerous overlapping variables we have not undertaken a statistical analysis which held variables constant and would justify our reaching conclusions about causation. However, the availability of data from more than one source in most cases, and particularly from 120 family members gives us some confidence in the conclusions we reach in this section and at the end of each chapter. This is especially so when we consider our outcome measure of whether or not the service to protect the child and help the family succeeded in involving them in the process. We did wonder at the start of the study whether family members might consider they had been fully involved when we, as researchers, were aware that they had been given only snippets of information to placate or manipulate them. We need not have worried. Except for the one practical point when several parents thought they had received full minutes when in fact they had only received a summary of the conclusions, family members were well aware of the difference between involvement and placation. This difference was often not so much in what was actually said or done, but in the **way** it was said or done and the intentions, values and attitudes which were behind words and actions.

We chose for our study those teams where we knew that thought had been put into attempts to work in partnership with family members, but which were going about it in different ways. It could be seen as disappointing that such a small proportion (16 per cent) of the 385 family members took a full part or were partners in the work. However, our close analysis of the cases shows that there are many reasons for this. Some family members (30 per cent of those from whom we had a direct response) did not want a service so would be unlikely to want to work in partnership. In many of these cases there was no agreement about what had gone on, who was responsible and how serious an impact it might have on the child. In some cases discrepant views persisted and there were some where it seemed likely to the researchers that the version of the parents and child was the correct one. Working in partnership, as Howe (1992) has pointed out, is not possible if one party is not willing to become engaged in the work. However, the worker **can** and some certainly did, keep these family members fully informed, be honest with them, consult them when important decisions were to be made, and give careful consideration to their wishes. Thus the aim of 'involvement' is a more appropriate aim for the early stages of cases where child protection is at issue, and our 42 per cent success rate using this outcome measure gives more room for optimism.

In Chapter 8 we considered the variables which appeared to be associated with family involvement. We concluded that although some parents and children had such severe problems that it was not possible to involve them at all, these were very few in number. Even when the degree of difficulty in a case was such that a poor outcome for child and/or parent was almost inevitable some workers managed to involve some of these parents and young people in the work. We concluded that in a large majority of the cases a skilled and determined worker would be able to involve parents and older children, and move towards working in partnership as the case progressed. The proportion of cases where family members were involved or were partners could certainly have been higher, and chances were lost by insensitive or unskilled workers or agency policies which undermined parents who were willing and able to participate in plans to help and protect their child.

In short, whilst failure to **work in partnership** can sometimes be attributed to aspects of the case itself or characteristics of family members, differences between cases where family members were **informed, involved and consulted** and those where they were not were almost always attributable to either the agency policy and procedures or the social work practice or both together.

These differences need to be addressed as we found no evidence of poorer outcomes for children or parents resulting from attempts to work in partnership, and many cases where lack of success in involving parents and children appeared to have a negative influence on the ability to plan in a purposive way and provide services which would have benefited the child and other family members.

Implications for agencies

Although our study has concentrated on social services departments and social workers many of our conclusions are relevant to managers and workers in other agencies and professions. Certainly the changes in practice which result in increased family involvement can not be achieved without the active encouragement of the Area Child Protection Committees (ACPCs).

In Chapter 1 we considered previous research and noted that it had concentrated on the initiative of inviting family members to initial child protection conferences. Our study in a sense vindicates this interest in that if there is one single practice which aids or impedes family member involvement it is the inclusion of parents as valued **participants** and not just attenders at conferences. This is partly because of the contribution they make to the effectiveness of the conference, but also because their involvement at conferences changes the way all other aspects of the case are handled. It is an extremely effective quality control mechanism in that professional workers know that they will be held accountable by the parents and exposed to their colleagues if they have not done what they said they would do by the time of the next conference.

Few of the workers whose cases we scrutinised had undertaken training to imporve their skills when involving family members in their work. Some made avoidable mistakes especially before and during initial child protection conferences which resulted in avoidable discomfort or distress to a minority of family members. Many of the tips for practice of which we learned have already been incorporated in a Reader and training material funded by the Department of Health (Lewis et al., 1992). Others are contained in Department of Health guidance (DH, forthcoming). We pick out here just a few points which emerged strongly from our study.

- The chairpersons, workers and managers in the areas we studied who welcomed parents at the whole or most of the conferences at a time when this practice was relatively unusual had strong commitments to this style of working. Some organised training for themselves but it is fair to say that they were for the most part inventing policy and practice as they went along. Since 1990 there is far more guidance about procedures and practice which has resulted from these pioneers sharing their experience about what works well and what works less well. On the other hand not all those who now work with family members in conferences have the same enthusiasm for the change in policy or the essential skills. Training for all attenders is therefore essential so that the lessons already learned can be passed on, and workers can practice ways of saying things which might be hurtful or shocking when those concerned are present.

- Parents and older children who are to attend and their supporters also need to be well prepared. It is especially important that reports are discussed with them beforehand. There were cases in our study where parents were not clearly told what the meeting would be discussing, and were upset when incidents which they thought were long in the past were brought to the attention of the conference. This seemed to happen most often if a small incident such as a smacked bottom was the 'last straw' which pushed a family where there had been a series of concerns into the child protection arena.

- Some conferences were deferred because it was thought essential to convene them before full information was available on which to base a decision about risk and registration, but undesirable to take the serious step of placing on the register the details of a family who might subsequently be found to be blameless. This seemed an appropriate way of handling such situations. However, in other cases it was decided to defer a decision in order to achieve compliance by the parents with the preferred plan of the workers. In some such cases it was not at all clear that the child was 'likely to suffer significant harm', and usually the deferred conference decided not to register. This was undesirable for two reasons. Firstly it created resentment and made it harder to engage family members in the work; and secondly, as we have noted, even when there was no question of initiating care proceedings, parents were afraid that the child would be taken away from them. They thus remained in a state of anxiety until the next conference and high levels of anxiety detract from parenting competence. The degree of difficulty of some of the children and the problems their parents had to cope with meant that care was needed not to detract from their competence and self esteem as parents which was often already fragile.

- The 'emotional abuse' label was found by some parents to be particularly unhelpful and inappropriate to the position as they saw it. In discussions with them and in considering the cases it would appear that 'emotional neglect' would be a more appropriate categorisation of some of the cases registered as 'emotional abuse'. Some workers did indeed use the neglect category for cases which in other agencies would have come under the emotional abuse category. We did encounter cases which clearly were appropriately described as emotional abuse in that there was an element of deliberate cruelty and desire to harm, even though in some such cases a parent might not be able to prevent themselves from inflicting such harm because he or she was suffering from a mental illness or personality disorder.

- We noted that almost a third of the conferences took place three weeks or more after the initial incident, and that less than a third happened within the recommended ten days. It did not appear to us that this was to the detriment of the way the protection process proceeded, since in all cases of imminent danger the child was removed from home by emergency procedures. Whilst cases must always be pursued with urgency in view of the high level of anxiety and tension within the families when a conference is pending, it is also important to allow enough time to make the necessary inquiries and to prepare the family members who are to attend.

- There were few cases when young people were present at conferences. Some of those we spoke to would have liked to be there and others not. In the few cases in which they attended they were not well prepared, and more attention must be given to the circumstances when they should or should not be invited, and to the way they are prepared and helped to participate. A child protection meeting is a difficult, stressful and very much an adult occasion. The main point at issue concerns the behaviour and actions of parents and it is often not appropriate for children, especially those living at home, to hear some of the hard truths and distressing information that has to be discussed. A child protection meeting, unlike a review meeting for a child in care, can not be made into a 'child centred' event, even though the discussion must be essentially focused on the welfare and protection of the child.

- If children are not present there should always be a separate item on the agenda before each decision is taken about the opinions and wishes of the child, and these should be made known to the conference by someone who has consulted the child first. This item should be separated out from the agenda item on the opinions and wishes of the parents, and also from the professional opinions of anyone who is speaking on behalf of the child.

- Parents should normally be present throughout unless there are good reasons why this should not happen. Although social workers who are skilled at involving family members and determined to do so can get over the resentment engendered when they are asked to leave for no obvious reason, it is time consuming and unnecessary to make their job more difficult in this way.

- If a parent is suffering from the onset of an episode of mental illness, wherever possible the conference should be postponed or should ensure that the child is protected and then adjourn in the hope that the family member will be able to take a fuller part in the proceedings within a few weeks.

- Contrary to practice in many agencies, parents and children should specifically be asked to give their opinion about any positive or negative effects of registration on their family functioning. Parents do not expect to have the last word and a vote on this, but most of those we interviewed did have something useful to say about it which would have been helpful to conference members.

- Particular care is needed to explain the proceedings and provide translations and interpreters when family members are from a different race or culture from the majority of attenders, and especially if they use a different language.

- The now well established practice of chairpersons meeting briefly with parents before the meeting is a positive way of helping them to feel they have a part to play.

- A clear agenda and copy of the relevant paragraphs from 'Working Together' giving the criteria for registration should be given to all attenders and to parents and older children whether or not they attend.

- Introductions should be accompanied by clearly readable labels giving name and official designation.

- Chairs should ensure that decisions really are made at meetings and conferences do not merely rubber stamp previous conclusions. This is why it is especially important that the chair is neither a line manager for the case nor a person who has been heavily involved in providing consultation on it. The most common complaint was 'They'd made their mind up before we came in. They weren't listening' and as observers we sometimes concurred with this conclusion of the parents. We saw important contributions go unheeded if they introduced information which was not congruent with the opinions which conference members brought with them into the meeting. On other occasions we saw a chair pick up such a piece of new information introduced by a parent or relative which threw a different light on things and cause the conference to pause and take stock as a result. In the light of this it is essential that strategy discussions should limit themselves to the *Working Together* task of deciding how to conduct the investigation and are not allowed to become, as sometimes happens, preliminary discussions about the allegation held in the absence of the parents. If professionals have jointly chewed over the details of the allegation before the child protection conference it is more likely that family members will consider that it was all decided beforehand, and they will probably be right.

- The significant and usually positive part played by relatives in several of these cases suggests that there could be benefit in extending the practice of deferring some conferences to allow for a New Zealand style family group meeting to be held, as is already happening in some parts of England and Wales (Ryburn, 1992).

One further point arises from our finding in common with other researchers that it is rare for work **after** the conference to be truly multi-disciplinary. There is a danger that 'meetings' will become confused with 'work' or 'help'. Family members should be involved in meetings to review the plan and progress made, but joint work should also happen **between** meetings. We sometimes gained the impression, especially when children were in care, that parents and workers lurched from meeting to meeting and never saw each other in between except that the family was descended upon the day before by a barrage of professionals to be shown reports to be presented the next day. In such cases parents told the researchers of their irritation with workers who were not prepared to help and were 'only interested in doing their jobs properly'.

Other aspects of agency policy to which we would draw attention are:

- the provision of leaflets and other suitably recorded information in appropriate languages, which should be routinely sent to parents and older children, as well as and not instead of a personal explanation by the social worker;

- the provision of resources which will facilitate attendance at meetings including child care, transport, trained interpreters and support and equipment for people with diabilities when needed;

- ensuring that family members know who they can call on to accompany them to meetings and provide support before, during and after what will almost always be a stressful event;

- ensuring that the agency is wholehearted in its support of workers who attempt to involve parents and children in the work. Those social workers and conference chair persons who considered that their commitment to working to involve family members was shared throughout their agency had surprisingly high morale despite the stress engendered by their work.

Finally, agencies must ask whether they are using the child protection system appropriately. The wide discrepancy between teams and agencies in the situations considered by child protection conferences which we and other researchers have found suggests that resources are being wasted in some authorities and may indicate that protection plans are not adequate in others. We considered that registration was necessary and in keeping with the guidelines in 50 per cent of these cases (as compared with the 62 per cent actually registered) which reached conferences. In some of the others it was necessary to hold a child protection conference in order to determine that registration was **not** necessary, even though a child or family member might still need help. We are conscious that our conclusions are based on a cohort of cases which, whilst it included some very serious and indeed life threatening episodes of abuse or neglect, also included some very needy families who had been crying out for help for some time, and others whose children had been harmed by an acquaintance or partner who had been promptly ejected by a caring and appropriately protective parent. In neither type of case was the protection system necessary in order to provide the help that was needed. In some cases the system operated so smoothly that it was welcomed as conveying concern and practical and emotional help; in other cases it was resented and did harm to people whose self esteem was already at rock bottom. Far more resources were then needed to help build them up again and maximise their competence as parents than would have been necessary if the services and support had been provided when they had first been requested. Because of the very wide range of cases coming into the system it is hard to make it appropriately responsive to the most serious episodes which might lead to child deaths or irreparable damage. We heard evidence from workers and family members to support the findings of other researchers that one reason for the discrepancies between areas is that some workers and managers are still using entry into the child protection system as a gateway to resources. One of the resources sometimes sought in this way is an inter-agency assessment and service which should now be available for children 'in need' under the provisions of Part III of the Children Act.

Social work practice

Family members fell into two groups. A minority of around a third found themselves caught up in the child protection system, whether through their own actions or those of others, who did not want help for themselves although they might have wanted it for their children. Once involved, they wanted the process to make sure they knew what was happening and to treat them in an open honest and efficient way. These parents did not particularly mind whether it was a social worker or another professional who dealt with their case, and some, especially those who had not previously been known to the welfare services and could rely on support from friends or relatives, preferred the more direct and down to earth approach they received from the specialist police officers.

Around two thirds, however, did want help before and after the confer-ence, and whether or not the child was registered. Some did not want it from a particular social worker whose attitudes and approach at the time of the allegation or in the past they had not found helpful. Others however developed a relationship of trust over the crisis of the referral and were upset and resentful at having to have a new worker, especially if the change was hurried or they were left without a worker until one could be allocated. The least desirable option for those who know they and their children need help is to be passed from investigating team to assessing team all of whom keep their emotional distance, doing a competent job except for the one ingredient which parents and children valued most, being cared about as individuals and having their strengths acknowledged as well as their weaknesses understood. If they are lucky, they will eventually reach a long term team worker who starts providing the help they have been asking for from the first mention of abuse or even long before. In other cases the family members, including the child who needs help, will develop strategies to outwit the assessors and get themselves off the books as soon as possible.

Clearly case allocation systems are needed, but if partnership means anything there must be some flexibility about the timing of a change of worker and the possibility of the worker who undertook the investigation remaining if it will be difficult for a parent or child to establish trust in a new worker. Equally a request for a change of worker should be taken seriously and acted upon if trust really has broken down or not been established. Even if changes of worker are necessary for administrative reasons, there should always be a key worker who will offer continuity and a supportive or therapeutic relationship as well as marshalling and coordinating the packages of help and any monitoring of the child's well being. This mother clearly lacked such a sense of continuity:

> *For me, it was a bad experience. I don't think Kevin benefited, and having different social workers' faces each time and going through it all over again wasn't good. He wasn't happy about them coming round again. He was more worried that Alan [his step-father who was accused of physically abusing him] might be put away.*

Sometimes parents and child will need different workers, and an absent parent alleged to be involved in the abuse will need a different source of support and therapy. This would appropriately be provided by the probation service if a criminal charge is pending.

If this element of continuity and coordination is in place our study suggests that additional workers can with advantage be brought in **alongside** the key worker to provide short term specialist assessment or therapeutic services. Family centres or specialist children's services teams appeared to be particularly effective. They could work with different family members or the family as a group, either in their own home or the centre and also had a range of practical and recreational resources at their disposal. Such resources are especially likely to engage family members if they provide opportunities for them to become involved in running the centre and using their talents and experiences to help others. But whether the service is a long or short term one, the workers must establish themselves as people who value and care about those they are seeking to help. If we are left with one comment ringing in our ears, it is the plea not to be treated as 'just another job lot'.

Bibliography

ARNSTEIN, S. R., 'A Ladder of Citizen Participation', *Journal of the American Institute of Planners*, Vol.35, Part 4, 1969, pp.216–224.

BARNES, M. and WISTOW, G., *Researching User Involvement*, Nuffield Institute, 1992.

BELL, M., *Parental Involvement in Initial Child Protection Conferences in Leeds*, University of York, 1993.

Berkshire Social Services Department, *Parents/Carers invited to Child Protection and Case Conferences*, The Bracknell Pilot Project, Chairman's Interim and Final Reports, 1990.

BIEHAL, N. and SAINSBURY, E., 'From values to rights in social work', *British Journal of Social Work*, 21, 1991, pp.245–257.

BIRCHALL, E., in Stevenson, O., (ed.), *Child abuse – public policy and professional practice*, (Chapter 1) Hemel Hempstead: Harvester Wheatsheaf, 1989.

BROWN, C., *Child Abuse Parents Speaking – parents' impressions of social workers and of the social work process*, Working Paper 63, Bristol: School of Advanced Urban Studies, University of Bristol, 1984.

BROWN, T. and WATERS, J., *Parental Participation in Case Conferences*, Rochdale: BASPCAN, 1986

BULLOCK, R., LITTLE, M. and MILLHAM, S., *Going Home*, Aldershot: Dartmouth, 1993.

BURNS, L., *Partnership with Families: a study of 65 child protection case conferences in Gloucestershire to which the family was invited*, 1991

CALDERDALE ACPC, *Child Protection Case Conferences – Family Involvement – Research Project*, 1992.

Central Council for Education and Training in Social Work, *Good Enough Parenting*, London: CCETSW, 1978.

Chartered Institute of Public Finance and Accountancy, *Statistical Information Service*, 1992.

CREIGHTON, S., *Child Abuse Trends in England and Wales, 1988–1990*, London: NSPCC, 1992.

CREIGHTON, S. and GALLAGHER, B., *Child Abuse Deaths*, Information Briefing No. 5 (revised), London: NSPCC, 1988.

CLEAVER, H. and FREEMAN, P., *Parental perspectives in cases of suspected child abuse*, London: HMSO, 1995.

Cleveland Social Services Department, *Report of a project designed to evaluate Parents' views on case conferences*, 1991.

CROFT, S. and BERESFORD, P., *From paternalism to participation: Involving people in Social Services*, York: Joseph Rowntree Foundation, 1990.

Department of Health and Social Security, *Report of the Committee of Inquiry into the Care and Supervision provided in relation to Maria Colwell*, London: HMSO, 1974.

Department of Health, *Social Work Decisions in Child Care*, London: HMSO, 1985.

Department of Health, *Principles and Practice in Regulations and Guidance*, London: HMSO, 1989.

Department of Health, *Protecting Children. A guide for social workers undertaking a comprehensive assessment*, London: HMSO, 1988.

Department of Health, *Working Together*, London: HMSO, 1988.

Department of Health, *Working Together under the Children Act 1989: A guide to arrangements for inter-agency cooperation for the protection of children from abuse*, London: HMSO, 1991.

Department of Health, *Patterns and Outcomes in Child Placement*, London: HMSO, 1991.

Department of Health, *Children and Young People on Child Protection Registers, Year Ending 31 March 1991*, London: HMSO, 1992.

Department of Health, *The Challenge of Partnership: A guide for practitioners*, London: HMSO, 1994.

DOEL, M. and MARSH, P., *Task-centred Social Work*, Aldershot: Ashgate, 1992.

DRISCOLL, J. and EVANS, L., *An Evaluation of the Participation of Parents and those with Parental Responsibility in the Child Protection Process in Suffolk*, Ipswich: Suffolk Social Services Department, 1992.

Dudley Social Services, Child Protection Team, *Involving Clients in Child Protection Review Conferences – a preliminary report*, 1991.

ELY, D., *The Parents' Perspective on their Involvement in Case Conferences*, St. Gabriel's Family Centre, Brighton, 1991.

Family Rights Group, *The Children Act 1989: Working in Partnership with Families*, London: FRG, 1991.

FARMER, E., OWEN, M. and PARKER, R., *Child Protection Practices: Private Risks and Public Remedies*, London: HMSO, 1994.

FISHER, M. *Parental Participation in Case Conferences*, Social Work in Partnership, University of Bradford, 1990.

FISHER, M., MARSH, P. and PHILLIPS, D., with SAINSBURY, E., *In and Out of Care*, London: Batsford, 1986.

Fox-Harding, L., *Perspectives in Child Care Policy*, London: Longman, 1991.

Gardner, R., *Who Says? Choice and Control in Care*, London: NCB, 1987.

Gibbons, J., Conroy, S. and Bell, C., *The Operation of Child Protection Registers.* London: HMSO, 1994.

Guernsey's Local Support Group for Families with Children in Care or in Difficulties, *Families in Care*, Bulletin No. 4, Guernsey: October 1991.

Hallett, C. and Birchall, E., *Coordination Policies and Practices in Child Protection*, London: HMSO, 1994.

Hardiker, P., Exton, K. and Barker, M., *Policies and Practices in Preventive Child Care*, Aldershot: Avebury, 1991.

Housiaux, S.T., *Parental Attendance at Child Abuse Case Conferences*, Coventry: NSPCC, 1984.

Howe, D., 'Theories of Helping, Empowerment and Participation' in Thoburn, J. (ed.) *Participation in Practice: A Reader*, Norwich: University of East Anglia, 1992

Lewis, A., Shemmings, D. and Thoburn, J., *Participation in Practice: A Reader*, Norwich: University of East Anglia, 1992.

Lonsdale, G., *A Survey of Parental Participation at Initial Child Protection Case Conferences*, 1991.

McGloin, P. and Turnbull, A., *Parental Participation in Child Abuse Review Conferences*, London: London Borough of Greenwich, 1986.

Marsh, P. and Fisher, M., *Good Intentions: Developing Partnership in Social Services*, York: Joseph Rowntree Trust, 1992.

Merchant, A. and Luckham, S., *A Study of Parental and Child Participation in CP Conferences in Mid-Essex*, 1991.

Millham, S., Bullock, R., Hosie, K. and Haak, M., *Lost in Care*, Aldershot: Gower, 1986.

Millham, S., Bullock, R., Hosie, K. and Little, M., *Access Disputes in Child-Care*, Aldershot: Gower, 1989.

Morrison, T., Blakey, C., Butler, A., Fallon, S. and Leith A., *Children and Parental Participation in Case Conferences*, London: NSPCC, 1990.

North Yorkshire ACPC *Family Participation in Child Protection Case Conferences*, 1991.

Office of Population, Censuses and Surveys, *Population Trends 1963–66*, 1991.

Office of Population, Censuses and Surveys, *1990 Mortality Statistics. Childhood. England and Wales*, Series DH6 No. 3, London: HMSO, 1991.

Office of Population, Censuses and Surveys, *1991 Census: Report*, London: HMSO, 1993.

O'HAGAN, K.P., *Working with Child Sexual Abuse*, Milton Keynes: Open University Press, 1989.

OWEN, M., *Social Justice and Children in Care*, Aldershot: Avebury, 1992.

PACKMAN, J. with RANDALL, J. and JACQUES, N., *Who needs care? Social Work Decisions about Children*, Oxford: Blackwell, 1986.

PARSLOE, P., DAINES, R. and LYONS, K., *Aiming for Partnership*, London: Barnardo's, 1990.

PHILLIPS, J., Introduction in Brown, T. and Waters, J. (ed.), *Parental Participation in Case Conferences*, Rochdale: BASPCAN, 1986.

PHILLIPS, J. and EVANS, M., *Participating Parents*, Bradford: ADB Publications, 1986.

RYBURN, M. 'Family Group Conferences' in Thoburn, J. (ed.) *Participation in Practice: A Reader*, Norwich: University of East Anglia, 1992.

Salford ACPC, *Family Participation in Child Protection Conferences*, ACPC policy documents.

SHEMMINGS, D., *Family Participation in Child Protection Conferences – Report of a Pilot Project in Lewisham Social Services Department*, Norwich: University of East Anglia, 1991.

SHEMMINGS, D. and THOBURN, J., *Parental Participation in Child Protection Conferences: Report of a Pilot Project in Hackney Social Services Department*, Norwich: University of East Anglia, 1990.

SINCLAIR, R., *Decision-making in Statutory Reviews on Children in Care*, Aldershot: Gower, 1984.

SMITH, N., *Learning from Parents*, Cumbria Social Services Department Child Protection Unit, 1990.

Social Security Statistics, Department of Social Security, London: HMSO, 1991.

Social Services Inspectorate, *Inspection of Child Protection Services in Rochdale*, London: Department of Health, 1990.

Social Services Inspectorate, *Inspection of Child Protection Services in Manchester*, London: Department of Health, 1990.

Social Services Inspectorate, *Inspecting for Quality: Evaluating Performance in Child Protection*, London: HMSO, 1993.

TAYLOR, S. and GODFREY, M., *Parental Involvement in Child Protection Case Conferences*, an evaluation of the pilot project, North Tyneside Social Services Department, 1991.

WILSON, E., *Children/Young Persons' Attendance at Child Protection Case Conferences*, Resources Pack, Bath/Wansdyke Pilot Project, 1992.

WOODHILL, R. and ASHWORTH, P., *Parental Participation in Case Conferences*, Sheffield Hallam University 1989.

Researcher Rating Protocols

Researcher rating protocols were drawn up after data collection was almost completed and following discussions between the three researchers and colleagues working on similar studies. In the early stages of coding reliability cross-checks were made by a second researcher and any differences of approach discussed. At later stages discussions took place when the researcher coding a case had difficulty reaching a conclusion.

Allocation to best, middle or worst scenario group

Cases were allocated to one or other of these groups according to the researchers' assessment as to the likelihood that it would be possible to work in partnership with this family member. Allocation to the different groups was based on the following variables at the time of the conference, alone or in combination.

Best scenario

Abuse is: single episode of physical abuse; neglect – not deliberate; sexual abuse where abuser has left home; a result of parent's mental illness or some other recognisable stress factor.

Parents: not implicated in the alleged abuse or neglect; not believed to have failed to protect the child; accept there is a problem; they and social worker agree about the nature and degree of the abuse/neglect; welcome social work help.

Worst scenario

Alleged abuse is: sexual and the alleged abuser still lives at home; persistent; severe or organised.

Parents: have a record of violence or threatening behaviour; deny that abuse has occurred; take no responsibility for abuse or neglect; reject social work help; they and social worker cannot agree on what has happened.

Middle scenario cases have some best and some worst scenario characteristics.

Rating of whether policy and practice with adults was participatory

If most of these apply for most of the time the case is allocated to the 'partnership' group. If some apply, it is allocated to the 'involvement' group.

Evidence for the ratings was gained when possible from the family member, the social worker and the case file, with most weight being given to the view of the family member if that was available.

- Comprehensive and comprehensible information was made available at appropriate times, both verbally and in recorded form suitable to the needs, language, and disabilities of the family member. Recorded **and** verbal information should have been given on **most** of the following: how to keep the child safe; child care and family support services; the child protection process; the child protection register; recording procedures and access to recorded information; complaints procedures and the possibility of a change of social worker; voluntary care if it might be appropriate; care orders and the court process if their use was seriously considered.

- A key worker was clearly identified to the family member as being available to provide information, help and support. This worker conveyed to the family member her/his concern for him or her as a person and also for the well-being of the child. He or she treated the family member with respect and courtesy.

- Key worker and conference chair respected the individuality of the person, and took care to understand the impact of any external or internal pressures, cultural, religious, language or racial aspects of the situation or any disabilities or emotional difficulties of parent and/or child.

- Family members and any supporters were well prepared for conferences and other decision-making meeting, and had the practical and emotional support needed to attend.

- Family members' views were carefully ascertained about all big decisions, the services to be offered and the social work method, the identity of the social worker(s), the place of visits, the detail of the investigation and assessments. Preferences were followed when possible, and clear explanations given if they could not be followed.

- Social worker was willing to attempt to negotiate with family members if there were disagreements and find alternative ways of protecting the child which were acceptable to family members.

- Family member was enabled to retain as much control of the decisions and plans as was consistent with protection of the child and securing his or her long-term well-being. All agreements were carefully negotiated with family members' opinions and wishes included.

- There was a discussion with the family member about records kept, and how these and reports would be made available to family member. Family member sees and signs all reports unless they have said they do not wish to do. Family member is asked to check accuracy of important reports and minutes, and received a copy.

Rating of whether policy and practice with child was participatory

Generally as for adult, but in addition:

- was the child seen on his or her own?

- was information given specifically to the child in an age appropriate way?

- did the social worker check that the child knew what was happening and invite the child's views about how the investigation should proceed?

- was the child or young person invited to give their views to the conference and consulted about how these views should be put across in the conference?

- if attending the conference or other meetings, was the young person adequately prepared for this and supported during the meetings?

Interim Outcome for child

Any assessment of outcome only six months following the child protection conference must of necessity be tentative. However, it was part of our research design that a case should not be seen as satisfactory if there was evidence that the outcome for the child was poorer as a result of the involvement of family members in the process. The researchers allocated cases to the good, poor, or no change outcome groups according to answers to the following questions:

- Do the child's living and parenting arrangements appear to be settled?

- Is the child either living with or in contact with parents and other adults who are important to him/her, and is this contact arranged in a way which makes it a positive experience?

- Are there any indications that the child is making developmental progress or is slipping backwards?

- Are there indications that any emotional or behavioral problems are diminishing or increasing?

- Does it appear that the protection plan is offering protection for the child?

- Does the protection plan appear to be working as intended for the overall benefit of the child?

- Is the professional contact for the child and carers at an appropriate level in view of the problems identified?

The "no change" category was only used when it was not possible to allocate a case to the 'good' or 'poor' categories. It was usually when a child remained living at home and the child protection process appeared to have had little impact on the child's well-being and circumstances.

Rating of adequacy of social work service

- This rating was based on 'Working Together' (1988) and Social Services Inspectorate Reports. It was close to the recently published SSI 'Guidelines for Inspectors' (DH, 1993). To be rated as adequate, the work needed to combine understanding of and empathy with the family members with practice which appeared to be well planned and competently carried out. Those who did not request help or declined it when it was offered might be rated as receiving an adequate service provided the worker kept them fully informed and behaved with courtesy and respect towards them, and efficiently followed the procedures. However, in the majority of cases family members expected a worker to indicate that he or she cared about them as people, and to offer help over a range of difficulties, and not only those which were associated with the child protection inquiry. For workers to efficiently follow the procedures was not sufficient to be rated by the parents or the researchers as providing a satisfactory service if it failed to provide at least some of the help requested or needed. The family member would need to be kept at least fairly well informed and involved at least to some extent for the service to be rated as adequate.

Researcher rating of whether the child protection conference was necessary (based on 'Working Together' (1988), Cleveland Report and other SSI Reports)

If all these three apply for at least one child being considered, a conference will be rated as being necessary.

- Was evidence or information brought to the conference which, if substantiated, would lead to the conclusion that a child had been abused, neglected or otherwise harmed in such a way that met, or if substantiated would meet, one or more of the criteria for registration under the child protection procedures of the ACPC?

- Was the abuse, neglect or harm attributable, or was information brought to the conference of suspicion that it was attributable to the actions or lack of actions by parents or other adults in a caring role?

- Was there evidence that an agency protection plan under the ACPC procedures might be necessary to protect the child from future harm?

Researcher rating of whether registration was in line with the Department of Health guidance

If all these apply for at least one child being considered, registration will be rated as being necessary.

- Was evidence given to the conference which supported the conclusion that one or more of the criteria for registration was met in respect of each child registered?

- Did the evidence presented to the conference support the conclusion that the abuse, neglect or other harm resulted from the actions or inaction of parents or other main carers?

- Did the evidence presented to the conference justify the conclusion that a plan was needed to provide protection and promote the well-being of any child in the family?

- Did the evidence presented to the conference justify the conclusion that the protection plan needed to be a multi-disciplinary plan under the auspices of the ACPC child protection system?

Index

Printed in the United Kingdom for HMSO
Dd299963 5/95 C7 G559 10170